Economic
Relations
with the USSR

The California Seminar on International Security and Foreign Policy, founded in 1970, has an active program of research, discussion, and publication on issues faced by governments in foreign policy and arms control. It is jointly sponsored by the California Institute of Technology and The Rand Corporation. Funding for the preparation of this book came largely from the Sarah Scaife Foundation.

The Seminar welcomes and encourages diversity in the viewpoints and backgrounds of contributors. It does not take an institutional position on the issues it considers. The views expressed in this book are those of the authors.

Economic Relations with the USSR

Issues for the Western Alliance

Edited by

Abraham S. Becker

A Policy Study of the California
Seminar on International
Security and Foreign Policy

LexingtonBooks
D.C. Heath and Company
Lexington, Massachusetts
Toronto

Library of Congress Cataloging in Publication Data

Main entry under title:
Economic relations with the USSR.

(A Policy study of the California Seminar on International Security and Foreign Policy)
"LexingtonBooks."
Includes index.
Contents: Introduction: East-West economic relations as an alliance problem/Abraham S. Becker—The Role of trade and technology transfer in the Soviet Union/Philip Hanson—Soviet energy prospects and their implications for East-West trade/Ed. A. Hewett—[etc.]

1. East-West trade (1945-   )—Addresses, essays, lectures. 2. United States—Foreign economic relations—Soviet Union—Addresses, essays, lectures. 3. Soviet Union—Foreign economic relations—United States—Addresses, essays, lectures. 4. Europe—Foreign economic relations—Soviet Union—Addresses, essays, lectures. 5. Soviet Union—Foreign economic relations—Europe—Addresses, essays, lectures.
I. Becker, Abraham Samuel, 1927-   . II. Title: Economic relations with the U.S.S.R. III. Series.
HF1411.E264   1983   337.73047   83-47991
ISBN 0-669-06794-6

Published simultaneously in Canada

Printed in the United States of America

International Standard Book Number: 0-669-06794-6

Library of Congress Catalog Card Number: 83-47991

Contents

Figures and Tables

**Part I
Overview**

1

Introduction: East–West Economic Relations as an Alliance Problem

Abraham S. Becker

The major papers presented at a conference, "Economic Interchange with the USSR in the 1980s," held in April 1982 at the Belmont Conference Center in Elkridge, Maryland, are collected in parts II and III of this book. The conference marked the culmination of a project on the "USSR in the International Economy" organized by the California Seminar on International Security and Foreign Policy and financed under a grant from the Sarah Scaife Foundation. In addition to this book, the project produced four papers.[1]

What distinguished this conference from others with similar titles was the attention to issues for the Western alliance. By early 1981, when the conference was being planned, it had become clear that the state of the alliance had become pivotal to the entire system of East-West economic relations. The first two years of the Reagan administration suggest that the future of these relations is likely to hinge more on what happens to the alliance in general than on its East-West economic policies. At the conference this issue was the focus of the opening address by Richard Perle, assistant secretary of defense for international security policy. It was a central feature of the discussions on the papers by Jean-Marie Guillaume, Marshall Goldman, and John Hardt and Kate Tomlinson. It was also prominent in the group's consideration of the two papers on the Soviet economy by Philip Hanson and Ed. Hewett. The conference concluded with a panel discussion seeking the elements of a common alliance strategy of East-West economic relations.

Part I presents an overview of the alliance problem as considered by the Belmont conference. This chapter first provides some background for the conference and then summarizes the general tenor of the discussion. In chapter 2, Josef Joffe reflects on the alliance problem from his viewpoint as a European with strong connections to and knowledge of the American scene.

The Context

How did Atlantic relations become a critical factor in Europe's and America's East-West economic policy? (References to Europe here generally include Japan as well.) From the mid-1970s onward, U.S. public opinion had

3

been turning sour on détente, in part because of Soviet activities in the
Third World (such as Soviet encouragement of the Arab oil embargo in
1973-1974 and the expansionary thrust into Angola, Ethiopia, and Yemen),
in part because of the slowly growing perception of the cumulative scope
and seriousness of the Soviet military buildup, which nurtured concomitant
doubts about the meaning and results of the strategic arms limitation talks
(SALT) agreements. European views of these events and of Soviet purposes
in the global arena were changing much more slowly, if at all. On the whole,
Europeans continued to see détente as a viable and desirable framework of
relations between East and West; they tended to explain away Soviet activities in the Third World as peripheral, in a strategic as well as a
geographic sense, to the global conflict, which they saw as still centered on
Europe.

A second major contributor to the widening gap of perceptions between
Europe and America was the evolution of East-West trade. Basic asym-
metries between trade patterns with the East of the United States and
Western Europe tended to make the Europeans more and the United States
less interested in improving economic (and political) relations with Moscow
and its European allies. First, compared with the United States the European Economic Community (EEC) countries had higher absolute and
relative levels of trade with the East. It is true that East-West trade still constituted small proportions of total trade turnover and still smaller shares of
GNP in all these countries. Nevertheless the proportions were considerably
higher in Europe than in the United States. In addition, there were structural differences in the trade flows. As Jean-Marie Guillaume points out,
the United States was primarily a food exporter to the East, while the EEC
states exported capital goods, generating long-term contracts with a few
large, often quite influential enterprises. With the economic downturn of
the late 1970s and the sharpening trade competition among Europe,
America, and Japan, East-West trade in Europe became coupled to the problem of employment maintenance, particularly in the Federal Republic of
Germany. Guillaume also notes that the United States consistently earned
trade surpluses in the 1970s, whereas toward the end of that decade the EEC
was running a deficit as a result of the large volume of high-cost energy imports from the Soviet Union. Finally the Europeans were continuing to increase their lending exposure to Eastern Europe despite the mounting
economic difficulties in those countries, especially in Poland, whereas the
United States had begun to cut back its lending activity to Eastern Europe
by the mid-1970s.

In 1979 two crises further strained U.S. relations with its allies, presenting tests of the allies' ability to harmonize their divergent interests and
cooperate in the use of economic sanctions against a third party. In an effort to free the hostages imprisoned in the takeover of the U.S. embassy

in Teheran in November 1979, the Carter administration froze some $12 billion of Iranian assets under U.S. control. This action involved extraterritorial extension of U.S. controls to overseas branches of U.S. banks. America's allies were disquieted by these actions; they did not attempt to undercut the controls, but neither did they reinforce the American effort by rigorous sanctions of their own.

The more important test and evident failure of the allied coordination process came after the Soviet invasion of Afghanistan. The Soviet incursion shocked not only President Carter but also the American public, perhaps considerably more than it shocked the Europeans. One unpleasant surprise was the American discovery that trucks built in the Kama River factory, which the United States had helped to finance, were used as troop carriers in the invasion.

In this case, the major U.S. sanction was a partial grain embargo. Probably Moscow was unable to circumvent the embargo completely; moreover the costs of the partial circumvention were not negligible. Nevertheless the willingness of other producers—Argentina, Australia, and Canada in particular—and of European transshippers to fill the gap considerably reduced the embargo's political effectiveness and surely reduced the likelihood that it would be used again for foreign-policy purposes. With respect to other measures taken by the United States at the time, most notably the boycott of the Olympic games in Moscow, cooperation from U.S. allies was selective and generally grudging. In no case did Europe or Japan reinforce the American action by stringent independent measures of their own.

The combination of Reagan administration policy and the Polish crisis exacerbated the U.S.-European conflict. In its early stages, the administration's anti-Soviet rhetoric, apparent hostility to arms control, and occasional reference to the possibility of successfully waging nuclear war alarmed many Europeans. On East-West economic issues specifically, Washington was now pressing hard to curb the flow of militarily relevant technology to the Soviet Union and to strengthen COCOM (the Coordinating Committee on Export Control of the Atlantic alliance plus Japan) in order to tighten the net controlling technology transfer to the USSR. After some initial hesitation, the administration forcefully opposed the gas-pipeline deal involving West European sales of pipe and other gas-transmission technology to the Soviet Union in exchange for large volumes of gas to be shipped in the mid- and late 1980s.

The institution of martial law in Poland in December 1981 triggered new American sanctions against the Soviet Union, among them a stricter ban on energy-technology transfer.[2] Left unresolved was the threat of extension of the ban to extraterritorial transactions, by foreign subsidiaries of U.S. companies and even by foreign companies using American-licensed technology. At the same time a crisis arose over the Polish debt, which had reached Latin American-like proportions and appeared totally unmanageable under the conditions of near collapse of the Polish economy. Washington considered forcing a default among the sanctions against Poland, but this was sharply opposed in Europe. The Polish debt and gas-pipeline issues also stirred intense debate on the extent and justification of Western subsidization of trade with the East, a debate aggravated by the cross-Atlantic quarrel over the desirability of punishing the USSR as well as Poland for the events of December 1981. In the United States there was a growing resentment toward the allies for their unwillingness to take action against Moscow's latest act of aggression. The allies bridled at American pressure, which they perceived as threatening not only a valued channel of trade (at a time of deepening economic recession) but also the stability of the West's relations with the USSR.

The Belmont Discussions

It was in this environment and against the background of these events that the conferees opened their deliberations at Belmont.

The conflict between the United States and its allies on East-West economic issues is evidently a matter of both strategy and tactics, strategy being understood in the broader sense that includes objectives and definitions of the state of the world. The conference dealt with both components, although in varying depth and detail. It did not examine the contrasting perspectives on the scope of Soviet ambitions, the nature of communist society, and the like, but there was debate at the second level of strategy on the political uses of economic measures in East-West relations. And considerable attention was given to the uses and misuses of particular measures of sanction and leverage.

Because the central theme of the American position on East-West economics is the security cost of these relations—to which a European response emphasizes their putative contribution to both economic well-being and détente—the conferees explored the relative roles of politics and economics in East-West trade. As Marshall Goldman affirmed, politics clearly shapes U.S. economic involvement with the Soviet bloc. Nor are political considerations absent from Moscow's policy, it was pointed out—and not only in reciprocal relations with Washington but also in negotiations with other Western governments and firms. As for Europe and Japan, had not Western private-sector investment in Eastern Europe followed the strong lead of governments, expressed in example and encouragement and even more in guarantees? Jean-Marie Guillaume calls attention to a more subtle form of politicization of Western trade dealings with the East through the structure of that trade itself. As its exports became tied to future imports from the East through such major deals as the gas pipeline, Europe became less willing to accept politically inspired trade fluctuations. Other participants noted the difficulty of superimposing national or alliance security objectives on the goals of strong domestic interest groups.

Thus the play of politics in Europe operated to discriminate in favor of East-West trade. So Washington would argue and many Europeans would agree. For this reason (but also because of its free-enterprise orientation), the Reagan administration contends that East-West trade ought to be left to the play of market forces. Purged of the superstructure of guarantees, subsidies, and political encouragement and in a period of high real interest rates and high East Eurpean debt burdens, trade and investment flows to the East would be redirected to more profitable markets. The European conferees had mixed views on this argument. They were prepared to see some validity in it but were also convinced that politics and economics were inextricably intertwined in international trade generally, as well as in East-West trade particularly. A U.S. scholar raised the question whether East-West trade was too important to be left to the market. This is in fact a vulnerability of the Reagan administration's position, inasmuch as the administration is pressing hard for more stringent government controls on technology transfer in all forms.

If, as both America and Europe seem to agree (though for different reasons), a pure market approach is not possible and politics and economics must jointly rule, by what criteria can their relative roles be defined? What are the objectives of the policy?

At a first level of analysis, the Reagan administration offered at least an articulated perspective: the Kremlin was likely to continue to invest in military capability at rates approximating those of the past ten to twenty years; NATO for economic and political reasons was unlikely to be able to keep pace, much less to catch up; through legal or illegal channels, East-West trade has been contributing significantly to Soviet military capability; it was therefore necessary to do everything possible to limit the aid the West was offering to the Soviet military buildup. The prescriptive conclusion of this syllogism, carried one step further, suggested that an effective program of constraints would not only limit Soviet access to specific key goods, services, and knowledge—for example, the much-discussed critical technologies—but would also control the aggregate flow of resources to the USSR. The former constraint related to technology transfer, but the latter supplied the justification for opposing trade and credit subsidization and, most notably, the Siberian gas-pipeline deal. The projected hard-currency earnings from that deal would enable Moscow to continue to draw heavily on Western food and technology without having to cut back on military expenditures. Thus the Reagan administration sees Soviet economic troubles as an opportunity to complicate further their resource-allocation dilemma in the hope that the additional pressure would result in a reallocation of resources away from defense or (a secondary line of reasoning) would push the economy in the direction of economic and political reforms.

This raises the question of the vulnerability of the Soviet economy to Western economic pressure and of the role of technology imports in Soviet development prospects of the 1980s. The two chapters on Soviet problems address these questions, among others. Ed. Hewett maintains that the energy sector will not offer a promising fulcrum despite Moscow's heavy bet on the development of Siberian oil and gas. Other participants disagreed, pointing to the requirements for Western energy equipment and knowledge in all phases of energy production and distribution, from exploration to transmission. Apart from energy technology, to what degree would Soviet planners seek to sidestep obstacles to raising productivity, to overcome systemic barriers to innovation and diffusion, by importing Western technology in large volume? Philip Hanson pondered the meaning of the leveling off and decline of Soviet technology imports in the late 1970s and offered several different explanations, some of which might suggest less reliance on this factor in the 1980s (for example, the dependence of import policy on the initiative and support of Alexei Kosygin). Other participants argued, however, that the falloff had more to do with temporary problems of assimilation and that Soviet leaders continued to recognize their needs for foreign technology so that imports would have to be resumed in the straitened circumstances of the 1980s. One or two of the Europeans were skeptical of this argument. They seemed inclined to believe that Soviet ability to import would tail off because of diminishing export prospects and that the late-1970s' development represented a policy change toward less dependence on the West, if not indeed a revived search for greater autarky. (One suspects that other Europeans, more impressed by the continuing promise of East-West trade, would strongly disagree.)

Assuming that Soviet economic needs would maintain or create dependencies on the West, what would be appropriate tactics of sanction and leverage? The participants looked at the record of the recent past and probed the likelihood of future success. Leverage is in fact not a single but a multiple issue: Are the various measures likely to cost the adversary more than those who apply them? Under what circumstances would Moscow yield to such pressure? Could the alliance achieve the degree of cooperation required to implement credible sanctions? Each of the component subissues is controversial.

Some participants believed that leverage-linkage had been effective in selected cases in the past: by West Germany with respect to the emigration of ethnic Germans, by the United States with respect to Jewish emigration from the USSR. (There was some dispute about the causal connection between the Jackson-Vanik Amendment and Soviet policy on Jewish emigration.) For them the clear implication of this measured success was the necessity of maintaining a level of economic relations sufficient to provide an instrument of leverage. It also was suggested that leverage worked only where the objective exacted a fairly minor concession from Moscow, although emigration from the USSR is hardly a trivial issue to the Politburo. Levers, it was noted, could be negative or positive (in which case they become carrots) and directed to the past or to the future. There was little support for negative past-oriented levers—that is, sanctions that punish for past transgressions—although the relation to deterrence of such future actions was not examined. A former high U.S. government official suggested, however, that if we could not agree with our allies on the circumstances that ought to trigger particular sanctions against the USSR, we might at least seek assent on an ordinal ranking of such sanctions. In general the Europeans present seemed to doubt that Soviet choices could be affected except at the margin.

Amid the debate on leverage exerted against the Soviet bloc, some participants raised the danger of reverse leverage on the Europeans. In the early stages of the transatlantic debate on the Siberian gas pipeline, there was fear of the political costs of excessive European, particularly German, dependence on Soviet gas supplies. This argument has since faded, replaced by emphasis on the import-augmenting potential of the hard-currency proceeds to be earned from gas sales to Western Europe. Probably because of this likely Soviet interest, the significance of German dependence was downgraded. A European conferee maintained that the argument could be generalized: the Soviets would have powerful economic reasons for refraining from any attempt to exploit East-West trade for political advantage. And there was general agreement on the desirability of limiting Western vulnerability to Eastern pressure by such measures as building up strategic reserves, arranging for emergency alternative supplies, and diversifying supply sources.

Whatever the needs of the Soviet economy for access to Western markets and to Western technology, the ultimate question of Soviet vulnerability to Western pressure centered on the likelihood that the Kremlin would yield to external pressures. Would the Soviets allow economic requirements to dictate military-resource allocation? Could constraints on resource inflow to the Soviet Union lead to systemic change? At best the expectations advanced by proponents of this view were modest. Many, if not most, of the conferees were doubtful, and some rejected the prospect as unrealistic.

A related set of issues arose in connection with John Hardt and Kate Tomlinson's assessment of the role of Eastern Europe in East-West trade. These authors urged Western assistance to Eastern Europe as a policy course in the best interests of both groups of states. Most discussants did not see a Western interest in bringing about or contributing to the collapse of East

European economies; indeed there may have been a majority supporting a differentiated policy discriminating in favor of Eastern Europe and against the USSR. (One of the conferees warned, however, that differentiation would be difficult to implement inasmuch as Europe opposed sanctions against Moscow and the U.S. government was hardly prepared to subsidize Eastern Europe.) But little confidence was expressed that aid and trade would lead to beneficial political changes in Eastern Europe.

This apparent consensus for skepticism probably would have been broken had the conference enjoyed more European representation, especially from Germany, where faith in the continued viability of the classic assumptions of economic détente, especially with respect to Eastern Europe, is still strong. Thus the Washington perspective did not encounter at this conference a sharply contrasting alternative; the American participants by and large tended to take intermediate positions along this spectrum.

Neither side of the Atlantic debate constitutes a homogeneous view, however. London, Paris, and Bonn also exhibit divergences in strategic perspective. One European conferee held that if there are two polar views of the Soviet Union in the alliance, that of the United States (especially the Department of Defense) and that of Germany (presumably the speaker had in mind the mainstream of the Social Democrats), the government of France shares the American view but behaves like Germany in East-West economic matters. Guillaume admits the ambiguity in French policy, which he sees as intended to avoid sending out the wrong political signals. An American commentator thought that the more appropriate characterization was ambivalence with respect to the goals of alliance relations and security, on the one side, and the value of East-West trade, on the other. One might extend this appellation to much German foreign-policy behavior as well.

The conferees were impressed by the difficulty of achieving alliance consensus; they traced this to irreversible changes in the power structure of the alliance such that decisions can no longer be made or enforced by a single dominant state. A current U.S. government official thought that agreement on tightening the net around Western technology transfers would not be difficult to achieve once the governments were better informed as to how much security damage had been caused and the costs of compensating for that damage compared with the costs of forgoing the relevant trade. It was suggested that it might be easier to agree on an alliance credit policy if the focus of discussion were moved from interest rates to principal amounts. One participant argued that the existence of a true world market in grain meant that the United States could undertake a grain embargo without fear of economic damage. Even if other states replaced the prohibited American sales to the USSR, the former customers of these states would, directly or indirectly, buy up the product of U.S. farmers. (Neither the U.S. farm bloc nor the Reagan administration seems to accept that logic.)

Would these fractionating issues continue to bedevil the alliance for the indefinite future? The conferees speculated on the degree to which the alliance might enjoy a respite from internal conflict on East-West economics during the 1980s as a consequence of change in the economic environment. If the extraordinary growth of Eastern bloc debt was traceable, at least in part, to the flood of petrodollars into international credit markets in the mid- and late 1970s, the current softness in energy prices and the unlikelihood of major price rises in the medium term would cut off the source of future lending extravagance. Similarly the Soviet bloc's eagerness to import from the West in the 1970s would be tempered in the 1980s by debt-management problems, economic retardation, and fear of dependence on the West. If such a development were to reduce the scope for Western leverage, it would also limit the cases generating alliance policy dispute. Others saw East-West trade becoming less profitable as credits tightened and energy prices softened. Thus the market might bring about at least a partial resolution of alliance conflict on this issue, where diplomacy had failed. Others were not so confident of the beneficence of market automaticity. In the camouflage of subsidies surrounding Western credits, guarantees, and product prices, the true scale of profitability was difficult to discern; as Europe worried increasingly about its competitive position in world trade, the Eastern market, with its administered stability (and perhaps imperfect quality discrimination) might look even more promising.

One of the prime sources of cross-Atlantic acrimony on East-West trade was the European perception of an asymmetry of Western state involvement and inequality of sacrifice in levying sanctions against the East. It was easy for Washington to oppose the gas pipeline when the U.S. economic stake was minuscule compared with that of Europe; U.S. imports from the communist bloc were traditionally insignificant, and above all there was the U.S. grain policy. President Reagan abolished the U.S. grain embargo as soon as he came into office, placating the important farm interest and removing potentially one of the most effective sanctions, but he insisted that Europeans should submerge their national economic interests for the greater alliance good. So ran the European argument.

It is interesting that although burden sharing has been a traditional item on the agenda of alliance defense planning, there has been little discussion of the analogue in East-West trade policy. The absence of negotiations on the subject must be due in part to the American government's argument that selling grain to the Soviets is intrinsically different from selling them technology. But if Washington should agree that a burden issue exists, an American participant ventured, the administration would be hindered by weak leverage—against the Europeans, not the Soviets. U.S. unwillingness to extend public-sector credits and guarantees on exports to the East deprived the White House of leverage in bargaining with the Europeans.

The concluding session of the conference was a panel discussion of the requirements for and possibilities of a consensual alliance strategy. To no one's surprise, the panel did not come up with a blueprint ready for application. Given the divergence of interests, the uncertainties attaching to analysis of Soviet behavior (and even that of Western governments), and the complexity of the set of interactions among all the relevant actors, it probably could not be otherwise. The necessity for seeking common ground and avoiding damage to the vital interests of the alliance was, of course, generally appreciated. A former U.S. government official called for the creation of a high-level East-West economic coordinating committee. Marshall Goldman suggests the creation of an economic coordinating committee in the U.S. government to bridge the gaps between and among Congress and the relevant parts of the administration. Even in hard-line circles in Washington, there is little inclination to scuttle the alliance. The more sensible expression of that view seeks to find a policy balance between serious damage to the alliance by contentious unilateral action and acquiescence to the lowest common denominator of inaction. At the conference one European spoke of the desirability of effecting "an orderly withdrawal" from East-West trade. That does not seem to be a popular view in European capitals. More characteristic, probably, would be an effort to find the complement of the American balance: a balance between causing serious damage to the alliance by refusal to cooperate with Washington and being "dragged into adventurism."

Epilogue

Hopes for an accommodation of the varying perspectives within the alliance were badly jarred shortly after the Belmont conference. Following the failure of the Versailles economic summit, the Reagan administration extended the ban on energy-technology shipments to the USSR to extraterritorial reaches, infuriating allied governments, which saw this action as an infringement of their sovereign rights. Several months of acidulous dispute were required before an agreement was reached to withdraw the extraterritorial ban in exchange for study of the major issues of East-West economics.

Currently the conflict within the alliance that flared up so dangerously in the summer of 1982 does not appear headed for imminent resolution. There remain several issues of long-term significance:

1. The gas pipeline is clearly a reality, and the Reagan administration has resigned itself to the implementation of that fact. This deal, however, was supposed to be only the first phase of a possibly more extensive arrangement between Western Europe and the Soviet Union. Will Europe remain interested in additional sections of the line and in an increased volume of gas imports? Will the recent softening of oil prices cut down on the size

of the European take, alter European governments' perceptions of the profitability of the deal, or affect their interest in diversifying energy sources for the 1990s?

2. Technology transfer remains a vexing question, if only because of the issue of dual-use technology. The alliance has always agreed to prohibit exporting equipment of direct military application. The conflicts have arisen over (primarily) American attempts to constrain transfers of machinery having both a civil and a military use. The Reagan administration is pressing for a narrower interpretation of civil use and a broader sense of what is strategic. How abrasive this issue will be depends considerably on the extent of Soviet and East European technology imports. There are contending forecasts of these magnitudes.

3. The conflict over credit subsidies is likely to be only partly resolved. Because of the complexity of credit arrangements, it would be difficult to plug all the possible loopholes, even if there was the requisite political will. The readiness to curb subsidies in Europe and even in the United States probably will depend on the state of the respective economies. High levels of unemployment in European industries with political visibility and potential export markets in the East provide a powerful inducement for West European governments to subsidize. Moreover, U.S. allies consider trade subsidies a traditional instrument of international economic competition. Even with substantial recovery from the present recession, that competition would provide a rationale for subsidies and fuel for alliance conflict over their relative national levels.

4. Underlying all of these specific differences is the most important difference of all: the fundamental divergence between Europe and America in political perspectives—on the viability of détente, on an appropriate strategy for East-West relations, and on the legitimacy of using economic sanctions against the USSR or Eastern Europe in the framework of that strategy. The year 1983 has been dominated by the debate on the intermediate nuclear force (INF) arms-control talks and the deployment of intermediate-range missiles. The outcome of that debate is likely to affect the entire range of East-West issues for a number of years.

No resolution of these differences is in sight. Whether market development or Soviet behavior or allied governmental changes, or perhaps still other factors, will bring a resolution, is unknown. Perhaps it is partly faith in the power of inertia that suggests we are more likely to muddle through than to reach either a harmonization of interests or a breakup of the alliance. But there is adequate scope for prudent action by all governments concerned.

Notes

1. H. Stephen Gardner, *Soviet International Economic Relations: Recent Trends in Policy and Performance*, Discussion Paper No. 90 (February

1981); Robert Campbell, *Soviet Technology Imports: The Gas Pipeline Case*, Discussion Paper No. 91 (February 1981); Philip Hanson, *Soviet Strategies and Policy Implementation in the Import of Chemical Technology from the West, 1958-1978*, Discussion Paper No. 92 (March 1981); and John Kiser, *Barriers to Increasing the Export of Manufactures from the USSR: Prospects for Change*, Discussion Paper No. 95 (May 1981); all published by the California Seminar on International Security and Foreign Policy, Santa Monica, California.

2. In response to the Soviet invasion of Afghanistan, the Carter administration initially froze exports to the USSR of high technology plus oil and gas machinery. After several months, it permitted the export of oil and gas equipment but not the export of high technology. President Reagan suspended all license applications for oil and gas equipment and expanded controls to cover energy-refining and -transmission equipment.

2 Mixing Money and Politics: Dollars and Détente

Josef Joffe

Machiavelli, speculating on the relationship between money and power, thought it was better to be strong than to be rich. In his view, it was easier to acquire wealth with the help of good soldiers than to acquire good soldiers, hence power, with the help of money.

From the late 1960s onward, the West lived by the obverse of Machiavelli's rule, calculating that trade, credits, and technology transfers to the East would yield influence over the East. At the threshold of détente, around 1969, the West started out with a theory in hand. Together, the nations of the Atlantic alliance would cast a net of interdependence around the Soviets, enmeshing them in trade and technology ties, credit lines, and arms-control agreements. Having acquired a stake in cooperative relations with the West, the Soviet Union would behave according to Western standards—like any reasonable power that values peace and prosperity more highly than the costly pleasures of aggrandizement. The Kremlin, so the linkage theory went, would not risk the horn of capitalist plenty for a quick geopolitical grab here or there.

The West European, in particular the West German, linkage approach was even more ambitious. Whereas the Nixon-Kissinger version of détente essentially sought to stabilize a multiple status quo around the world (with the added inducement of economic and financial benefits), the West Europeans aimed for a status quo plus, with stability begetting its opposite: change and evolution. The all-but-final recognition of the Soviet Union's postwar gains by way of Ostpolitik and the Conference on Security and Cooperation in Europe (CSCE) would provide the indispensable foundation. Secure in its possessions and lured by the steady promise of economic subsidies, the Soviet Union would relax its heavy grip on its vassals, opening the way toward the progressive reassociation of the two Germanies and peaceful change in Eastern Europe.

The expectations invested in economic détente were staggering. Facing the task of containing and socializing the Soviet Union in the 1970s and beyond but lacking the will or the wherewithal to apply more traditional forms of power, the West fell back on its liberal vision of politics and its experience as postimperial, civilian societies. The Europeans, sobered by two world wars, sought to substitute economic power (of which they had aplenty) for military power (where they were hopelessly outclassed by their

15

Soviet neighbors to the East). The United States did have the resources, but there was also the more recent experience of the Vietnam war. With Congress in revolt, large parts of the populace disaffected and Watergate casting its lengthening shadow over the presidency, Nixon and Kissinger had little choice but to go for a "hegemony on the cheap." There would be "regional policemen" (such as the Shah of Iran) who would help to uphold the global order, and there would be "linkage," which would entangle the Soviet Union in a finely spun web of material incentives and penalties. In short, the market would have to act where might was lacking.

A dozen years later, it cannot be said that our hopes have blossomed into reality. The Soviets did not live up to the good-conduct code in Angola, Ethiopia, and Afghanistan. Where they faced concentrated Western power (as in Europe) they behaved with prudence; where Western commitments were neither clear nor backed by force, they acted as great powers always do: with opportunism and some propensity for risk taking.

As the impressive Soviet arms buildup throughout the 1970s showed, prospering great powers do not necessarily turn into responsible citizens; they just carry a bigger punch. In 1961 during the decisive stage of the Congolese war, the Soviet Union could do very little to help its ally, Patrice Lumumba. In 1975, the Soviets did have the planes and the ships to project their power (by Cuban proxy) into the civil war in Angola, and this time their side won.

In Eastern Europe, dollars and deutsche marks did not make for devolution; indeed they may have exacerbated the problem of liberalization. As events in Poland throughout the 1970s showed, the heavy subsidization of a planned economy leads not only to mismanagement but also to a classic revolutionary gap between promise and performance. Unable to satisfy the burgeoning economic expectations of the populace, the regime has to squelch rising demand by periodically cutting real income. By 1980, economic repression in Poland led to full-scale political disaffection, ultimately triggering military repression by the imposition of martial law in December of 1981. As Susan Sontag said in a much-publicized speech, it was "tanks *and* banks" that did Poland in.[1]

The failure of détente, at least in terms of more ambitious expectations, has many reasons, and most of them have little to do with the lackluster productivity of dollar-and-deutsche mark diplomacy. Great powers, especially when confronted with the task of upholding political and pontifical supremacy, are not easily swayed by mundane mercantile considerations. To vary a famous saying of Lenin, trade is good, control is better— which is precisely echoed by Philip Hanson's contribution to this book: "The worsening of political relations has increased [Soviet] worries about dependence and fears of economic leverage."

For the Soviet Union, the gain of a lucrative contract (or credit line) is evidently dwarfed by the political losses that might follow the loosening of its imperial grip. When it comes to high politics, the bottom line is marked in terms of power, not profits. To return to Machiavelli's precept, the exchange rate between the currencies of economic and politico-military power is not very favorable, and when the chips are down, money's fungibility disappears completely.

Still, linkage is the very essence of diplomacy; even the ancients knew about this tool as reflected in the more traditional Latin terms of *do ut des* and *quid pro quo*. There is even some evidence, as Marshall Goldman points out in his analysis of the Jackson-Vanik Amendment, that economic pressure did encourage the Soviets to yield on politics. As the tortuous history of the Jackson-Vanik Amendment suggests, there may indeed be some limited issues where the Soviets value the loss of control less than the prospect of economic gain.

Yet even if there is such a differential in costs and benefits, hence the making of political Pareto optimality, linkage requires a second condition: a differential in dependence. Linkage assumes that Western welfare and cost curves are shaped in such a way that it could more easily give up the gains of trade than the Soviets. For otherwise, the West could not credibly threaten what the linkage theory requires: to cut links whenever the Soviets do not live up to Western standards of proper behavior.

The judicious application of sticks and carrots requires an ability for fine-tuning that is not exactly a strong suit of Western society. Western societies labor under a twin handicap. Their institutions are not identical with those of the state or the party, and their governments depend on the consent of the governed. Hence firms and farmers do not yield gladly to subtly calibrated control from above, which is indispensable for a political trade policy. Linkage requires the freedom to cut links. That freedom is heavily constrained by vested economic interests, the prospect of lost jobs and the pains of structural adjustment. Nor is this a peculiarly European disease, as the topsy-turvy history of the American grain embargo has shown. The sanctions imposed by President Jimmy Carter in the aftermath of Afghanistan were swiftly rescinded by his successor who was less oblivious to the electoral clout of the corn belt. Farming cycles do not smoothly follow the rapid oscillations of foreign policy, and thus the immediate punishment inflicted on American farmers looms far larger than the more distant consequences suffered by the Soviets.

The second problem of a political trade policy stems from the nature of our adversary's society. As the contribution by John P. Hardt and Kate S. Tomlinson shows, there is at least a strong correlation between the increase in economic intercourse and economic growth in the Soviet Union and the countries of Eastern Europe. Similarly, the dwindling of trade and credit flows at the threshold of the 1980s is paralleled by a decline in the Council for Mutual Economic Assistance (CMEA) growth rates. However, the authors seem quite agnostic when it comes to the critical question: the "difference between the likely performance without the sanctions and actual performance with the sanctions."

Presumably the West's subsidization of the Warsaw Pact's economies did reduce the adversaries' opportunity costs; presumably the cheap grain does set free scarce factors that might be channeled into the production of guns. On the other hand, we do not really know the shape of the Soviet Union's opportunity cost curves, and there is at least a strong suspicion that Soviet grain and Soviet guns are produced in two tightly separated compartments, with opportunity costs looming much larger in the civilian than in the military sector. There may be links between both, but what does seem clear is the large degree of freedom that authoritarian regimes enjoy when it comes to imposing priorities between guns and butter. Indeed outside pressure historically has pushed the ruled and the rulers closer together.

In the Olympic summer of 1980, Muscovites did not turn out in droves to protest their government's adventure in Afghanistan. When the League of Nations imposed sanctions on fascist Italy, the "man in the street" responded by donating his wedding ring to the nation's cause, and even old-style Liberals like the philosopher Benedetto Croce at that point closed ranks with the Duce. The league thus helped to rout the last remaining opposition to the Mussolini regime. Nor was Khomeini toppled by American sanctions in the aftermath of the embassy occupation. Moreover, Western nations will always be caught in an irreducible moral dilemma: do we want to punish the regime or the people? We cannot hit the one without hitting the other even harder, and that is not a pleasant choice.

The third problem stems from the necessity of acting in common. There is little profit in punishing American grain farmers while presenting their Canadian and Argentinian colleagues with a handsome windfall made in USSR. If boycotts work at all, then it is only if all work together (or if one nation holds an unbreakable monopoly). To get even allied nations (who are also commercial competitors) to march in tandem requires an extraordinary expenditure of power on the part of the alliance leader. The intra-alliance pipeline war of 1982 revealed a highly unfavorable return on American political capital: the sanctions inflicted on European firms drove NATO to the brink of its worst crisis without affecting the Soviet Union.[2] Whether the Europeans have acted wisely in tying that particular energy knot with the Soviet Union is yet another issue. It is clear, however, that even so powerful a nation as the United States should not squander its political assets so lightly on ventures that promise so remote a return.

Alliance cohesion will always be a difficult objective because nations will always find themselves in positions of differing vulnerabilities. As Jean-Marie Guillaume has pointed out in his chapter, there are vast gaps between Europe and the United States when it comes to the impact of trade restrictions on the members of the alliance. In dollar terms EEC trade with the East in 1980 was ten times higher than that of the United States; as a share of total trade it was almost four times higher; and as a share of GNP it was ten times higher. Comparing individual West European countries with the United States makes for even more blatant discrepancies. Thus the West German ratio of Eastern trade to total trade was six times higher than the American one; as a share of GNP, Eastern trade was 14.5 times greater in the Federal Republic than in the United States.

These remarkable gaps bespeak drastic differences in vulnerabilities and hence interest. Nor are they likely to disappear soon because, for historical and geographical reasons, the Europeans will always have a much bigger stake than the United States in East-West trade. It should not come as a surprise, then, that the Europeans will not flock to the flag whenever the United States calls for economic warfare. Where costs and benefits are so unevenly distributed, the United States might regularly end up with the worst of all possible worlds: no change in the adversary's stance plus maximum resentment on the part of its allies.

In sum, it is difficult to escape the conclusions rendered by a study of the Congressional Office of Technology Assessment released in the spring of 1983:

> OTA found that trade leverage usually works under very limited conditions, and that past precedents have demonstrated its weakness when used against the Soviet Union. The aftermath of U.S. attempts to embargo grain and energy equipment exports to the USSR dramatically demonstrate the limitations on U.S. power to successfully conduct a trade leverage policy. Although both embargoes were directed at vulnerable areas of the Soviet economy, their results were inconclusive at best. U.S. sanctions and embargoes may well have hurt the USSR, but it is unlikely that they have hurt enough to make a real economic difference.[3]

U.S. experience with the limited productivity of both carrots and sticks should make for more modest expectations in the future. Money, to recall Machiavelli's dictum, does not make up for deficiencies in power. If Congress cuts off military aid to our side in Angola, a cutoff of grain years later will hardly reverse the verdict of war. If the United States neglects its military arsenal for the greater part of the 1970s, a credit squeeze in the 1980s will not by itself reestablish the balance of power. Yet if money cannot substitute for might, is there at least economic profit in East-West trade?

The bottom line does not look overwhelming. Classical economic theory tells us that there is not much gain to be had from selling to a monopsonist like the Soviet Union because competition among many suppliers will necessarily drive down the rate of return. In many cases, we have even paid dearly for the privilege of trading with the Russians—by subsidized interest rates, for instance, that create jobs for some but impose costs on all, the taxpayers.

If East-West trade, as experience suggests, is politically sterile, then mutual advantage should be the only guide. Yet that criterion should preclude subsidies—a rule both Americans and Europeans have regularly forsaken. Throughout the protracted, worldwide recession and monetary contraction of the early 1980s, the market imposed a discipline on East-West trade that bankers, business persons, and bureaucrats had been unwilling to accept before. As the global economy gathers steam again in the mid-1980s, will the West once more throw good management to the winds and invest its resources in areas where profits are risky at best and negative at worst?

Notes

1. On February 6, 1982, reprinted in the *Nation*, February 27, 1982, pp. 230-231.

2. For a more extended account of the pipeline war, see Josef Joffe, "Europe and America: The Politics of Resentment," *Foreign Affairs—America and the World, 1982* 61, no. 3 (1983):569.

3. Office of Technology Assessment, U.S. Congress. *Technology and East-West Trade: An Update* (Washington, D.C.: U.S. Government Printing Office, 1983), p. 8.

**Part II
The Soviet Economy and
East–West Trade**

3

The Role of Trade and Technology Transfer in the Soviet Economy

Philip Hanson

Even the behaviour of sharks is still a matter of guesswork for science. And the Soviet Union is more complex than a shark.—Alexander Zinoviev, *Kommunizm kak real'nost' [Communism as Reality]* (1981)

In the early 1960s and early 1970s the importance of East-West trade to the Soviet economy increased. In the late 1970s and early 1980s there has been no clear further increase; in some respects the Soviet Union could even be said to have reduced its economic involvement with the Western world. So far as future prospects are concerned, it is likely that Soviet trade with the West will be held at rather modest levels during the rest of the decade.

This chapter is largely devoted to setting out the grounds for this judgment, with particular emphasis on the constraints imposed by external finance. There is, however, a subsidiary theme: that Soviet trade with the West since the mid-1970s has been much affected by policy decisions that I characterize as discretionary in character. For example, Soviet buying of Western machinery and equipment in the 1960s and early 1970s fits fairly well into a primitive model whose rationale is "buy as much as you can afford."[1] Between 1978 and 1980, however, even if variations in the values of gold reserves and of net hard-currency debt are brought into the picture along with hard-currency export earnings and the grain-import bill, the low level of machinery ordering cannot be accounted for on financial grounds. Political considerations, with perhaps an admixture of domestic economic policy considerations, seem to have become the binding constraint.

A number of Soviet speeches and press articles that appeared from 1979 to 1981 stressed disadvantages and errors in Soviet use of commercially acquired Western technology.[2] After President Reagan's announcement of economic measures against the Soviet Union in the wake of the imposition of martial law in Poland, there was a particularly clear and authoritative Soviet statement. It came in an interview on Hungarian radio on January 23 with V. Zagladin, the deputy head of the CPSU (Communist Party of the Soviet Union) Central Committee's foreign affairs department. Zagladin said that the USSR would take countermeasures against Western economic

I am grateful to participants in the Belmont conference, especially Gregory Grossman and Herbert S. Levine, for comments on an earlier draft.

23

sanctions, including a drive toward self-sufficiency. "We are going to produce everything that is necessary for us unaided and by the development of relations and cooperation with the socialist countries."[3]

When words like these are being bandied about, extrapolations of Soviet-Western trade from past relationships cannot inspire a great deal of confidence. Changes in East-West political relations have always affected Soviet-Western trade, and such changes cannot be incorporated in an economic model. To make matters worse, large, unpredicted shifts in key economic variables have also tended to undermine recent past projections. In a period when relative prices in world trade have changed sharply, with dramatic effects on such Soviet staple exports as oil and gold, this is not surprising. All the same, it needs stressing.

Even in the discussion of issues and policy viewpoints that follows, therefore, it is as well to bear in mind the difficulty of getting so much as the direction of change right in this particular segment of world trade. The influence of decisions that are constrained only within a very broad range by economic factors is particularly large in East-West trade. (Those are chiefly OPEC oil-price decisions, Soviet government decisions on the level of nongrain imports, and, to an apparently lesser extent, Western government decisions on East-West trade policy.)

Soviet-Western Trade and Payments, 1975-1981

The influence of external financial constraints on Soviet trade with the West has been, and remains, a fundamental one. But other constraints seem to have become binding in recent years. I have argued in detail for this interpretation elsewhere, focusing on the import of machinery (typically around a third of hard-currency imports in most of the 1970s).[4]

Table 3-1 provides the best estimates of main items in the Soviet hard-currency balance of payments in 1970 and from 1975 through 1979, plus my own estimates for 1980 and 1981.[5]

Table 3-2 assembles five series that should help to identify key influences and outcomes in Soviet decision making on hard-currency merchandise. If grain (or total food) imports have a high priority, as they seem to have had, hard-currency export earnings each year, less the hard currency preempted by grain (or total food) buying in that year, may be pictured as a major influence on nongrain (or nonfood) hard-currency import decisions made in that year.[6] Thus rows 1 and 2 present two alternative series of disposable income in this sense. In row 1 the grain bill, and in row 2 the total food bill, is deducted from current reported merchandise export earnings. Rows 3, 4, and 5 show three alternative measures of the embodied-technology import decisions made in each year: reported machinery orders

Table 3-1
Soviet Hard-Currency Trade and Payments, 1970 and 1975-1981
(millions of dollars)

	1970	1975	1976	1977	1978	1979	1980	1981
1. Reported merchandise imports	-2,701	-14,247	-15,316	-14,645	-16,951	-21,593	-25,428	NA
2. Reported merchandise exports	2,201	7,835	9,721	11,345	13,157	19,524	23,009	NA
3. Gold sales (estimated)	0	725	1,369	1,597	2,673	2,200	1,800	2,700
4. Arms sales for hard currency (estimated)	100	793	1,108	1,500	1,644	} 3,980	(3,700-5,600)	(3,900-5,900)
5. Net invisibles (estimated)	422	190	187	954	763		(-350)	100
6. Current account balance (estimated)	22	-4,714	-2,931	751	1,266	4,111	(2,700-4,500)	-1,300
7. Net outstanding debt, end year	NA	7,451	10,115	11,230	11,217	10,200	7,500	(14,500)
8. Debt service as percent of total export earnings	NA	15	15	16	17	19	NA	NA
9. End-year gold reserves, value	1,835	7,350	5,590	6,665	7,894	15,736	26,354	-8,687

Sources: For 1970 and 1975-1978, rows 1-8 come from P.G. Ericson and R.S. Miller, "Soviet Foreign Economic Behavior: A Balance of Payments Perspective," in U.S. Congress, Joint Economic Committee, *Soviet Economy in a Time of Change* (Washington, D.C.: U.S. Government Printing Office, 1979), 2:208-244.

For 1979, rows 1-8 come from CIA, *The Soviet Economy in 1978-79 and Prospects for 1980*, ER 80-10378 (June 1980), table 10.

Row 9 is derived as follows. End-year gold-reserve volumes for 1970-1979 come from CIA, *Handbook of Economic Statistics 1980*, table 46. Volume figures for 1980 and 1981 are derived from estimates by J. Aron of New York (*Financial Times*, January 15, 1982). Valuation is at $35 an ounce for 1970 and at 75 percent of the average London price in the last quarter of the year for the other years. The size of Soviet gold reserves (in tons) admittedly is problematic, but I believe that the direction and rough order of magnitude of year-to-year changes in row 9 are reliable. The London gold price and approximate volume of Soviet sales are known, and the rival estimates of production (CIA and Kaser/Consolidated Goldfields) are now closer than they were.

For 1980, I have calculated rows 1 and 2 from the Soviet trade returns, *Vneshniaia torgovlia SSR v 1980g* (Moscow, 1981), using the average of Gosbank ruble-dollar exchange rates for the year and using the Ericson and Miller list of multilateral trade partners of the USSR.

For 1980 and 1981 the estimates of gold sales were obtained by following the J. Aron estimates of sales volume (*Financial Times*, January 15, 1982) at the average London gold prices of the years concerned ($613 and $420 per ounce, respectively).

The net invisibles figures for 1980 are set arbitrarily at the 1978 sum of net shipping, net tourism, and net interest given by Ericson and Miller. The arms sales figures for 1980 and 1981 and the invisibles, gold sales, and current-account figures for 1981 are derived from Wharton Econometric Associates (WEFA), "Soviet Foreign Trade Performance in 1981," April 12, 1982, p. 5. My view is that the WEFA estimates of hard-currency earnings from arms sales may be on the high side in the light of CIA estimates for earlier years.

The end-1980 net debt figure is as estimated by G. Fink, *An Assessment of European CMEA Countries' Hard-Currency Debt* (Wiener Institute fur Internationale Wirtschaftsvergleiche, Forschungsberichte, No. 72, September 1981). The 1981 estimate is based on a gross debt figure of $19 billion (*Economist*, January 30, 1982) less the $4.5 billion of Soviet deposits with BIS reporting banks at September 30, 1981 (*London Times*, February 15, 1982).

Note: Figures in parentheses are rough estimates of lower reliability than estimates not so designated.

Table 3-2
Selected Elements in Soviet Hard-Currency Merchandise Trade, 1970-1981
(millions of dollars)

	1970	1971	1972	1973	1974	1975	1976	1977	1978	1979	1980	1981
1. Hard-currency merchandise exports less hard-currency grain imports	2,672	2,839	2,420	5,275	8,775	6,495	8,389	8,161	11,369	16,224	18,756	
2. Hard-currency merchandise exports less hard-currency food imports	2,493	2,619	2,209	5,857	8,283	5,499	7,615	7,103	10,554	12,956	13,217	
3. Reported machinery orders in the West	500	850	1,700	2,600	4,300	4,650	5,990	3,800	2,800	2,600	2,400	5,024
4. Actual machinery imports from OECD in following year (year $t+1$ shown as year t)	903	1,207	1,729	2,309	4,576	4,909	5,375	5,816	5,346	5,388		
5. Machinery and pipe imports from OECD in the following year	1,122	1,458	2,157	2,964	6,085	6,494	7,064	7,371	7,266	6,952		

Sources: Rows 1 and 2, Ericson and Miller, "Soviet Foreign Economic Behavior," through 1978. Author's calculations are from *Vneshniaia torgovlia SSR* for 1979 and 1980.
    Row 3, Ericson and Miller through 1978. CIA ER-10328 for 1979. For 1980 and 1981, author's compilations of $1,664 million and $2,854 million, respectively, have been scaled up in the ratio of CIA 1979 to Economist Intelligence Unit's *Quarterly Economic Review of the USSR*.
    Row 4, Standard International Trade Classifications (SITC) 7 data from OECD *Statistics of Foreign Trade* (Paris).
    Row 5, Row 4 plus data for SITC 678 and 679.2.

in that year, actual machinery imports of the following year, and machinery and pipe imports of the following year. The lag between orders and deliveries varies a great deal by product, but the view that the lag in the case of Soviet imports of Western machinery averages about one year is consistent with the figures in rows 3 and 4 through, but not beyond, 1976.[7]

Table 3-3 pictures Soviet technology-buying behavior (in the sense of purchases of Western machinery and pipe) in the 1970s as a story of changing propensities to import Western hardware out of current merchandise export earnings of hard currency, with two indicators of financial strength (gold reserves to net debt and gold reserves to hard-currency imports) juxtaposed (rows 4 and 5).

The story that emerges seems reasonably clear from 1970 through 1976 but thereafter rather murky. In general, it does not seem to make much difference whether one takes hard-currency spending on total food or on grain alone as having a priority call on current earnings. The two move fairly closely together, so that the A and B measures of the varying propensities (machinery ordering, machinery importing, and hardware importing) also move closely together. On each of these measures, the period 1970 through 1976 shows a rising propensity for the commercial acquisition of Western technology, with the 1972 harvest failure producing an abrupt but brief leap above the general medium-term tendency of these figures. This development is one that fits our general understanding of Soviet policy in the détente period. It was not, however, a development that initially involved any relaxation of financial caution (rows 4 and 5); Soviet hard-currency liquidity was maintained by the sharply rising gold price from 1970 through 1974.

It is in 1975-1976 that financial problems arise, when another harvest failure (1975) coincides with a growth of debt and a halt in the rise of the world prices of energy and gold. The cutback in orders that follows is large and clear (table 3-3, row 3); it is less clear in the imports series (row 4)—in other words, the apparent one-year average lag of 1970 through 1976 seems to vanish—but there is nonetheless an absolute fall. This is less clear if pipe is added to machinery (row 5), but even here the current-price inflow ceases to rise. These developments are reflected (table 3-3) in a decline in the various propensity series, a decline that is clearest in relation to reported machinery orders.

This cutback in commercial acquisition of Western technology was maintained through 1980. Meanwhile grain imports were not noticeably curbed: hard-currency grain imports were at least $3,300 million in 1979 and $4,253 million in 1980.[8]

From 1978 through 1980 net debt was considerably reduced (table 3-1) against the trend in the rest of the Council for Mutual Economic Assistance (CMEA). This was primarily because nongrain imports, notably machinery,

Table 3-3
Machinery-Import Propensities and Liquidity Measures in Soviet Hard-Currency Trade, 1970-1981

	1970	1971	1972	1973	1974	1975	1976	1977	1978	1979	1980	1981
1. Machinery-ordering propensities												
A. Table 3-2, row 3 divided by row 1	0.187	0.299	0.702	0.493	0.490	0.716	0.714	0.466	0.246	0.160	0.128	
B. Table 3-2, row 3 divided by row 2	.201	.325	.770	.535	.519	.846	.787	.535	.265	.201	.182	
2. Machinery-import propensity												
A. Table 3-2, row 4 divided by row 1	.338	.425	.714	.438	.521	.756	.641	.713	.488	.332		
B. Table 3-2, row 4 divided by row 2	.362	.461	.783	.475	.552	.893	.706	.819	.525	.416		
3. Hardware-import propensity												
A. Table 3-2, row 5 divided by row 1	.420	.514	.891	.562	.692	1.000	.842	.903	.639	.429		
B. Table 3-2, row 5 divided by row 2	.450	.557	.976	.610	.735	1.181	.928	1.038	.688	.537		
4. Gold reserves divided by net debt end year		3.093	4.730	3.602	4.353	.986	.553	.593	.704	1.543	3.514	1.289
5. End-year gold reserves divided by hard-currency imports	.679	.612	.631	.642	.852	.516	.365	.455	.729	1.036	1.145	

Sources: Rows 4 and 5: table 3-1 and Ericson and Miller, "Soviet Foreign Economic Behavior."

Note: The gold reserves series used is not entirely consistent, since valuation from 1971 through 1975 is at 75 percent of the average price for the whole year. The difference should be small.

continued to be held down while the second energy-price jump in 1979-1980 brought further windfall gains in hard-currency export earnings, and gold and hard-currency arms sales were at high levels (table 3-1). As a result the machinery-ordering propensity fell to low levels, and the current account recovered from deficit to surplus. As a result of that and the resumption of a rapid rise in the gold price through most of 1980, the liquidity measures also returned to the high levels of the early 1970s.

Despite these signs of financial recovery, however, machinery ordering stayed at low levels through 1980. Of course, the maintenance of those low levels was itself one of the reasons for the recovery. Nonetheless, if machinery imports from the West, as recorded in the Soviet trade returns, had been as much as 50 percent higher in 1979 than they actually were ($10.4 billion instead of $6.9 billion) and other things had remained equal, there would still, according to the table 3-1 estimates, have been a surplus on the hard-currency current account and the gold reserves would still have covered about nine and one-half months' hard-currency imports instead of about twelve and a half.[9] Similarly, the surge in the value of gold reserves in the following year, combined with the apparent reduction in net debt, did nothing to stimulate a renewed surge of ordering during that year.

It is true that table 3-1 does show a marked recovery in machinery ordering in 1981. Well over half that total, however, consists of machinery ordered for the giant Urengoi-Western Europe natural-gas pipeline project. That project is a special case in two important respects. First, it is a self-financing, product-payback project, which will also (over and above repayment) be capable of making up for at least part of the generally expected fall in hard-currency export earnings from oil in the mid- and late 1980s. Second, it is a project in which the scope for economic leverage by the West is at least matched by the capability for leverage against the West with which it endows the Soviet Union; and such leverage as it provides for Moscow is in the especially useful form of leverage tending to widen cracks in the Atlantic alliance. It is unlikely that there are many more projects with these particular features. For these reasons, and pending further evidence, I am inclined to treat the Uregnoi project as unique and not as evidence of a return to the early 1970s enthusiasm for Western technology imports.

In short, I suggest that Soviet behavior in East-West trade has changed since the mid-1970s. Grain imports remain an item of apparently overriding priority.[10] There has been, however, a retreat from technology importation, which, unlike earlier and briefer retreats between 1955 and 1975, cannot readily be accounted for on financial grounds. The initial cutback in ordering could be explained in this way, and any further cutbacks in 1982 might also be explained by financial stringency, since balance-of-payments difficulties seem to have recurred in 1981-1982 and to have coincided with a slide in the gold price. It is the period 1978 through 1980 that prompts recourse to other sorts of explanation.

There is no shortage of alternative or additional explanations. Soviet-U.S. political relations have been tending downhill since the Nixon administration. The markers on the downward slope have included the Jackson-Vanik Amendment, President Carter's human-rights policies, Angola, the Horn of Africa, Afghanistan, and Poland. And there are signs that, however limited the U.S. role in Soviet nongrain trade, the state of relations with Washington dominates Soviet official thinking about East-West trade. (Given the political influence of the United States in the West and the economic and technological influence of U.S. multinationals, there need be nothing irrational about this focusing on the opposing superpower.)

The political background, however, will be taken here as given. It is the official Soviet perception of the pros and cons of East-West trade that is the subject of the next section. The emphasis will be on discussions relating to technology transfer. Capital-goods and know-how imports, as distinct from the narrower category of machinery and transport equipment, formed 40 to 50 percent of Soviet imports from the West from 1971 through 1976;[11] if food imports retain their apparently fixed priority, Soviet official policies on technology imports can be expected to be the main source of change in Soviet East-West trade policies generally.

Changing Soviet Views on East-West Trade and Technology Transfer

From the mid-1950s to the mid-1970s imported Western capital goods rose from about 2 to 2.5 percent of Soviet equipment investment to a high point of about 8 to 9 percent.[12] The rise was not continuous, but fluctuations seem to be broadly attributable to the exigencies of the hard-currency balance of payments. I have traced elsewhere the evolution of Soviet official thinking that prompted and accompanied this development.[13] Briefly, it can be summarized as a growing perception, diffused in due course to the top leadership, of the benefits forgone in the traditional Stalinist strategy for technological developments. That strategy relied on absorbing Western technology chiefly through channels that minimized personal and commercial contacts and relied heavily on literature screening and the reverse engineering of Soviet designs from individual Western machines. Purchasing Western complete plants, machinery, and know-how on a substantial scale could (at least up to a point) be more cost-effective. The mix of technology-transfer channels used by the Soviet planners duly shifted in that direction as East-West political relations eased. Soviet institutions were modified to facilitate transfer by commercial channels (for example, by the setting up of a specialist foreign-trade organization to engage in license trade and by Soviet adherence to the Paris Convention on the Protection of Industrial Property).

The late Soviet prime minister, Aleksei Kosygin, was easily the most conspicuous top-level spokesman favoring this shift. He argued strongly at the Twenty-third Party Congress in 1966 for a greater use of foreign licenses as a way of economizing on domestic research, development, and innovation (RDI) resources.[14] But he can be identified with such views at least as far back as 1959. The conversion of other members of the leadership to his views (or at least to acceptance of their consequences) was gradual. One may guess that by no means all of the leaderships were ever entirely persuaded, but there is evidence that in about 1968 Brezhnev suspended important reservations at which he had previously hinted.

Since 1979, evidence has accrued that those who are opposed to this development strategy, or who at least counsel the greatest caution in pursuing it, have gained ground. This has culminated in important statements by Brezhnev himself, as well as by Zagladin. Financial difficulties in the mid-1970s, for both the USSR and its East European allies, almost certainly hastened this reappraisal, lending ammunition to the skeptics. The concomitant deterioration in East-West political relations can only have assisted the process.

In the summer of 1979, two articles appeared in *Sotsialisticheskaia industriia* that were outspoken in their criticism of particular decisions to import Western chemical technology.[15] In each case it was asserted that a product or process (specifically paints and varnishes and an ionol manufacturing process) that had been developed by a domestic R&D organization was being unjustifiably neglected in favor of buying foreign technology. The point here is not whether these particular assertions were well founded but that this public airing of critical views about particular technology import deals was unusual.

This note of technological chauvinism has been sounded in a number of Soviet press articles and other publications since mid-1979. An unnamed British firm, for example, was described as demanding over 3 million rubles in gold for an automotive industry license, but a domestic substitute was said to have been used and to have proved to be superior.[16]

In two cases relating to the steel industry, Soviet engineers had developed a superior item of equipment to the stage of a successful prototype; it was not introduced into series production, however, and foreign substitutes were acquired instead that were either more expensive or technically inferior, or both. One of these items of equipment was a press for stamping alloy shapes by the hydroextrusion method, for which it was claimed that Soviet engineering ministries were paying three times as much as they would have had to pay for the homemade version.[17] The second was equipment used in continuous casting, for which the Ministry of Ferrous

Metallurgy "paid in gold, yet it turned out worse than the Uralmash equipment. . . . Of course, it is time to abandon the idea that 'there are no prophets in one's own fatherland.' It is also time to treat the state gold reserves carefully."[18]

None of these articles contains systematic argument about general issues. They indicate, rather, a frame of mind, an attitude of skepticism about the cost-effectiveness of technology imports, which apparently has been encouraged to surface in the press. Insofar as these articles could be said to represent the interests of any particular professional group and not just a general stance of hostility and suspicion toward the outside world, that professional group would be the domestic R&D personnel whose work is neglected in favor of buying foreign know-how. The direction of the implicit argument is not clear, however. It seems to be that the results of domestic R&D are being neglected for one or both of two reasons. The first is the deeply ingrained Russian sense of technological inferiority to the developed, cultivated West. This has been summed up by Zinoviev:

> On top of everything else, there's abroad. Oh, if only it didn't exist! Then we'd be through in two ticks. But Over There they keep on inventing things, and we're obliged to keep up with the competition, to prove our superiority. We hardly have time to steal one machine from them before we have to start thinking about the next. By the time we've introduced something, it's out of date already![19]

The second is the systematic Soviet weakness in moving from the development stage to innovation and diffusion of new technologies.

Two alternative lessons could be drawn from these anecdotes. One is that various influential officials need only to be shaken out of some economically inexplicable sloth and distrust of indigenous know-how for all to be put right. In this case, the message would be that everybody must start thinking positively about home-grown technology, exert themselves to get it introduced and diffused, and not have to pay foreigners for it, simultaneously freeing the Soviet Union from foreign influence in its economy. The other is that domestic technology tends to be only weakly implemented for systemic reasons, and a radical economic reform would raise the cost-effectiveness of domestic RDI relative to that of buying foreign technology. In the absence of such a reform, the maximum financially feasible import of technology remains desirable. In more specialist writings, this conclusion is almost explicitly drawn. In the daily press, on the whole, it is not.

Some other press articles have criticized particular technology-import decisions on different grounds: that import decisions that in principle may have been well founded were in practice badly implemented. Thus there is a story (one of several such) of over half a million rubles' worth of imported equipment lying uninstalled for twelve years in Novopolotsk.[20] A similar tale of imported equipment and chemical reagents for the oil industry that had been abandoned to the elements was presented as a result of culpable negligence and corruption; because of this a deputy minister of the petroleum industry had lost his job.[21] A subtler variation on this theme was the criticism of a decision to import five plants for the manufacture of silos for fodder storage. The special commission that planned the imports was criticized for proceeding at once to the purchase of five plants instead of trying one out first. They were also criticized for not acquiring a special gum that was needed for sealing the inside of the silos. As a result of these errors only 226 instead of 1,200 silos delivered from these plants to Ukranian farms between 1971 and 1980 were said to be in use.[22] In these instances there is neither an explicit nor even a clearly implied criticism of foreign technology as such.

To suggest that all Soviet published sources referring to technology imports have moved massively in this direction would be misleading. There have been exceptions. One of the most notable was an article in *Pravda* in March 1981 by Dzherman Gvishiani, a son-in-law of the late Prime Minister Kosygin and a deputy chairman of the State Committee for Science and Technology.[23] Gvishiani has long been associated with the promotion of technological cooperation agreements with Western firms and with a critical attitude toward domestic Soviet RDI performance.

Gvishiani on this occasion again criticized Soviet RDI organization and performance strongly and went on to reaffirm the early 1970s orthodoxy with which he has been so closely linked: the broadening of trade with capitalist countries was an important factor in increasing the effectiveness of Soviet RDI. He then said something that appeared to be addressed to Western advocates of trade sanctions: "Any artificial hindrances to [the sort] of trade which serves as a means of transfer of the latest technology inevitably inflict damage on the effectiveness [of RDI]." The remark, however, is not given a specific address indicating to whom it is directed.

However this passage is read, it has antichauvinist implications. If the 'artificial hindrances' are to be interpreted as emanating from Washington, then Gvishiani is acknowledging that they can have a deleterious effect on Soviet production. In other words, he is stressing the loss of allocative efficiency arising from the withholding of a particular kind of gain from international trade; he is not stressing the opposing X-efficiency argument to which critics, both East and West, of technology embargoes are inclined to give such emphasis: that the withholding of the benefits of technology transfer only spurs the Soviet RDI system somehow to do better (by inclination, from given resources). This remark by Gvishiani could also be read, however, as being addressed to the Politburo colleagues of his late father-in-law.

More specialist writings still treat the impact of Western technology as a fact of life, which it will continue to be even if the policymakers persist in holding the rate of inflow to relatively modest levels. A particularly illuminating discussion of this and related issues in the context of the machine-tool industry has recently appeared.[24] The participants in this discussion included a deputy minister for the machine-tool industry, the USSR Gosplan official in charge of planning for the industry, several enterprise directors and design engineers, well-known economists S.A. Kheinman and A.G. Aganbegyan, and an official of Stankoimport, the foreign-trade organization responsible for handling both imports and exports of machine tools.

The discussion reveals a consensus on several matters. First, the existing stock of machine tools is grossly maldistributed among users so far as the attainment of maximum output is concerned. Second, the stock has, from the same standpoint, a grossly distorted composition by type of machine. Third, the product mix of machine-tool output is similarly distorted, with particular shortages of high-quality precision and automatic machines and of forging and pressing equipment. Fourth, there are severe defects in the quality of numerically controlled (nc) machine tools, by world standards, with the electronic control elements being the main target for criticism. For all these reasons, the participants in the discussion agree, imports of the more sophisticated kinds of machine tools will have to remain substantial during the Eleventh Five-year Plan (1981-1985).

It is worth noting that the electronics systems for nc machine tools are described as coming both from the Ministry of Instrument-making, Means of Automation and Control Systems (Minpribor) and from the Ministry of the Electronics Industry. The former is oriented mainly toward civilian customers but has been headed for many years by K. Rudnev, an official with a defense-industry background. The Ministry of the Electronics Industry, on the other hand, is mainly concerned with defense production. Its NTs-31 nc system is described (by a Minpribor representative) as "no masterpiece."[25] A machine-tool industry technologist, having criticized Minpribor's attempts at making nc systems, agrees and suggests that the electronics industry developed it by the "thoughtless" repetition of "experimental variants produced by Western firms."[26]

The machine-tool discussion probably could be repeated for most branches of Soviet industry. It illustrates how specific industrial weaknesses continue to generate pressure from enterprises and branch ministries for technology imports. It also illustrates the fact that managers and officials who have to live with these problems and pressures are well aware that the technological weaknesses are rooted in the economic system. The deputy minister of the machine tool industry observes in the course of the discussion that a factory manager who tries to introduce new and improved products will succeed only in worsening his enterprise's success indicators (and therefore losing bonus payments) for three or four years and getting a reprimand for his pains.[27] The senior Gosplan official participating in the roundtable discussion observes (in a separate interview) that the supply system generates requests for inputs (including machines) that are not "responsible" and provides no reliable indication of real requirements.[28] The only person explicitly to draw a drastic conclusion from all this, however, is the Stankoimport official. He states that things will not improve until enterprises can make their own choices among alternative suppliers; output cannot simply be allocated, "as it is in our material-technical supply system."[29]

The Soviet press, then, currently reveals a variety of attitudes toward technology imports. There is the unreconstructed détente view, expressed by Gvishiani, that increasing technology-based trade necessarily brings gains to output through increased participation in international specialization. By implication, there are gains for all involved, though Gvishiani's criticism of Soviet domestic RDI implies that these gains may be especially great for the USSR. There is the practical viewpoint of those engaged in implementing specific plans that such-and-such an increase in capacity by such-and-such a date is possible only if hard currency is spent on acquiring Western equipment to form part of that capacity. On the other hand, there is the view that import decisions of this kind can be and have been unhelpful because the details of acquisition and assimilation are badly worked out. There is also the view (particularly prominent in recent press articles) that such decisions can be and have been wrong in principle because equally good or better indigenous technology is being spurned.

So far as Soviet policy is concerned, the main conclusion I would draw from these press articles and discussions is that a more critical and skeptical view of technology imports is now being encouraged. I would also contend, however, that the objective grounds and professional-group motivation for such criticism have been there all along and that there remains a widely diffused professional interest among Soviet industrial planners and managers in the commercial acquisition of Western technology.

The idea that there is a backlash against technology imports that has top-level support nonetheless is persuasive. The retirement and death of Kosygin in 1980 was preceded by several prolonged spells of enforced inactivity on his part because of ill health. It may be argued plausibly that the semiretirement of the most influential advocate of increased technology imports would have gravely weakened any opposition at the highest level to a shift to more autarkic policies. This happened, moreover, at a time when East-West political animosities were growing fast. However ineffective Western embargo efforts may have seemed to many Western commentators, they were at least sufficiently conspicuous to provide ammunition for those Soviet leaders and senior officials who had never much liked the idea of doing business with the West. Financial difficulties in Eastern Europe could only have fueled such arguments.

This view is amply supported by high-level statements. At the Twenty-fifth Party Congress in February 1976 Brezhnev was still talking Kosygin's language:

> We, like other governments, try to make use of the advantages provided by external economic links for the purposes of mobilising additional opportunities for the successful resolution of economic tasks and the gaining of time, for raising the effectiveness of production and accelerating the progress of science and technology.[30]

In a speech to the Central Committee Plenum of November 1979, however, Brezhnev castigated Gosplan and the minister of the chemical industry, Leonid Kostandov (subsequently promoted), for going ahead "at great cost" with the building of mineral fertilizer plants for which raw materials were lacking when they came on-stream.[31] He did not say that a great many of these plants were imported, but all concerned would have known this.

By this time Brezhnev was in the habit of reading out a short list of key problem areas of the Soviet economy, usually energy, steel, and transport. At the next Party Central Committee Plenum in June 1980, he amended the list to include energy, transport, the use of agricultural equipment and the "import of equipment."[32] This passing reference was expanded in his report to the Twenty-sixth Congress in February 1981:

> We must go into the reasons why we sometimes lose our lead [in technology], spend large sums of money on purchasing abroad equipment and technology that we are fully able to make for ourselves, often indeed at a higher level of quality.[33]

Here Brezhnev is not far from saying the opposite of what he had said at the previous congress. Certainly the implication of the statement is the opposite of Kosygin's call at the 1966 party congress for greater use of foreign licenses in order to avoid wasteful R&D exercises. Of course, the statements do not necessarily and literally contradict one another. They could be interpreted as cautions against going too far from a balanced mix of home-grown and commercially imported technology: first against excessive autarky and then against excessive buying. But the emphasis, at least, has been reversed.

This new emphasis appears also in authoritative statements on foreign trade plans for 1981 through 1985. In 1981 a member of the collegium of the Ministry of Foreign Trade wrote of the foreign-trade plans for this period:

> Stricter attention should be paid to our ability to manufacture certain goods and equipment, so as to avoid spending foreign exchange on purchases of those foreign-made goods and technologies that can be developed and produced in the Soviet Union.[34]

The short passage on foreign trade in the Gosplan chairman's speech to the USSR Supreme Soviet in November 1981 is not inconsistent with this.[35] It can be deduced from the figures he quoted that Soviet merchandise trade turnover with the rest of CMEA is planned to rise at 5.6 percent a year, 1980 through 1985, while non-CMEA trade is to rise at only 2.3 percent a year. These are presumably volume, not value, calculations, and it is unclear whether the implicit non-CMEA trade plan has any operational significance. On the one hand the 1971-1975 plan for Soviet-other CMEA volume growth (of about 9 percent a year) was almost exactly fulfilled, while the implicit plan for non-CMEA trade volume was grossly overfulfilled (percent per annum growth rates of 2.3 plan and 10.7 actual). On the other hand, the only figure for trade volume growth indicated in the 1976-1980 plan was for a 5.4 to 6.2 percent per annum increase in total trade, and the outcome was just within that range, at 5.4.[36] So all we can say is that nothing in the plan figures contradicts the view that official policy is now to hold down the growth of East-West trade.

The main reasons why Soviet policymakers are adopting this stance (if indeed they are) have been indicated. The worsening of political relations has increased worries about dependence and fears of Western economic leverage. The financial troubles of the CMEA group as a whole (rather than the USSR considered separately) also must have played a part. And there has perhaps been some genuine disappointment with the limited gains from technology imports. The reasons for these limited gains are such as will have redirected attention to the shortcomings of the domestic RDI mechanism, which hinder both indigenous innovations and the assimilation and diffusion of imported technology.[37]

Domestic political considerations may also have played a part. Actual or fancied popular perceptions of a greater Western presence in Soviet industry may well have worried the KGB and others in authority. A glimpse of certain popular attitudes, actual or imagined, is provided in a 1979 book. The author describes a visit to the Fiat-designed Tolyatti automobile complex and eventually expounds what I have categorized as the unreconstructed détente view of technology imports. On the way to this exposition he recounts conversations that purport to illustrate some popular misconceptions about the place. " 'Have you heard about Tolyatti? . . . The Italians are in charge of everything there.' " The speaker goes on to describe how on a Saturday the workers' pay envelopes contain not only their pay but also a note that says either that the worker is doing well or, " 'Sorry, you're not shaping up, you're not needed any more . . . thank you and *ciao*.' " The author also describes how rather more sophisticated acquaintances had said to him that a great deal of attention was being paid to the VAZ complex, described as a splendid factory, but there was really nothing to be proud of because the equipment, the plant design, and the product design were all foreign.[38]

The Soviet published source that comes nearest to listing in any systematic way the arguments for a cautious and skeptical approach to East-West trade is a book review in the journal *Voprosy ekonomiki* in the autumn of 1981.[39] The book under review, *Socialism and International Economic Relations*, was written by Nikolai Shmelev of the Institute of Economics of the World Socialist System and published in 1979. In a generally favorable notice, the reviewer acknowledges the gains to be had from increased East-West trade. He goes on, however, to call attention to "the negative phenomena" emerging in economic relations in the second half of the 1970s, particularly, the "sometimes excessive dependence" of some branches of the economy. Other "negative phenomena" that developed in recent years, the reviewer adds, include "the import of inflation" from the capitalist world into some of the socialist countries, "not uncommon" instances of lack of coordinated action by the CMEA countries in Western markets, and "growth of indebtedness of some [CMEA] countries to Western partners." The author therefore is reproached for not having spent more time on the question of containing the size of debt. In general, the reviewer is arguing that the growth of East-West trade has brought some unwelcome results—undue dependence, imported inflation, some weakening of CMEA unity, and the complications of uncontrolled external debt—and needs reappraisal. If the mood of Soviet policymakers has changed in favor of a return to greater self-sufficiency, such views are likely to be well received. It need not follow that any such retreat to semiautarky will be prolonged. It does not appear, however, that Soviet policymakers do not envisage a return to the rapid increase in East-West trade that characterized the early 1970s, at least as long as political relations with the West remain poor.

This section was written as though Western technology was commercially available to the USSR and the chief question was whether (within its financial limits) Moscow would take it or leave it. The role of the West in this trade was viewed, by implication, as a passive one. Broadly, this is a realistic view. Despite a great deal of talk about economic sanctions, the totality of Western firms, banks, and governments has done little to reduce the range and quality of technology and other purchasable items on offer to the USSR. For countries like Poland and Rumania, whose credit ratings have collapsed, the story has been quite different. The fear of not getting paid inhibits suppliers powerfully. Nothing of similar persuasiveness has so far inhibited them with respect to the USSR. (The recent apparent worsening of Soviet liquidity, however, seems to have reinforced the banks' worries about lending to CMEA countries generally and may be making Soviet access to Western credit more difficult and costly.)

The chief effect of the various calls for sanctions (over human rights, Afghanistan, and Poland) has probably been to strengthen the hand of those Soviet leaders and high officials who were opposed to an expansion of East-West trade and to reduce the U.S. share of Soviet-Western trade. It could, in addition, be argued that the attempts to embargo grain exports to the USSR have contributed to the maintenance of a large resource allocation to Soviet agriculture in the face of strong domestic pressures to reduce that allocation. Insofar as this in the medium term inhibits military spending, it is a consequence favorable to the West.

Costs and Benefits of Trade with the West

The Soviet policymakers, then, are pictured here as cutting back on imports from the West in a manner that is discretionary in the sense that it is not enforced, though it may be encouraged, by Western embargoes or Soviet balance-of-payments constraints. What are the Soviets forgoing in acting this way?

Western studies of Soviet-Western trade and technology transfer have achieved a certain amount of common ground among specialists assessing Soviet net benefits from East-West trade. Most analytical effort has gone into the appraisal of technology transfers. Much less attention has been paid to tracing the effects of agricultural imports, but they cannot be disregarded. It should be borne in mind that 12 percent of domestic grain supplies from 1976 through 1980 is a more than marginal contribution from net imports to Soviet consumption and that other food imports are also significant. So far these food imports appear to have enjoyed a higher priority than technology imports. (This is not to say that this priority could not be reappraised, nor does it entail adherence to the particular pattern of food imports observed in the past; substitution of feed grain for livestock products or vice-versa should not be precluded.)

The assessments of the impact of technology imports have varied considerably in scope, aims, methods, and conclusions. It is important therefore to sort them out into several noncompeting groups in order to avoid exaggerating the extent of substantive disagreement. First, there have been attempts at assessing the impact of imports of Western machinery on the output of various parts of the Soviet economy—chiefly the industrial sector—by the use of more-or-less aggregate production function analysis.[40] Second, there have been efforts to predict the same impact through the use of a Kalecki-type growth model.[41] In both cases the point of the exercise is that the imported machines may be expected to embody technologies more advanced, and therefore capable of generating more output from given resources, than the nearest available types of Soviet or East European machinery.

The first approach sets out to measure any increase in output that may in fact arise. The second approach assumes that the superior technology embodied in the imported machines necessarily aids labor productivity in the user industry that reflects the difference between incremental labor productivity (labor productivity on new-vintage machinery) between the exporting and the importing country. The predicted impact then depends chiefly on what that international labor productivity differential is, how large a share the imported machines occupy in total equipment investment in the importing country, how rapidly the latter's capital stock is increasing, and what the time lags are in the process of importation and utilization.

Both of these approaches confront the difficulty that the potential impact of technology imported in embodied form is both direct and indirect. The direct impact is the increase in output arising directly from the use of superior technologies in production with the imported hardware. Indirect benefits may also accrue insofar as (1) the imported machines are used to make producer goods that themselves have productivity-augmenting effects in use, compared with the nearest domestically available equivalents, (2) the technology embodied in the imports is diffused by being copied in domestically made machinery, and (3) organizational slack in industries supplying inputs to the processes using imported technology is reduced by the stimulating effect of having to meet more stringent quality requirements. (The competitive economy of the neoclassical textbook would incorporate indirect effect 1 in the market valuation of direct effort and would allow no room for 3. This does not, of course, render the search for such indirect effects in the Soviet economy redundant.) The production function approach in principle could capture indirect as well as direct effects. The Gomulka approach in principle predicts only direct effects, though the model can be extended to predict certain indirect effects as well.

The third approach has been a disaggregated case-study analysis of particular industrial branches and production complexes. This has been applied chiefly to the chemical, the automobile, and the oil and natural-gas industries.[42] Here the analysis is part qualitative and part quantitative, though not econometric. By elucidating, for example, the questions of lead times in Soviet utilization of imported machinery and of the extent and lead times of subsequent domestic diffusion of imported technologies, these studies can improve the assumptions used in econometric studies.

All of the three approaches have in common a concern with the effect of technology imports on Soviet output. This entails no special concern for high technology as such—either in the sense of products and know-how from research-intensive industries or in the sense of technology capable of improving Soviet military capabilities. The characteristic of the imported technology that is relevant to its impact on Soviet production is the extent to which it is more productive than the nearest equivalent technology available (within a given time frame) from domestic or East European sources. The impact in this sense can be greater in a low-technology area than in a high-technology area if the gap between Soviet and Western attainments is greater in the former than in the latter. There are many instances of large gaps in relatively low-technology areas: mineral fertilizer production, car production, and the manufacture of large-diameter pipe, for example.

The fourth main approach is aimed at assessing the impact of imported Western technology on Soviet military capabilities. Interpreted broadly, this could incorporate all of the previous kinds of analyses and indeed all analyses of East-West trade; it can always be argued that the import of anything, so long as it is more cost-effective than domestic production of that item, must increase total domestic supply of goods and services with given national resources and must therefore reduce the opportunity cost of a given resource allocation to military purposes. Interpreted more narrowly, however, this approach is concerned with the more-or-less direct improvement of military capabilities by the acquisition of technologies that have military applications.[43] There have also been some studies that do not fit into the categories but nonetheless have a bearing here.[44]

From the case studies and from Hardt's writings, there emerge two potential negative indirect effects of technology imports on Soviet policymakers' attainment of their objectives. One is the possibility that a heavy reliance on imported technology in a particular industry in the long run may adversely affect that industry's development insofar as it operates to keep the branch RDI system in a stunted or embryonic state of development. There is some evidence that this may have happened in the Soviet chemical industry. Whether it outweighs the gains from the transformation of that industry over the past quarter of a century with the aid of a large and continuing injection of foreign complete plants and equipment, is a moot point.[45]

The second of the boomerang effects has been suggested by Hardt: that the import of technology for a primarily civilian industry such as car making induces, through linkages presumably not foreseen by the planners, pressures to divert resources to related civilian investment projects (such as the building of roads and service stations), which tend to impede the previously planned allocation of resources. Skillfully as Hardt has argued this case, I remain unconvinced. It seems to require a degree of ineptitude on the part of the Soviet planners and policymakers that even their severest critics would hesitate to assume. It also posits a readiness on the part of the Soviet military and military industries to concede resources to civilian uses, a readiness hard to reconcile with other evidence. Moreover, to fulfill their laudable peace mission, these resource-demanding effects would not have merely to exist; they would have to outweigh the resource-releasing effects that conventional economic analysis would predict for technology imports.

What, then, do the various kinds of studies tell us about the contribution of technology imports from the West to the achievement of Soviet leaders' aims?

The macroeconometric production function approach has been in-conclusive. Using the same data series for the Soviet industrial sector for the 1960-1974 and 1960-1975 periods, Green and Levine, on the one hand, and Weitzman, on the other, reached conflicting assessments. A key Green-Levine estimate was that of the annual growth of 6.6 percent in the official measure of Soviet industrial output, 1966 through 1974, as much as 1.2 per-cent could be attributed to the productivity-augmenting effect of the superior technologies embodied in Western machinery installed in Soviet in-dustry in that period. In view of the small share of Western machinery in the Soviet capital stock, this meant that the imported machines were credited with an exceptionally high marginal product. Weitzman, however, found that the available data could not be used to demonstrate a statistically significant difference between the productivity of imported Western ma-chines and that of indigenous machinery (in which East European machines were in principle included). I have discussed the reasons for these differ-ences at length elsewhere; they stem from differences in the specifications of the production function that were adopted, and here Weitzman's specifica-tions have stronger theoretical justification. But both estimates were in any case vulnerable to severe deficiencies in the data used (affecting, for exam-ple, the direction of change of the stock of imported machinery in some in-dustries as a proportion of the total machinery stock).

The Gomulka approach has the attraction of generating a figure for the contribution of imported machinery to Soviet industrial growth (about 0.5 percent per annum in the mid-1970s) roughly halfway between the assess-ments of Green-Levine and Weitzman (though Weitzman should really be read as demonstrating agnosticism rather than zero effect). It rests, however, on an assumption about the automatic determination of labor-productivity levels by the technological vintage of the machinery used, regardless of other influences. Interpreted loosely as an indication of the maximum extent of direct impact rather than as a precise prediction of the outcome, this may be acceptable. But case-study evidence from the Soviet chemical industry suggests that in that industry at least, labor productivity in imported plants was typically of the order of two-thirds of that of West European labor in similar plants.[46] A difference as large as this, if it were generally the case in Soviet production, would entail a lack of realism in one of the key assumptions of the Gomulka model sufficiently great to cast doubt even on the orders of magnitude of the effects it predicts.

From all these studies, one fact is clear: the share of Western machinery in the Soviet machinery stock has been, and remains, small, almost certainly below 10 percent for the economy as a whole. Unless the indirect effects of imported technology are relatively large, therefore, the limits to the total impact of these imports on Soviet production must be fairly severe.

The case studies tend to modify the picture so far given of a highly un-certain and possibly negligible role for imported Western technology in Soviet development since about 1960. The chemical, motor, and gas-transport in-dustries have been transformed in scale and (in the case of the first two) prod-uct mix by capital-goods and know-how imports. Diffusion of the imported technology emerges generally as very weak and limited, but the imported equipment has generally been put into use and has helped to widen some im-portant bottlenecks, for example, in nutrient supplies to crops, in road-transport capacity, and in energy supply. Assessments for the mineral fer-tilizer industry and for natual-gas pipelines indicate high rates of return to the expenditure on imported capital goods.[47] It is possible, moreover, that the benefits of technology transfer have been such as to carry a larger weight in the fulfillment of Soviet policymakers' objectives than any conventional out-put measure can indicate. In my broad judgment, the benefits have probably been greatest for consumption end uses, typified by cars, plastics, and crop production. I suggest that Soviet leaders have been most willing to rely on technology imports in areas that were not of direct strategic importance, thus helping to maintain the flows of indigenous resources, and indigenous RDI effort in particular, to military-related lines of production.

The case-study findings are nonetheless consistent with Gustafson's analysis of technology imports from the standpont of security concerns. He argues that Soviet capabilities for absorbing, diffusing, and building on im-ported technologies should be a major consideration in Western policies. In general these capabilities are highest in the high-priority, defense-related areas. These areas, to which the traditional rationale of the COCOM list applies, therefore merit the preservation of vigilant control. In other areas, however, the most-effective barriers to technology transfer are those erected by the Soviets against themselves. These areas are also harder for the United States unilaterally to control since a Western consensus outside the strictly and directly military-related embargo is hard to achieve. Since the Soviet ability to profit from this is limited, however, Gustafson concludes that attempts to widen the scope of U.S. export controls should be embarked on only after the most careful consideration and preparation; the United States may well sim-ply lose business to competitors while the Soviets gain rather little from the imports in question.

In general, Gustafson's emphasis on Soviet systemic weaknesses in ex-ploiting commercially imported technology fits well with other analyses. In my view, however, he does not give sufficient weight to the gains that can ac-crue from imported technology even if that technology is only weakly diffused and is not further developed at all. The lesson of the industry case studies is that the Soviet civilian economy has derived benefits from technology im-ports that are large enough to carry some weight with Soviet policymakers.

Conclusions

The information and incentive problems of the Soviet economic system are such that it performs particularly poorly, compared with the West, in two activities in which entrepreneurship is especially important: agricultural production and the introduction and diffusion of new products and processes. The impact of the latter weakness on Soviet military capabilities is minimized in part by the allocation of relatively large quantities of resources to defense and in part by endowing the military with a customer power unique in the Soviet system, so that military production tends to be more cost-effective than civilian.[48] The economy in total, meanwhile, stands to benefit from a kind of systemic comparative advantage in Soviet trade with the West. Soviet exports of gold, fuel, raw materials, and arms (the last named being in part for hard currency, though not directly to the West) are exchanged for agricultural products, capital-goods embodying technology superior to that available within the USSR, and (to a modest extent) licenses and know-how.

It is common sense, and not merely neoclassicism, to suppose that most trade is mutually advantageous in most respects. This seems to be the case for Soviet trade with the West. The Soviet state, however, despite some internal inconsistencies and disagreements, takes part in trade as a unitary actor. Western firms and governments are pursuing aims that often conflict, and they are in many respects in competition with one another. The upshot in the recent past has been that sharpening East-West hostility has not much affected the readiness in practice of the West as a whole to trade with the USSR, though it has affected the readiness of the United States to do so. The deterioration of relations has, however, appeared to prompt a partial Soviet recoil from a fifteen to twenty year process of expanding economic links with the West. Financial concerns have played a part, but they have not been a sufficient explanation of this partial Soviet withdrawal. This change in Soviet policy seems on balance to be contrary to Soviet economic interests, at least in the medium term.

The projection of Soviet-Western economic relations through the rest of the 1980s is a hazardous exercise. Soviet GNP growth, constrained by slowing growth of labor force, energy, and capital inputs, is almost certain to be very slow.[49] Potential benefits from imports of Western food, energy-sector technology, and technology for the steel, engineering, and electronics industries might therefore be expected to loom large in Soviet policymakers' calculations when they are related to supply increments available from other sources.

The pressures on Soviet policymakers to return, insofar as it is financially feasible, to policies involving growing imports of Western technologies therefore should be strong. The fact remains that their recent behavior seems to amount to unenforced abstinence from the benefit of technology imports. If they have shown no such inclination to forgo food imports, that surely indicates where the potential for Western economic pressure is greatest.

Notes

1. See P. Hanson, *Trade and Technology in Soviet-Western Relations* (New York: Columbia University Press, 1981), chap. 7.

2. Surveyed in P. Hanson, *A Backlash against Technology Imports?* Radio Liberty Research Report RL 453/81 (November 12, 1981).

3. *Times* (London), January 25, 1982, p. 4.

4. P. Hanson, "Foreign Economic Relations," in A. Brown and M.C. Kaser, eds., *Soviet Policy for the 1980s* (London: Macmillan, forthcoming).

5. Full details for each year are provided in P.G. Ericson and R.S. Miller, "Soviet Foreign Economic Behavior: A Balance of Payments Perspective," U.S. Congress, Joint Economic Committee, *Soviet Economy in a Time of Change* (Washington, D.C.: U.S. Government Printing Office, 1979), 2:208-244. For all years, however, row 9 (gold reserves) is a series I added, though based on the CIA volume series (extrapolated through 1981 by the percentage increases in a separate series from J. Aron of New York).

6. D.L. Bond and H.S. Levine, "Energy and Grain in Soviet Hard Currency Trade," in U.S. Congress, *Soviet Economy*, 2:244-290.

7. Ericson and Miller, "Soviet Foreign Economic Behavior," table 1.

8. These are the totals for grain imports reported from the United States, Canada, Australia, Argentina, France, and Sweden in *Vneshniaia torgovlia SSR v 1980 g.*, converted to dollars at the annual averages of Gosbank's ruble-dollar rates. I estimate that net grain imports from all sources accounted from 1976 through 1980 for about 12 percent of total, usable, domestic grain supply and that about half of gross imports came from the United States. Hanson, "Foreign Economic Relations," n. 22.

9. I am referring here to totals derived from Soviet trade returns Common Foreign Trade Nomenclature (CTN) 1. These are consistently higher than the OECD data for Standard International Trade Classification (SITC) 7 used in the tables.

10. Not just grain, in fact, but agricultural imports generally. Meat imports for hard currency in 1981 are thought to have exceeded $1 billion. *London Daily Telegraph*, February 9, 1982.

11. Hanson, *Trade and Technology*, p. 132.

12. This section summarizes and updates Hanson, *Backlash*. Hanson, *Trade and Technology*, chap. 8.

13. Hanson, *Trade and Technology*, chap. 5.

14. Quoted in ibid., where the other points in this paragraph are also documented.

15. V. Seliunin, "Podpis' pod kontraktom" [Signature on a Contract], *Sotsialisticheskaia industriia*, June 7, 1979, p. 2; K. Ikramov, "Dvoinaia igra" [Double game], *Sotsialisticheskaia industriia*, July 6, 1979, p. 3. The Western suppliers were not named.

16. *Pravda*, June 14, 1980, p. 3.

17. Iu. Kuz'ko, "Kupit' prosche?" [Buying Simpler?], *Pravda*, June 2, 1981, p. 3.

18. V. Parfenov, "Inzhenery" [Engineers], *Pravda*, June 29, 1981, p. 2.

19. A. Zinoviev, *The Yawning Heights* (Harmondsworth, Middlesex: Penguin, 1981), pp. 513-514. Zinoviev wrote this book in 1974.

20. *Pravda*, August 20, 1981, p. 3.

21. V. Sevast'ianov, "Izderzhki popustitel'stva" [The Costs of Toleration], *Sotsialisticheskaia industriia*, October 4, 1981, p. 2.

22. V. Vasilets, "Bashennaia likhoradka" [Tower Fever], *Pravda*, January 16, 1982, p. 2.

23. Dzh. Gvishiani, "Glavnyi put' povysheniia effektivnosti proizvodstva" [Chief Path to Raising Production Efficiency], *Pravda*, March 27, 1981, pp. 2-3.

24. "Vokrug stanka" [About the Machine], *Ekonomika i organizatsiia promyshlennogo proizvodstva (EKO)*, no. 1 (1982), pp. 47-87. The same issue also contains an article on the industry by Kheinman (pp. 25-47) and an interview with the Gosplan official (pp. 125-135).

25. Ibid., p. 69.

26. Ibid., p. 72.

27. Ibid., pp. 63-64.

28. "Gosplan: planirovat' s otkrytymi glazami" [Gosplan: Planning with Open Eyes], *EKO*, no. 1 (1982):128, 132.

29. "Vokrug stanka," p. 66.

30. *Pravda*, February 25, 1976, p. 3.

31. Ibid., November 28, 1979, p. 2.

32. *Ekonomicheskaia gazeta*, 1980, no. 26, p. 3.

33. *Pravda*, February 24, 1981, p. 5.

34. V. Klochek, "Soviet Foreign Trade on the Threshold of the Eleventh Five-Year Plan Period," *Foreign Trade*, no. 5 (1981):14.

35. *Pravda*, November 18, 1981, p. 3.

36. P. Hanson, *USSR: Foreign Trade Implications of the 1976-80 Plan* Special Report No. 36 (London: Economist Intelligence Unit, 1976), and *Vneshniaia torgovlia SSSR v 1980 g.*

37. Hanson, *Trade and Technology*, chaps. 9-12. An alternative policy conclusion that could be drawn from these limited gains is that too rapid an increase in technology imports was attempted in the early 1970s, in the

sense that a longer lead time was needed for assimilation of this technology than the planner had originally supposed. Thus the Tenth Five-year Plan (10 FYP) could have been intended as a period of digestion following a spell of rapid acquisition in the 9 FYP, a sequence analogous to that of the 1 and 2 FYPs with respect to total investment. I am indebted to Gregory Grossman for this suggested interpretation. As a clue to future Soviet policies (in the 11 FYP) it may fit in with the marked slowdown planned in the growth of Soviet investment. It could be argued, of course, that Western credits can be used to moderate the slowdown in investment growth and raise the share of Western machinery in a slower-growing investment effort. The imports from the West, however, have been strongly associated with new-plant investment and therefore have had fairly rigid requirements for complementary domestic construction inputs. Insofar as the investment program as a whole is strongly constrained by the limitations on construction-industry capacity, this in itself could be a significant domestic economic reason for holding down imports of Western embodied technology. I am indebted to discussions with Don Green and John Hardt for this argument.

38. Pavel Volin, *Volzhskoe pritiazhenie* [*Volga Attraction*] (Moscow, 1979), pp. 11-13. I am grateful to Michael Berry for drawing my attention to this book.

39. A. Boichenko reviewing *Sotsializm i mezhdunarodnye ekonomicheskie otnosheniia* [*Socialism and International Economic Relations*] in *Voprosy ekonomiki*, no. 9 (1981):145-147.

40. The main articles are D.W. Green and H.S. Levine, "Macroeconometric Evidence on the Value of Machinery Imports to the Soviet Union," in J.R. Thomas and U. Kruse-Vaucienne, eds., *Soviet Science and Technology* (Washington, D.C.: George Washington University, 1977), pp. 394-425, and M.L. Weitzman, "Technology Transfer to the USSR: An Econometric Analysis," *Journal of Comparative Economics* (June 1979). A fuller listing is given in Hanson, *Trade and Technology*, p. 156; the same source, pp. 157-160, presents some production function estimates for the Soviet chemical industry in which I have tried, without attaining statistically satisfactory results, to avoid some of the methodological weaknesses and data defects revealed in discussions of previous such estimates.

41. Notably S. Gomulka, "Import of Technology and Growth: Poland 1971-1980," *Cambridge Journal of Economics* (March 1978). An adaptation of Gomulka's formula to provide an estimate (prediction) of impact on the Soviet industrial sector is given in Hanson, *Trade and Technology*, pp. 154-155.

42. Chemical: Hanson, *Trade and Technology*, chaps. 10, 11. Automobile: G.D. Holliday, "Western Technology Transfer to the Soviet Union, 1928-37 and 1966-75: With a Case-Study in the Transfer of Auto-

motive Technology'' (Ph.D. diss., George Washington University, 1978). Oil and natural gas: R.W. Campbell, *Soviet Technology Imports: The Gas Pipeline Case*, Discussion Paper No. 91 (Santa Monica, Calif.: California Seminar on International Security and Foreign Policy, February 1981); U.S. Congress, Office of Technology Assessment, *Technology and Soviet Energy Availability* (Washington, D.C., 1981).

43. The literature on this topic is extensive. The following book subsumes much earlier analysis. Thane Gustafson, *Selling the Russians the Rope? Soviet Technology Policy and U.S. Export Controls*, R-2649-ARPA (Santa Monica, Calif.: The Rand Corporation, April 1981).

44. John Kiser, *Report on the Potential for Technology Transfer from the USSR to the United States* (Washington, D.C.: Department of State, 1977); John P. Hardt, ''The Role of Western Technology in Soviet Economic Plans,'' in NATO Economic Directorate, *East-West Technological Cooperation* (Brussels: NATO, 1976), pp. 315-329.

45. P. Hanson, *Soviet Strategies and Policy Implementation in the Import of Chemical Technology from the West, 1958-1978*, Discussion Paper No. 92 (Santa Monica, Calif.: California Seminar on International Security and Foreign Policy, March 1981).

46. Hanson, *Trade and Technology*, chap. 11.

47. Ibid., chap. 10; Campbell, *Soviet Technology Imports*.

48. For an assessment of these two influences on the Soviet defense burden, see Abraham S. Becker, *The Burden of Soviet Defense: A Political-Economic Essay* R-2752-AF (Santa Monica, Calif.: The Rand Corporation, October 1981).

49. See Abram Bergson, ''Soviet Economic Slowdown and the 1981-85 Plan,'' *Problems of Communism* (May-June 1981):24-37; Hanson, ''Economic Constraints on Soviet Policies in the 1980s,'' *International Affairs* (Winter 1980-1981):21-43. Something of the order of 2 percent a year seems possible, though some analysts are going so far as to suggest that Soviet real GNP growth has already halted. See Peter Wiles, ''The Soviet Investment Deflator Again,'' *Soviet Studies* 34, no. 4 (1982):616. I make the increase in standard coal equivalent (sce) of Soviet output of the three main fuels in 1981 only 2.0 percent (derived from *Pravda*, January 24, 1982), and conclude that per capita production of meat and dairy produce has not been rising (Economist Intelligence Unit, *Quarterly Economic Review of the USSR*, 1982, No. 2).

4

Soviet Energy Prospects and Their Implications for East–West Trade

Ed. A. Hewett

Soviet leaders face a number of very difficult political-economic problems that even in the best of circumstances mean that Soviet economic performance in the 1980s will be the worst it has been in the postwar period. Within the Soviet Union, demographic problems, a secular decline in productivity growth rates, and continuing difficulties in agriculture will probably keep the GNP growth rate below 3 percent per annum. Barring the unlikely event of a quick resolution of U.S.-Soviet strategic-arms issues, Soviet military expenditures will have to grow faster than GNP, and consumption and investment will suffer, with possible economic and political consequences.

Economic prospects are no better in other socialist countries. Eastern Europe is only now initiating serious attempts at adjustment to an energy-expensive world, an adjustment they must make in the face of a Soviet refusal to increase exports of key industrial materials at subsidized prices. What must worry the Soviet leaders the most is that these adjustments will at best cause East European living standards to stagnate; they could well fall, posing a substantive threat to political stability in Eastern Europe.

Other problems surround Soviet economic, and particularly political, relations with the West. In the last few years U.S. defense policy and U.S. foreign policy have taken a turn unanticipated and unwelcomed in the USSR. Now in Soviet leaders' calculations on how to deal with problems in their domestic economy and in the empire, they must factor in a perceived resurgence in the military threat from the West, led by the United States.

Soviet energy prospects are a common thread interconnecting these areas of concern to Soviet leaders. Energy plays a role in the Soviet economy, not only for industry but also as a source of approximately 70 percent of all hard-currency earnings from merchandise exports. Those earnings are spent on food and raw-material imports necessary to sustain current living standards and output and machinery imports useful in increasing industrial productivity, including productivity in the fuel industry.

In the critical arena of Soviet-East European relations, energy has been a key Soviet export for two decades. In the period following the OPEC price increases, Soviet energy-export prices to Eastern Europe lagged far behind

I am grateful to Robert Campbell for his helpful comments on an earlier draft of this chapter.

those prevailing on world markets, so much so that in 1980, Soviet oil exports to Eastern Europe sold (at official exchange rates) for under one-half of the world market price.[1] The Soviet Union is endeavoring to increase those prices considerably (and reduce the subsidies) and simultaneously to reduce East European purchases of Soviet oil and free up oil for hard-currency earnings. Yet they are seriously constrained by the fear that a major increase in Soviet oil-export prices to Eastern Europe would create economic difficulties in that region, which would almost certainly generate political problems. In the near term Soviet energy and economic problems are likely to grow worse and pressures on Eastern Europe will grow, increasing the likelihood of serious political-economic problems in that region.

The general state of East-West political and economic relations can be influenced by, and in turn can influence, all of the above factors. Economic problems and political unrest in Eastern Europe will tend to increase tensions in East-West relations. On the other hand Western loans and equipment sales to the USSR now, in exchange for gas in the mid-1980s, could contribute to releasing some tension in the entire system by alleviating some of the pressure on Soviet energy balances, which could alleviate some of the Soviet pressure on Eastern Europe.

Therefore although energy is not the exclusive determinant of near-term prospects for Soviet economic performance, Soviet-East European relations, and East-West relations, it is an important variable determining how each of those areas will develop and interact in the future. This chapter explores the prospects for Soviet energy and the policy issues the United States faces regarding those energy prospects.

Soviet Energy Prospects through the Mid-1980s

The important issue concerning Soviet energy in the 1980s is not whether the Soviet Union may in the near term become a net importer of energy—that is highly unlikely—but how much energy will be available for export. The focus thus is on the energy balance; both total energy supplies and total energy demands in the future are important. If all energy-supply plans are met in the Soviet economy except for oil, and the shortfall there is, say, 0.9 million barrels per day (mbd), the significance of that shortfall is in large measure a function of whether Soviet planners manage simultaneously to save an equivalent of 0.9 mbd of energy on the demand side (without reducing output below plan). If they have not managed that, then the oil production shortfall will be important; if they have managed, then they have met the most important energy target—the balance—without sacrificing output. If they manage all of this by the extensive use of other resources—by substituting labor for machines at a tremendous cost to other sectors—then they will have met their energy plan at a cost to the economy overall, and they will violate other parts of the output plan.

Even when the current discussion on Soviet energy is couched in terms of the energy balance, there is still a tendency to be preoccupied with the uncertainties on the supply side. There are legitimate areas of disagreement there, but nevertheless the sum total of the difference between most of the pessimists and most of the optimists is really a difference between meeting the supply plan and missing it by, say, 1 mbd of oil equivalent (mbdoe).

In fact there is probably at least as much uncertainty, probably much more, on the demand side. Suppose the USSR achieves 2.5 percent GNP growth on average over this five-year plan period. If it continues to have the energy-GNP elasticity of previous years (approximately 1.25), then energy demand will go up about 4 mbdoe relative to 1980. If, on the other hand, it achieves an energy-GNP elasticity of 0.75, which is still far above what Western countries have exhibited in recent years (for example the United States and Japan have achieved elasticities of approximately 0.33), energy demand will rise only 2 mbdoe. The difference, 2 mbdoe, is a significant amount of uncertainty (equal to about one-half of 1980 Soviet energy exports), far more than probably currently exists on the supply side. Therefore a serious attempt at estimating the Soviet energy balance must devote at least equal attention to supply and demand. And any effort to reduce uncertainty should go on the demand side.

Prospects for Soviet Energy Supplies

Soviet primary energy production in 1980 and official plans for 1985 are presented in table 4-1. The first and third columns of the table give data in natural units; the second and fourth columns convert the data to mbdoe in order to render them internally comparable. As the table shows, petroleum is, and will remain, the most important source of primary energy in the USSR, but natural gas is growing rapidly in importance. Coal is an important source of energy but a stagnating one, and nuclear and hydro power are relatively insignificant energy sources.

The last column of this table illustrates how critical natural gas is to the near-term energy prospects for Soviet energy. Of the planned increment of 4.98 mbdoe of energy production during the period 1981 to 1985, 3.20 mbdoe, or 64 percent of the total, will be natural gas. For coal and petroleum the planned increments are quite modest, with planned levels for 1985 below what had been planned a few years ago for 1980. The planned nuclear increment is probably overly ambitious, but in any event nuclear is still such a small portion of the balance that shortfalls here are relatively unimportant for the overall balance, although they can be quite important for electricity supplies in the European USSR.

Table 4-1

Soviet Energy Supplies: Actual for 1980 and Planned for 1985

	Actual 1980		Planned 1985		Increment 1985-1980
	Natural Units[a]	mbdoe[b]	Natural Units[a]	mbdoe[b]	mbdoe
Petroleum	603	12.03	630	12.60	0.54
Natural gas	435	7.10	630	10.32	3.20
Coal	716	6.98	775	7.20	.22
Nuclear	73	.30	220[c]	1.02	.72
Hydro	184	.76	230	1.06	.30
Total[d]		27.17		32.20	4.98

Sources: Actual data are from *Narodnoe khoziastvo,* 1980; plan data are from the final version of the Eleventh Five-Year Plan, published in *Pravda,* November 18, 1981.

[a]Petroleum and coal are measured in millions of tons; natural gas in billion cubic meters; and electricity in billion kilowatt hours.

[b]Million barrels per day of oil equivalent.

[c]Estimated. The final plan figures give only a joint figure for nuclear and hydro.

[d]Excludes minor primary sources, such as firewood and peat.

In assessing the realism of these supply plans, they must be viewed as a whole for several reasons. First, the ultimate source of interest in Soviet energy balances is not the adequacy of domestic energy supplies overall (that is not in doubt) but rather the availability of exportable energy supplies. For that reason the coal-output plan is just as important to Soviet oil exports as the oil-output plan. If, for example, the Soviets meet their oil-output plan but fall short of their coal plan by 75 million tons (0.7 mbdoe), that is virtually the same as meeting the coal plan and falling 0.7 mbd short on the oil plan. Either way boilers will draw 0.7 mbd of *mazut* (crude oil) that otherwise would have been available for export.

Another reason to view the energy-supply plans as a whole is that the constraints on meeting the plans are in part economic, relating to capital scarcities in the near term. Whether these plans can be attained will be determined in part by Soviet economic performance and in particular by investment resources made available to the energy sector in the context of a very tight investment budget for 1981 through 1985. Although it is conceivable that Soviet planners could meet plans for any one of these energy carriers by devoting enough capital and labor to that industry, the important question is if they can simultaneously find enough capital and labor to meet the plans in all the energy industry, with enough left over to meet demands in other parts of the economy, including the military.

Until and if more data on investment plans become available, it will be difficult to say how this will turn out. If Soviet planners are forced to choose among the energy carriers, they will choose natural gas, at least in the near term. The reason for the growing preference for natural gas is easily seen in the data contained in figures 4-1 through 4-3, which record monthly outputs, respectively, of coal, oil, and natural gas, along with the annual plan targets. In each figure, the relatively smooth line is a trend for monthly output of the energy carrier, estimated by regressing a second degree polynomial in time on the log of output of that energy carrier. The fluctuations of actual output around the trend are indicated by the shaded areas (above the trend) and the areas filled with diagonal lines (below the trend). The straight lines at twelve-month intervals are annual plan targets. As an approximation one would expect either rising or falling output to cut through the target about midyear in order for the plan to be fulfilled.

In the coal industry the annual plan has not been fulfilled since 1976, and in fact in recent years plans have been underfulfilled even though they have been modified downward over time. At the beginning of the Tenth Five-year Plan, the intention was to be producing 790 million to 810 million tons of coal by 1980, which would have been 2.16 million to 2.21 million tons per day. These projections were soon recognized as impossible, and so in fact was the final annual plan for 1980 of 745 million tons, or 2.04 million tons per day. Actual output was 716 million tons, or 1.96 million tons per day. Also the variance of coal output has increased noticeably in recent years, so that in 1981 the Soviet economy set monthly coal-output records on the high side and the low side.

The problems in the coal industry are structural and will not soon be rectified without a considerable commitment of new investment funds (U.S. CIA 1980b). Apparently in recognition of these problems, planners switched in 1977-1978 away from a heavy emphasis on coal toward a more pronounced emphasis on hydrocarbons.[2] Figure 4-2 shows monthly output data for petroleum and condensate output in the Soviet Union since 1976. In 1977 as Soviet planners were beginning to be literally pushed away from coal, they also experienced their first small plan underfulfillment in oil (10.92 mbd versus a plan of 11.0 mbd), which coincided with the April 1977 CIA report alleging serious problems in the Soviet oil industry (U.S. CIA 1977). In the December 1977 plenum of the party, Brezhnev formalized the switch toward hydrocarbons with an emphasis on oil and followed his speech with a spring trip to Siberia, presumably to spur the oil workers on.

The 1978 oil plan, originally set at 11.6 mbd, was revised downward in late 1977 to 11.5, and still actual output was slightly below that, despite what appear to have been heroic efforts in the fourth quarter. The 1979 plan, even though significantly revised downward (from 12.2 mbd to 11.86 mbd) in recognition of the impossibility of the 1980 plan, was underfulfilled (actual was 11.71 mbd), as was the revised 1980 plan. And the 1981 plan, which was very modest indeed relative to 1980 (12.2 mbd), was still slightly underfulfilled at 12.18 mbd. The 1982 plan calls for output of 12.28 mbd— an increase over 1981 of 0.8 percent—but for the first quarter of 1982,

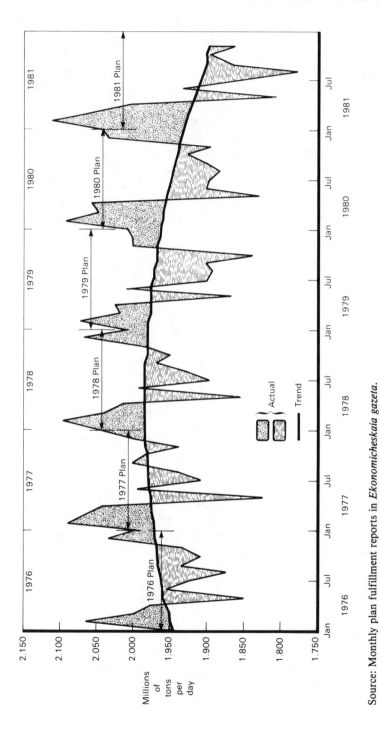

Source: Monthly plan fulfillment reports in *Ekonomicheskaia gazeta*.

Note: Trend is Log (X) = 0.666 + 0.00132T − 0.00002T^2.

Figure 4-1. Monthly Coal Output in the USSR, January 1976-December 1981: Trend and Actual

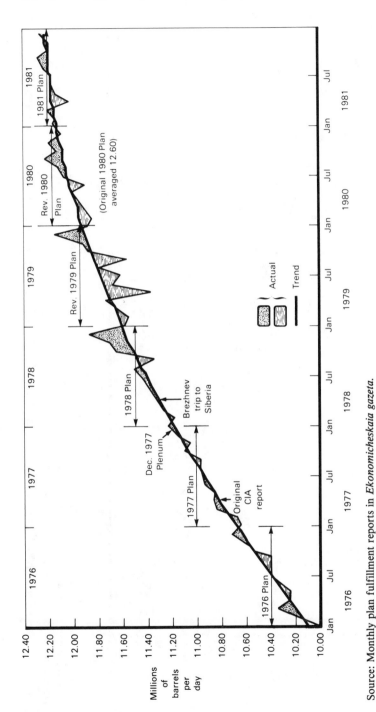

Source: Monthly plan fulfillment reports in *Ekonomicheskaia gazeta.*

Note: Trend is Log (X) = 2.308 + 0.0051T − 0.00003T².

Figure 4-2. Monthly Petroleum and Condensate Output in the USSR, January 1976-December 1981: Trend and Actual

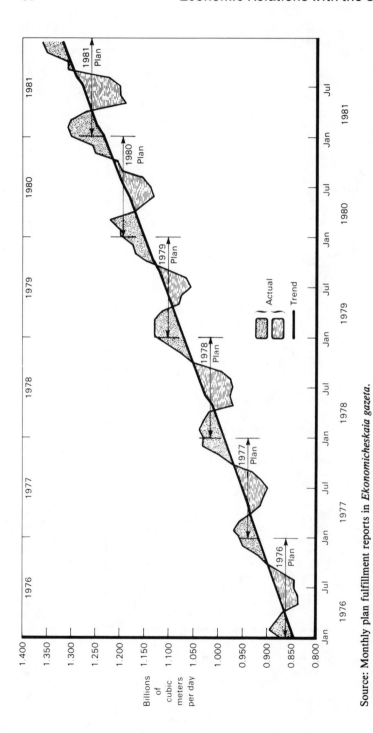

Source: Monthly plan fulfillment reports in *Ekonomicheskaia gazeta*.

Note: Trend is Log (X) = $0.173 + 0.0067T - 0.00001T^2$.

Figure 4-3. Monthly Gas Output in the USSR, January 1976-December 1981: Trend and Actual

output stagnated relative to the first quarter of 1981, indicating that oil output may have peaked.[3]

The continuing problem in the oil industry caused planners in the latter years of the Tenth Five-year Plan to shift their attention to the one truly successful energy carrier in the Soviet economy, natural gas. As figure 4-3 shows, gas output apparently is locked on an output escalator, as annual outputs consistently meet or exceed the plans set for them. This was not always the case. In fact, until the mid-1970s, the gas industry was missing plans more often than meeting them (Stern 1981). But the enormous reserves in northwest Siberia along with increasing problems in other energy carriers have gradually drawn planners into a full commitment to natural gas. This commitment is reflected in the fact that 64 percent of the planned increment to Soviet energy outputs will be in the form of natural gas. In fact it would not be at all surprising if natural gas accounted for 100 percent of actual net energy output increases through 1985.

The plans to increase gas production rest almost solely on plans to increase the output of the Urengoi gas field in northwest Siberia from an output of 50 billion cubic meters (bcm) in 1980 to an output of 250 bcm in 1985 (a change from 0.82 to 4.10 mbdoe). This increase will be accomplished by constructing six fifty-six-inch gas pipelines—five primarily for domestic use and one for export to Western Europe—of a total length of 20,000 kilometers. Construction of three of these lines (including the line to Western Europe) is already underway. There are no doubts about the enormity of gas reserves in the USSR or about the Urengoi field itself, whose estimated reserves of 6 trillion cubic meters place it among the largest gas fields in the world. The question of whether the 1985 plan of 630 bcm will be achieved is primarily a question of whether these lines will be put into operation on time.[4]

Soviet planners must grapple with two types of constraints in their attempt to meet the gas plan: equipment and organizational. The equipment constraints relate primarily to the fact that the Soviets do not produce sufficient fifty-six-inch pipe or the optimum types of compressors needed to keep pressure up in the pipes. This is a problem not just for the West European line but for the five other lines, and as a consequence the implication of Soviet gas-expansion plans is that they could be shopping on world markets for large amounts of compressor stations, pipe, and pipelaying equipment.

All of these items are easily obtainable from Western markets, and the credits probably will be available (in large part from European governments) to finance Soviet purchases. Therefore this equipment constraint is one that can be overcome if the Soviets are willing to increase considerably, for a decade or so, their net debt to Western governments and banks. This assumes that East-West tensions do not substantially deteriorate, for in that case credits could dry up.

The organizational constraint is much more serious because imports cannot assist the Soviets in overcoming it. Soviet plans call for laying the six new pipelines at a pace more than twice that of previous years, something they intend to achieve in part by dramatically increasing the productivity of pipelaying crews. Under these general conditions of taut plans and in the harsh climatic and geographical conditions characteristic of the starting sections of each pipe, it is important that pipelaying and other ancillary services be extremely well organized. That is not the case now or in the near future. Soviet planners are encountering tremendous difficulties in coordinating new investments in Siberia for oil and gas. Of the many difficulties, those that seem most intractable relate to the unwillingness of Soviet industry to produce and deliver on time machinery and equipment appropriate to arctic conditions; inability or unwillingness of construction ministries to build infrastructural facilities important to supporting pipeline construction and operations; only a very modest use of modern modular construction techniques in compressor stations; and a severe labor shortage. The Soviets are fully aware of these problems but have taken no steps to deal adequately with them; therefore it seems likely that pipeline construction will proceed behind schedule and so will gas output. They probably will not meet the plan of 630 bcm by 1985 but rather are more likely to produce about 600 bcm (a shortfall equivalent to 0.49 mbdoe).

It is also unlikely that plans for the other energy carriers will be met. Oil production is likely to stagnate, and thus even the modest planned increase to 12.6 mbd seems optimistic. A much more likely figure would be around 11.7 mbd.[5] Soviet planners are concerned about performance problems in the coal industry and are taking measures (for example, increased wages) to improve matters. Fulfilling the plan of 770 million metric tons (mmt) seems unlikely. My guess is 750 mmt, and that all of the increment will be low-calorie coal from West Siberia, which means that raw-coal tonnage may rise while coal output in mbdoe may stagnate. (This is a guess rather than a firm projection. The important variable here is the calorific content of the coal, not the raw tonnage; and it seems likely that calorific content will fall. Notes a and g to table 4-3 outline the assumptions used here.) The nuclear program is probably too optimistic, and the Office of Technology Assessment estimate of 200 billion kilowatt hours (BKWH) seems more reasonable (instead of the planned 220) and is a more likely outcome (Office of Technology Assessment 1981, pp. 137-138). I assume hydropower develops as planned.

To summarize, 1980 Soviet energy production in the major primary energy carriers was 27.17 mbdoe. Official plans call for production in 1985 of 32.20 mbdoe, which represents an increment to energy production of 4.89 mbdoe. In fact 1985 output is much more likely to be 30.25 mbdoe, an increment of 3.07 mbdoe. That total increment approximates the increment in natural-gas production (3.20 mbdoe), with the increments in hydro and nuclear counterbalancing the fall in oil and with coal production stagnating in calorific terms.

If in fact plans are underfulfilled in this way it will be an unpleasant surprise for planners but one that will unfold gradually over the entire five-year period (as, for example, is occurring now in the problems in oil and coal production). Whether this will dramatically affect export prospects cannot be ascertained without projecting energy demands in the USSR over the same period.

Prospects for Soviet Energy Demand
in the Mid-1980s

The Soviet Union most likely consumes much more energy than is typical of other countries operating at similar levels of economic activity, although that is more a matter of conventional wisdom (particularly among Soviet economists) than a well-established research finding. In fact in the early 1970s the USSR consumed no more energy than one would have expected (by world standards) of a country at its level of development, with its geographic size, structure of GNP, and relative reliance on coal (Hewett 1980). What is probably true is that in the early 1970s in industry, the Soviet economy was an unusually high consumer of energy, while in other sectors it was using possibly less than was typical of other countries. That is certainly what is suggested in the very high share of industry in Soviet energy use. Were similar calculations made for 1980, they could well show an even higher relative use of energy in industry and relatively high use in other sectors in the light of advances in energy conservation in the West.

This apparent overconsumption of energy in industry creates uncertainty in future demand projections for the USSR. Now that Soviet planners perceive that they have a problem in the energy sector, they appear to be taking energy conservation quite seriously, and any efforts could translate into tangible conservation gains.[6]

Research on USSR energy demand is not well enough advanced in the East or the West to offer more than tentative conclusions on what is possible on this side of the balance. The data in table 4-2 provide basic information on the structure of Soviet energy demand in the latter half of the 1970s in a world context and serve as a necessary starting point for projections. All of the energy data are in mbdoe; the growth rates are average annual growth rates taken using the end points. The first four rows of the table give total primary energy (TPE) requirements, which is gross energy production, plus net imports and stock changes. Total final consumption (TFC) data, which are in the remaining rows of the table, are TPE less losses from electricity generation, other energy-transformation processes, and the transportation of energy.

Table 4-2
Energy Consumption in the Soviet Union, Europe, and North America, 1973-1980

	IEA Europe			IEA North America			Soviet Union		
	1973	1979	Per Annum Growth Rate	1973	1979	Per Annum Growth Rate	1975	1980	Per Annum Growth Rate
	(mbdoe)			(mbdoe)			(mbdoe)		
TPE requirements	19.60	21.14	0.013	39.74	41.97	0.009	20.27	23.78	0.032
Solid fuels	4.58	4.64	.002	7.50	8.16	.014	7.67	7.64	-.001
Oil	11.34	11.14	-.003	17.96	19.17	.011	7.37	9.07	.042
Natural gas	2.18	3.24	.068	11.31	10.46	-.013	4.96	6.63	.060
TFC	14.80	15.66	.009	28.72	30.06	.008	15.16	18.15	.037
Industry	6.07	5.86	-.006	9.31	8.88	-.008	8.84	10.44	.034
Solid	1.22	1.28	.008	1.96	1.85	-.010	2.47	2.63	.013
Oil	2.97	2.34	-.039	1.94	2.41	.037	1.62	1.76	.017
Natural gas	.98	1.22	.037	3.89	2.96	-.045	1.82	2.51	.068
Electric	.90	1.00	.018	1.53	1.66	.014	2.40	2.98	.044
Transport	2.75	3.21	.026	8.89	9.49	.011	1.26	2.10	.108
Oil	2.67	3.15	.028	8.88	9.48	.011	.87	1.77	.153
Residential-commercial	5.32	5.87	.017	9.45	10.43	.017	2.55	2.58	.002
Solid	.83	.65	-.040	.12	.11	-.014	.92	.76	-.037
Oil	2.92	2.81	-.006	3.59	3.72	.006	.28	.20	-.065
Natural gas	.79	1.37	.096	3.80	4.22	.018	.63	.75	.035
Electric	.78	1.03	.047	1.95	2.38	.034	.65	.76	.032
Gross domestic product			.021			.026			.026

Sources: European and North American energy data are from International Energy Agency, *Energy Policies and Programs of IEA Countries, 1980 Review* (Paris: IEA, 1981); Soviet energy data are adapted from Robert W. Campbell, *Soviet Energy Balances*, The Rand Corporation, Report R-2257-DOE (December 1978), and Robert W. Campbell, "Energy in the USSR to the Year 2000" (paper presented to the Conference on the Soviet Economy to the Year 2000, Airlie House, Virginia, October 23-25, 1980; revised February 1981). The IEA North America growth rate is that for the United States and Canada taken from U.S. CIA, *Handbook of Economic Statistics 1980* (Washington, D.C.: Government Printing Office, 1981). The IEA Europe GDP growth rate is taken from the same source and is the EEC minus France. The Soviet GDP growth rate is a combination of indices for the CIA *Handbook* and Wharton Econometric Forecasting, *Centrally Planned Economic Outlook* (September 1981).

Note: The following abbreviations are used: TPE, total primary energy production plus net imports, bunkers, and stock changes; TFC, total final consumption (TPE minus losses in electricity production, other energy transformation, and energy transportation); IEA, International Energy Agency; mbdoe = million barrels per day oil equivalent.

In 1975 Soviet TPE and TFC were about on a level with that of the European members of the International Energy Agency (essentially Europe except France) and about one-half of North American TPE and TFC in 1973. But between 1973 and 1979 TPE and TFC barely rose in the West, averaging around 1 percent per annum, even though GNP grew at twice or more those rates. IEA North American, for example, had an energy-to-GNP elasticity on TFC of 0.008/0.026 = 0.31, which was down from an elasticity of about unity in the pre-OPEC period.

During approximately the same time period, the Soviet Union increased TPE by 3.2 percent per annum and TFC by 3.7 percent per annum, while GNP growth rates averaged only 2.7 percent per annum. On TFC this is an energy-to-GNP elasticity of 1.42, and on TPE it is an elasticity of 1.23, which is very similar to the energy-to-GNP elasticity in the Soviet Union over the last two decades. (Using data on Soviet TPE and Western estimates of Soviet GNP, I have estimated for 1960 through 1979 a total energy-to-GNP elasticity of 1.13; for 1970 through 1979, it is 1.26; these are coefficients in regressions of log energy against log GNP. For natural gas the elasticities for 1960 through 1979 and 1970 through 1979 are 2.24 and 1.91, respectively. For oil they are, respectively, 1.50 and 1.55.) In brief the OPEC price changes essentially left energy-use patterns in the USSR untouched into 1980.

Virtually all of the increased Soviet energy use in the last half of the 1970s was in hydrocarbons as solid-fuel use stagnated; and the fastest growing hydrocarbon was natural gas. In some sense this made the Soviet Union like Europe, which also was satisfying most of the increased demand with natural gas; but the difference is that European oil demand was stagnant while Soviet oil demand was rising at 1.5 times the growth rate of GNP.

One of the striking characteristics of the structure of TFC is that in both Europe and North America, the International Energy Agency (IEA) countries managed to increase GNP and industrial production while decreasing energy use in industry. In Europe this was accomplished by a virtual one-for-one switch of oil for gas, and in the United States the opposite occurred, presumably reflecting the retention of price controls on gas while they were gradually lifted on oil. In contrast in Soviet industry energy demand rose almost as rapidly as TFC, with the burden of the increase in natural gas and electricity. This means that Soviet industry remains an enormous consumer of energy by world standards. In 1980 58 percent of TFC went to industry in the Soviet Union, while the comparable 1979 numbers were 41 percent for IEA Europe and 32 percent for IEA North America. It is almost certainly in Soviet industry that the most significant possibilities for energy conservation lie, and they are still unrealized.

If we take 1.25 as the current energy-to-GNP elasticity (on TPE) in the Soviet economy, then how far can that be brought down? Can it be brought down to what Western economies have attained in recent years, say 0.3 to 0.5? Soviet plans do not explicitly discuss energy consumption targets, so there is no official Gosplan position, explicit or implied, on the energy-to-GNP elasticity. Some Soviet energy specialists who discuss this assume an elasticity relative to Marxian national income of 0.8 is possible, which basically projects no change at all.[7] Between 1976 and 1980 Soviet national income grew at 4.1 percent per annum on average, yielding an elasticity on TPE of 0.78.[8]

In fact there seems to be good reason to believe that the current Soviet economic system will be unable to emulate the efficiency gains realized in Western countries after the OPEC price increases. Until there is a careful study of the source of Western gains, one cannot be sure, but it would make sense that some significant portion of the gains in Western countries came simply from economic pressures, as all energy consumers were forced by higher prices to monitor their energy use more carefully. The Soviet economic system is quite inept at using price increases to reduce usage. Substantial gains from that corner will not be realized until significant economic reforms are undertaken.

The remainder of the energy-conservation gains were realized through substituting capital and labor for energy, both of which required new investments. For the many small investments made to conserve energy (new thermostats, insulation, new equipment, and so on) the Soviet system will have trouble replicating them. As Philip Hanson has observed, it is difficult to induce Soviet managers to modernize existing plants, presumably because they have little incentive to endure the disruption, and make the many small decisions involved, for efficiency gains that might not be fully appreciated by the supervising ministry (Hanson 1981, p. 66).

The one area where Soviet planners might be able to find efficiency gains within the existing system would be in large investments that can be effectively commanded from the center. Some such measures were taken some time ago (cogeneration, for example), but others might be possible (dieselization of trucks or further increases in power-station efficiencies). But even here the very important factor that must be considered is that during the 1980s, investment funds will grow very little and will be much in demand simply to expand existing capacity. Therefore there will be very little room for replacement investment of capital still operating.

In addition to all of these considerations, there will be important upward pressures on the Soviet energy-to-GNP elasticity over this decade. In the transportation sector, for example, Soviet energy demands from 1975 to 1980 grew at three times the rate of TFC, and such disproportionate growth rates for transport are likely to continue along with the expansion of automobile and truck use in the Soviet Union. Furthermore the plans to continue high investments in agriculture represent high growth rates in energy use for new capital and for such inputs as fertilizer.[9]

Much more research needs to be done before any firm assessment can be made of the net effect of these pressures for change in energy-to-GNP elasticities and the barriers to change. For the present there is no compelling reason to expect the elasticity to fall very soon; certainly it seems unlikely that it will fall substantially by 1985. Possibly later in the 1980s as new capital is commissioned and as pressure grows from hard-currency balance-of-payments problems, then further declines may show up. In fact, most discussions by Soviet analysts of energy-conservation possibilities take the decade, not the next few years, as the relevant time period.

The 1985 Energy Balance

Table 4-3 summarizes the discussion comparing the energy balance for 1980, the officially planned balance for 1985, and a projection for 1985. In 1980 actual production (excluding peat, shale, and firewood) was 26.92 mbdoe, of which 4.38 mbdoe was exported, mostly in the form of petroleum. Of these exports, 1.9 mbd of the oil and 0.49 mbdoe of the natural gas was shipped to CMEA countries, almost all of the remainder (a total of 2 mbdoe of the 4.38) being sold for hard currency.

Official plans for 1985 call for energy output to rise an average of 3.6 percent per annum through 1985, attaining 32.2 mbdoe in that year. Although there is no official estimate of energy consumption that year, I am using the OECD (1981) projection of 3.1 percent per annum, which seems a reasonable estimate of what Soviet planners hope to achieve, in which case consumption reaches 26.22 mbdoe in 1985. That leaves 5.98 mbdoe for export, a little over a third higher than 1980 exports.

If these are indeed the expectations, they might break down in planners' minds as oil exports of 3.5 mbdoe (which would imply a very slow growth in oil demand, by historical standards, of 1.75 percent per annum), natural-gas exports of 130 bcm (2.13 mbdoe, over double the 1980 levels), and a slight increase in coal exports. This reflects expectations in late 1980 and early 1981. Now that problems in the oil industry are emerging even more clearly than before and coal-industry problems appear to be persisting, both the supply and consumption plans may be falling.

The last three columns of table 4-3 give a projection for 1985. On the demand side, Soviet planners may not be far off on their projections, but only because they are assuming too high a growth rate. I assume here a growth rate of GNP of 2.75 percent per annum on average over 1981 through 1985, which is about the average of the 1976 through 1980 period but above that of the last few years; and I assume an energy-to-GNP elasticity of 1.25. That yields the total energy-consumption figure of 26.8 and exports of 3.5 mbdoe.

Table 4-3
Actual Soviet Energy Balances, 1980: Planned and Projected for 1985
(millions of barrels per day oil equivalent)

	1980 Actual			1985 Planned			1985 Projected		
	Production	Apparent Consumption	Exports	Production	Apparent Consumption	Exports	Production	Apparent Consumption	Exports
Petroleum	12.03	8.80	3.23[b]	12.60	ND	ND	11.70	9.85	1.85
Natural gas	7.10	6.20	.90	10.32	ND	ND	9.80	8.15	1.65
Coal	6.73	6.48	.25[c]	7.20	ND	ND	7.00[d]	7.00	0
Nuclear	.30	.30		1.02	ND	ND	.80	.80	0[e]
Hydro	.76	.76		1.06	ND	ND	1.00	1.00	0
Total[f]	26.92	22.54	4.38	32.20	26.22[g]	5.98	30.30	26.80	3.50

Sources: Actual production, consumption, and export data are based on OECD, official Soviet, and CIA data. Plan data are from Soviet documents concerning the 1981-1985 Eleventh Five-year Plan. Projections are the author's.

[a] Data from Lalaiants (1981a), who converts the plan data into tons of coal equivalent (standard fuel). For coal his conversion implies a drop of 2.5 percent in the average calorific content of all Soviet coal (from 0.673 ton of standard fuel in 1980). The CIA (1980, p. 15) estimates that the drop will be somewhat sharper, to 0.643 million tons standard fuel, by 1985.

[b] Gross; no data are published for petroleum imports, but they are probably small.

[c] Estimated.

[d] I used Lalaiants's conversion here but assume that output will be only 750 million tons natural. The CIA figure may be right (in which output of 750 million tons natural would be the equivalent of only 6.75 mbdoe), but I cannot reconcile it with observed trends in calorific content in recent years.

[e] Negligible.

[f] Excludes peat, shale, and firewood (approximately 1 mbdoe in 1980).

[g] Based on the OECD estimate that the Soviets are planning for per-annum energy-consumption growth rates in the range of 0.028 to 0.0335. I have used the average of 0.03075 to arrive at 26.22. The national income growth rates accompanying these projections are 0.0375 to 0.0405 per annum (OECD 1981, p. 14).

The last few years have been heavily influenced by the poor weather in 1979, 1980, and 1981, and good weather probably will allow the Soviet economy to approach the growth rates of the late 1970s. It is possible that growth will average even lower than 2.75 percent, depending on cyclical and secular factors that we do not fully understand in the West. But should that occur, it would probably mean not only reduced energy consumption but also reduced total investment growth rates, which would affect energy supplies. Therefore the total energy-consumption and -supply projections discussed here could be too high, but even so, the projected balance may still be close to correct.

Within that total consumption figure I surmise that the Soviets can hold down the growth rate of petroleum consumption to 2.3 percent per annum, which implies an oil-to-GNP elasticity of approximately 0.8, one-half of the recent 1.55. That will take some serious effort, and preliminary 1981 data suggest no progress in that direction. (Net oil exports for 1981 were approximately 2.9 mbd, possibly 3.0. Output was 12.12, implying a consumption of 9.12, using the 3.0 figure. That is 3.6 percent above 1980 consumption, at least twice the growth rate of GNP. While admitting that one-year energy-to-GNP elasticities mean little, this is hardly a good sign.) So this oil-export figure is very optimistic if the production projection is right. The growth rate of gas consumption is projected at 5.6 percent per annum, about twice the growth rate of GNP, which is the historical natural-gas elasticity with respect to GNP. It, too, is somewhat optimistic since the historical figure was accompanied by growing oil use. Now gas will have to take the brunt of the demands conservation cannot control and coal cannot meet. Finally, it is assumed the Soviets will consume all the coal they can produce.

If these export figures are correct, then barring Polish-type recessions throughout Eastern Europe or conservation miracles, all of the 1.85 mbdoe of Soviet oil will be needed for East European industry. Of the natural gas, Western Europe will be taking no more than 1 mbdoe (60 bcm) in 1985, the remaining 0.65 mbdoe (40 bcm) being available for CMEA (an increase from the current level of 30 bcm in Soviet exports to Eastern Europe).

The most important figure here is the total gas and oil—that is, hydrocarbon—exports available for 1985 of 3.5 mbdoe; the mix in exports to CMEA and to the West could be different from that forecast here without any significant change in the implied hard-currency receipts. If, for example, the Soviets cannot sell 1 mbdoe of natural gas to Europe by 1985 because West European demand has not grown sufficiently to absorb that amount, then Soviet planners would probably attempt to speed up gas for oil substitution in Eastern Europe. It would be possible, therefore, to see the Soviets increase natural-gas exports to Eastern Europe more than anticipated here (say from 30 bcm to 50 bcm) and reduce oil exports to Eastern

Europe by an equivalent amount, exporting the freed-up oil for hard currency. For Soviet hard-currency receipts, the result would be essentially the same in either case, the only difference being the differential at that time between crude-oil and natural-gas prices.

This balance leaves the USSR a net energy exporter, as will any reasonable supply-and-demand projection for the Soviet economy. The actual balance could be higher or lower, although this projection seems the most reasonable. For the best case from the Soviet point of view, the official plans are probably a good basis, although they now seem very optimistic. A worst case would assume more dramatic supply disappointments—for example, oil at the CIA midpoint (10.5), coal possibly at 6.75 (due to a fall in calorific content), and natural gas at 570 bcm (9.3 mbdoe). If all of that transpires simultaneously, an unlikely event, then output falls a further 2 mbd below the balance projected in table 4-3 and still leaves room for some exports.

One weakness in these projections is the lack of an explicit link between economic performance and the expansion of energy supplies. A rapid expansion or contraction of GNP growth rates not only will expand or contract the growth rate of energy consumption but will also have an effect on investment funds, possibly including funds devoted to investments in energy industries. A more sophisticated projection should take this into account.

Energy Prospects for the Latter Half of the 1980s

It is difficult to be very precise about prospects for the latter half of the 1980s. A great deal of uncertainty surrounds strategies now still in the early stages of formulation in the USSR, possible new geological finds, and progress in energy conservation.

On the supply side the prospects seem no better than they are for the first part of the decade; in fact they are probably worse. Oil output is likely to continue to fall throughout the latter half of the decade. The last published CIA projection was for 1990 oil output of 7 to 9 mbd (Licari 1981); the OECD projects 10.4 to 11.6 mbd. The basic fact driving these projections is the absence of new large fields similar to Samotlor, which can replace it as its output stagnates and then declines (while simultaneously the decline in the Volga-Urals fields accelerates). Whether the CIA or the OECD is closer to outlining what shall actually transpire is difficult to evaluate now; much more will be known in a few more years as Soviet planners are forced to react to continuing problems in the Soviet energy sector. It is likely that investment constraints and the relatively low costs of natural-gas output increments will at least push Soviet planners to choose the lower end of the OECD projection, say 10.5 mbd.

One of the abundant resources the Soviets can, and plan to, exploit in the longer term is coal, especially in the lower-calorie coals in Kanksk-Achinsk in southwestern Siberia. Soviet coal reserves there and in Ekibastuz (in northeastern Kazakhstan) are huge, but the technical problems associated with converting that coal into energy deliverable to where it is needed (European USSR) are very difficult and unlikely to be resolved in the 1980s (CIA 1980a). It is therefore improbable that the Soviet Union will be able in this decade to rely on its enormous Siberian and Kazakh coal reserves to replace energy lost from falling coal production in the European USSR, and from falling oil production. (The 1990s are another matter.) I shall assume that in calorific terms coal output will remain stagnant throughout the 1980s.

The other alternatives are natural gas and nuclear power. The reserves position in natural gas seems strong enough to sustain very high growth rates of production in that energy carrier throughout the 1980s, and the only question will be if there are constraints on the capital that can be devoted to expanding productive capacity there. Both foreign credits and domestic constraints could prove important, but nevertheless this seems to be the most promising energy carrier for Soviet energy supplies. Suppose as a rough guess that in the 1986 through 1990 period the Soviets can maintain the 6.6 percent per annum growth rate of natural-gas output I have projected for 1981 through 1985. That will provide an increment of 3.7 mbdoe (222 bcm) to Soviet energy supplies between 1986 and 1990 (the 1981 through 1985 increment is 2.6 mbdoe in my projection). Nuclear and hydro may provide another 1 mbdoe in incremental energy supplies.[10]

These projections sum up to energy supplies equal to 33.8 mbdoe in 1990 (oil, 10.5; gas, 13.5; coal, 7.0; nuclear and hydro, 2.8), a net increment of 3.5 mbdoe over projected energy supplies in 1985 (table 4-3), and an average growth rate in energy supplies of 2.2 percent per annum.

The uncertainties in the demand projection are just as formidable as those on the supply side. In the unlikely (but not impossible) event that the Soviet energy-to-GNP elasticity remains stuck at 1.25 and assuming also that GNP growth rates average 2.5 percent over the decade, then by 1990 Soviet energy consumption would be approximately 31.25 mbdoe, leaving no more than 2.5 mbdoe for exports. There are two reasons why this scenario seems unlikely. First, Soviet planners seem intent enough on pushing detailed energy-conserving investments that they will surely succeed in pulling down the energy-to-GNP elasticity by some amount by the end of the 1980s. Furthermore economic reforms, which are very likely to follow the leadership succession, will exert a downward pressure on energy consumption. On the other hand, those same reforms may increase GNP growth rates, and hence energy consumption.

The information available on both energy-conservation possibilities in the Soviet Union and on the prospects (and timetable) for economic reforms is insufficient to allow any precise conclusion. But it is not implausible to argue that the stimulative effects of economic reform (on growth rates) will counterbalance the effect of falling energy-to-GNP elasticities so that in the end energy consumption will still be about 31 mbd in 1990, a growth rate of 3.1 percent per annum. This and the supply projection would imply energy exports of 2.25 mbdoe in 1990, down from 4.4 mbdoe in 1980, and 3.5 (projected) in 1985.

The balance could easily be 1 mbd higher or lower because of developments different from those I have projected in energy supply or demand. It is very improbable that the Soviet Union will be a net energy importer in the 1980s, and it seems equally improbable that it will attain any time in the decade the level of energy exports (and hard-currency earnings from energy) of 1980.

Implications of Prospective Energy Developments through 1985 for East-West Trade

Soviet energy developments will exert two major influences on East-West trade in the near term, as well as having general consequences for the remainder of the 1980s. The most immediate effect of Soviet energy plans will be large West European and Japanese exports of gas-pipeline equipment critical to the realization of Soviet plans to expand their gas-production capacity. The Soviet gas-pipeline system is to be expanded by 40,000 kilometers between 1981 and 1985, moving to a total length of 170,000 kilometers in 1985. Within this expansion, one-half will be six fifty-six-inch pipelines and the compressors to go with them. It is here where most of the import needs will arise because the Soviets have had long-term difficulties in developing and producing in large quantities fifty-six-inch pipe and the 25 megawatt (Mw) compressors most appropriate for the compressor stations along such a pipeline. The large-diameter pipelines will probably be comprised of approximately 13 million tons of pipe and 160 compressor stations, each station optimally configured with three 25 Mw compressors in it. It is not clear what proportion of the pipe and turbine requirements Soviet planners will try to meet with Soviet-built equipment. The Urengoi-Uzhgorod export line apparently will be constructed with primarily Western equipment, but for the remaining five lines there is an obvious attempt to rely primarily on domestic turbines and pipe.[11] Nevertheless, based on available data, it seems reasonable to assume that although the Soviets can produce some of the necessary pipe and can equip some of the compressor stations with Soviet-made compressors, it will be necessary to import about 10 million tons of pipe and 125 compressor stations. Imports of those two items should not total more than $15 billion in 1981 prices. Other equipment (for example, pipelaying equipment, valves, and so on) will add several more billion dollars. The total hard-currency cost of the entire pipe-line-expansion program is unlikely to exceed $20 billion (even allowing for inflation). This is a significant sum but still far short of the estimates in the press that the West European line alone will cost $10 billion to $15 billion. In fact the West European line itself is likely to cost no more than $5 billion in hard currency. This is not the total cost of the line; it excludes large labor and material costs, which will be financed internally (Hewett 1982).

Assuming a figure for equipment imports related to the gas industry of $20 billion between 1981 and 1985, that is $4 billion per year, which means about a 20 percent increase over 1980 levels of Soviet imports from Europe and Japan. It also implies an annual increment to Soviet net debt of $4 billion, and for this reason alone Soviet debt to the West would rise from its 1980 level of $10 billion (net) to $30 billion by 1985. For an economy as large as the Soviet economy and for an investment as promising as Soviet natural gas, such a debt figure seems well within Soviet reach. Assume the loans are issued for repayments over ten years to begin in 1985 and the interest rate averages 7.5 percent. That implies interest payments beginning with the first loans in 1981 and rising to a maximum of $1.5 billion in 1985, at which point repayments of $2 billion ($20 billion repaid over ten years) commence and go through 1994. Total principal and interest payments are at their peak at $3.5 billion in 1985 and thereafter fall as interest payments are reduced. Total pipeline costs could well be 25 percent below this high estimate of $20 billion, making maximum principal and interest in 1985 only $2.6 billion.

The precise timing of increments of Soviet gas deliveries to Western Europe is still unclear. The Soviet Union is now exporting 25 bcm and in 1984 intends to increase those deliveries, reaching possibly 60 bcm by 1987 (due to the new West European line). Other pipelines now under construction might allow it to begin exporting all 60 bcm as early as 1985, if the West Europeans wanted to buy that much that soon, which it will be assumed is in fact what will happen. Total gas exports in 1985 should be 100 bcm, so the 40 bcm left over after Western European deliveries is assumed to go to Eastern Europe, which is up 10 bcm from current delivery levels.

The critical question is what price the Soviets will obtain for their gas exports to Western Europe. The Ruhrgas agreement in effect determined that, but the details of the complex formula are not public information. Based on press reports it seems that beginning in 1984-1985 Soviet gas will sell at least for a price of $5.70 per million Btu, or approximately $31 per barrel of oil equivalent. Assuming 7 percent world inflation between 1981 and 1985, that is the equivalent of $23.65 per barrel of oil equivalent in 1982, a lower price than the Soviets thought they could obtain but the best they could manage in the face of a rapidly softening market for gas in Europe (and even then they have been forced to accept cuts in the quantities sold to major customers).

At a 1985 price of $31 per barrel of oil equivalent, which is $226.30 per ton of oil equivalent, the 60 bcm of gas exports (49.2 mtoe) will yield dollar receipts of $11.1 billion (1985) dollars. After principal and interest, that still leaves about $7.6 billion net receipts available for hard-currency imports (grain, machinery, raw materials), or $5.80 billion in 1981 prices (at 7 percent inflation).

From the Soviet planners' point of view, the prospect of such hard-currency earnings is hardly reason for jubilation, but neither does it represent a catastrophe. In 1980 Soviet earnings from energy exports peaked at $15 billion to $17 billion, when they constituted 70 percent of all hard-currency earnings from merchandise exports. Net earnings from energy in 1985 would be about one-third of that after adjustment for the inflation that will occur between now and then, which puts earnings from energy exports back into the magnitudes the USSR had in the post-OPEC, but pre-Iran, period. Those earnings probably are sufficient (assuming nonenergy exports do not collapse), although it will mean some very hard choices between food and machinery imports and therefore between consumer satisfaction and increased productivity.

The level of energy exports implicit in this for Eastern Europe will put considerable pressure on those economies. The only increases in Soviet energy exports to Eastern Europe anticipated here are 10 bcm of natural gas, which is the eqiuvalent of 0.16 mbdoe. I have estimated elsewhere that only in the best of cases could Eastern Europe hope to keep its incremental energy needs down in the range of 0.20 mbdoe. More likely is an increase of approximately 0.7 mbdoe in net energy import needs, which, after additional Soviet shipments, would leave Eastern Europe searching world markets for approximately 0.5 mbdoe of additional energy (net imports in 1979 from the rest of the world were practically zero). Under current balance-of-payments conditions in Eastern Europe, it is difficult to see how they could finance those additional imports.[12]

For the period beyond 1985, too little is known to allow quantitative projections for hard-currency imports or exports related to Soviet energy. Further expansion of natural-gas production will surely involve substantive equipment imports from Western Europe, and the Soviets will be trying very hard to pay for that new equipment with new gas exports. (Eight fifty-six-inch pipelines operating at 75 atm are required to attain the projected 222 bcm increase in natural-gas output between 1986 and 1990. That plus the associated trunk lines could easily call for a 50,000 kilometer expansion of the pipe system, probably a conservative figure. If advanced techniques are used where the gas is shipped at higher pressures, the job would still require five or six pipes. It is doubtful that the Soviets will have the productive capacity between 1986 and 1990 to meet the qualitative and quantitative demands associated with such a program.) But unless there are some dramatic successes on the supply or demand side or a dramatic change in the Soviet-East Eurpoean economic relationship, it is difficult to see how in fact the Soviet economy will have any energy available for net hard-currency exports.

But if Soviet leaders have successfully reformed the economic system by the late 1980s, then the lost hard-currency earnings from energy could be counterbalanced by increased exports of other commodities and reduced imports (for example, of food). In fact the prospective loss of hard currency earnings for energy will induce economic reform measures in the search for improved foreign-trade performance.

There are several ways in which Soviet hard-currency earnings could differ substantially from the projections I have discussed here. One way is that West European demand for gas could continue to soften, in which case Soviet shipments to Western Europe might not attain the projected 60 bcm by 1985 but rather would reach that amount only in the late 1980s. The other way is that the price at which Soviet gas is sold is below the currently set floor price for 1985, something that could conceivably happen if the oil price continues to fall. It will be some time before it is possible to develop some notion of how likely these outcomes may be, but they do bear watching. If in fact Soviet energy earnings are even lower than projected here, the consequences for the Soviet economy, and therefore for Eastern Europe, could be serious.

Nevertheless there is in the current projection no hint of an energy and economic situation in the USSR so bleak as to push Soviet leaders beyond their traditional conservatism (so evident now in their dealing with Poland) to contemplate military actions in the Middle East. Whatever action the USSR may take in the Middle East, energy concerns seem unlikely as a major motivating factor.

U.S. Policy Options Concerning Soviet
Energy Developments

The Reagan administration has not succeeded in its attempt to block various agreements concerning the Soviet gas-export expansion plan to Western Europe. The Soviets have already commenced construction on that line, and the pipe and compressor contracts will most likely not be seriously affected by U.S. sanctions. In short, a key feature of Soviet energy plans regarding East-West trade is in process of implementation over the very strong and vocal objections of the United States. This entire episode has simultaneously raised questions and offered answers about Soviet energy and East-West trade, which deserve careful study in the United States.

First, it is obvious that Soviet plans for the gas industry expansion not only played a key role in Soviet plans for all energy supplies, they also were important elements in West European and Japanese leaders' plans for their industrial exports. The portion of the gas deal of most immediate appeal to Western Europe was the prospect of enormous pipe and compressor exports. The thrust of the Reagan administration's alternative plan (involving U.S. coal, nuclear power, and liquified natural gas) virtually ignored this critical element of the deal. The U.S. government was pressuring West European governments not only to ask some European firms to give up the idea of buying relatively cheap Soviet gas, but more important it was asking these governments to tell other European firms to give up huge export deals, and this in the wake of having just removed an embargo on grain, a key U.S. export. Understandably West Europeans took U.S. actions, not words, as a guide, and they refused to consider the hastily drawn-up alternatives offered to them. The lesson in this for the U.S. administration is that Western Europe and Japan have reasonably strong economic interests in developing their export capacities to the Soviet Union and Eastern Europe. These are similar to the specific interests exhibited in the United States concerning grain exports, the difference being that European interests span a far broader set of commodities, focused on manufactured goods. If the U.S. government underestimates the strength of those economic interests or the political lobbies that lie behind them, it risks a substantial (and further) erosion in its credibility concerning East-West trade policy.

Second, the major constraints on Soviet abilities to realize their energy plans are of two general sorts: their ability to borrow funds and use them to buy primarily middle-level technology with no obvious direct military applications and the organizational issues discussed previously. If all the Western nations were to agree on credit or machinery export limits, Soviet energy production in the next four or five years would be affected significantly. But such a policy is not possible, and to attempt to pursue it would probably do more harm to the Atlantic alliance than it would do to the Soviet Union and Eastern Europe. The more serious constraints to improving Soviet energy balances are organizational, and in those the West can be of very little help, or at least it will not be asked to help. Rather, the internal dynamics of Soviet economic and political institutions will determine the severity of this constraint.

This will be even more the case as Soviet planners increasingly emphasize measures designed to improve the energy balance through conservation. It is, of course, true that new capital equipment will play an important role in increasing energy efficiency of the Soviet economy. But virtually all of that capital equipment will be middle-level technology available in many other parts of the world, including the USSR. More important, the major source of energy conservation that the Soviet leaders can tap is economic reform, and Western countries have very little influence over whether that particular source is exploited.

In short there is very little the United States can do on its own to influence Soviet energy plans. The U.S. failure to stop the West European line illustrates the futility, and indeed the potential harm to relations with important allies, of pursuing such a policy. It would be far more reasonable to concede the coincidence of Soviet and West European-Japanese interests on this point and then work with U.S. allies to ensure that the proper precautions are taken to minimize the potential harm that might attend a Soviet gas cutoff.

The probability of such a cutoff seems quite low. While much has been made of increasing West European dependence on the USSR for energy, very little has been made of dependence of the USSR on Western Europe for hard currency although that dependence appears to be much stronger. Throughout the 1980s energy will be an important source of hard currency for the Soviet economy, most of it exported as gas. For the temporary chaos the Soviets would cause the Western Europeans by a natural-gas cutoff (temporary, assuming arrangements are made to increase gas production in the North Sea on short notice, switch dual-fired boilers to fuel oil, temporarily reduce use, and so on) the USSR would jeopardize its major source of hard-currency earnings for much of the 1980s. That seems an unlikely, and for the Soviets an uncharacteristic, policy unless the world is already on the verge of a major conflict.

Notes

1. Vañous (1981, p. 554) gives estimates for Soviet oil export prices in 1980 to Eastern Europe. The average price is 71.60 rubles per ton, which equals $110.29 per ton at the official ruble-to-dollar rate, or about 43 percent of world contract prices for crude in 1980.

2. Gustafson (1981) provides an excellent discussion of the shift.

3. Data on original and revised oil output plans through 1979 are from Lee and Lecky (1979, p. 583). Data on output through 1980 are from *Narodnoe khoziastvo 1980*. The remaining plan and output data are from various issues of *Ekonomicheskaia gazeta*.

4. Plans for the gas industry are discussed in more detail in Hewett (1982).

5. This is the midpoint of a recent, and careful, projection done by the OECD's International Energy Agency; the range is 11.2 mbd to 12.2 mbd; see OECD (1981, p. 9). It is higher than the CIA's last published projection of 10 to 11 mbd (Licari 1981) but lower than some of the more optimistic views that the Soviets will manage to fulfill the planned output levels of 12.6 (a view, for example, held by the U.S. Defense Intelligence Agency).

6. Although one can find energy-conservation decrees and discussions in the Soviet press reaching back almost a decade, recent decrees have been detailed and obviously seriously meant; see, for example, *Pravda*, July 4, 1981. Furthermore recent articles in economics journals suggest that a detailed analysis of energy-conservation possibilities is underway (for example, Lalaiants 1981).

7. OECD (1981, p. 14), discusses Soviet estimates.

8. Campbell (1981, pp. 31-32) cites Makarov and Vigdorchik's longer-term estimate of a 0.6 elasticity (presumably on national income), which might work out to approximately unitary elasticity on GNP.

9. A point made, for example, by Tikhonov in his speech to the Twenty-sixth Party Congress in February 1981. See *Ekonomicheskaia gazeta*, no. 10 (March 1981):10.

10. The nuclear projection follows OTA (1981, p. 138), which projects a possible doubling in nuclear capacity between 1985 and 1990, hence an increment of 0.8 mbdoe. The remaining 0.2 is for hydro, which is similar to the projected increment over 1981 through 1985.

11. Numerous articles have appeared in the Soviet press that indicate a strong commitment to a very heavy reliance on a Soviet-designed and -produced fifty-six-inch laminar pipe, and 16 Mw and 25 Mw turbines, also of Soviet design. See, for example, "Tsentral'naia stroika," and Zotov (1982). But these are still only intentions, and there is no evidence that either the laminar pipe or the 16 Mw and 25 Mw turbines are yet in serial production.

12. Further discussion of this can be found in OTA (1981, chap. 9), which is a shortened version of Hewett (1981).

References

Campbell, Robert W. "Energy in the USSR to the Year 2000." In A. Bergson and H. Levine, eds., *The Soviet Economy toward the Year 2000.* (London: George Allen and Unwin, forthcoming).

Gustafson, Thane. 1981. "Implications of the Latest Developments in Soviet Energy Policy: Constraints on Soviet Behavior, and Opportunities for the West?" Mimeographed. May.

Hanson, Philip. 1981. *Trade and Technology in Soviet-Western Relations.* New York: Columbia University.

Hewett, Ed. A. 1980. "Alternative Econometric Approaches for Studying the Link between Economic Systems and Economic Outcomes." *Journal of Comparative Economics* 4 (September 1980):274-294.

_____ . 1981. "East European Energy in the 1980's." Mimeographed. March.

_____. 1982. "Near Term Prospects in the Soviet Gas Industry, and the Implications for East-West Trade." In U.S. Joint Economic Committee, *Soviet Economy in the 1980s: Problems and Prospects*, 1:391-413. Washington, D.C.: U.S. Government Printing Office.

Lalaiants, A. "Problemy ekonomii toplivnoenergeticheskikh resursov v narodnom khoziastve" [Problems of economizing on fuel-energy resources in the economy]. *Planovoe khoziastvo* (January 1981a):34-44.

_____. 1981b. "Bazovyi kompleks." [The base complex.] *Pravda*, December 30, p. 2.

Lee, J. Richard, and Lecky, James R. 1979. "Soviet Oil Developments." In U.S. Joint Economic Committee, *Soviet Economy in a Time of Change*, 1:581-599. Washington, D.C.: U.S. Government Printing Office.

Licari, Joseph A. 1981. "Linkages between Soviet Energy and Growth Prospects for the 1980s." In NATO Economics Directorate, *CMEA Energy, 1980-1990*, pp. 265-276. Newtonville, Mass.: Oriental Research Partners.

Narodnoe khoziastvo SSSR za 1980 g. Statisticheskii ezhegodnik 1981. [*Economy of the USSR in 1980: Statistical yearbook*]. Moscow.

Office of Technology Assessment. U.S. Congress. 1981. *Technology and Soviet Energy Availability*. Washington, D.C.: U.S. Government Printing Office.

Organization for Economic Cooperation and Development (OECD). Committee for Energy Policy. 1981. "Energy Prospects of the USSR and Eastern Europe." Mimeographed. Paris, June.

Stern, Jonathan P. 1981. "Natural Gas: Resources, Production Possibilities and Demand in the 1980s." In NATO Economics Directorate, *CMEA Energy, 1980-1990*. Newtonville, Mass.: Oriental Research Partners.

"Tsentral'naia stroika piatuletka" [The central construction project of the Five Year Plan]. *Trud*, February 9, 1982.

U.S. Central Intelligence Agency (CIA). 1980a. "Central Siberian Brown Coal as a Potential Source of Power for European Russia." SW 80-10006. April.

_____. 1980b. "USSR Coal Industry Problems and Prospects." ER 80-10154. March.

_____. 1977. "Prospects for Soviet Oil Production." ER 77-10270. April.

Vaňous, Jan. 1981. "Eastern European and Soviet Fuel Trade." In U.S. Joint Economic Committee, *East European Economic Assessment*, part 2, pp. 541-560. Washington, D.C.: U.S. Government Printing Office.

Zotov, V. 1982. "Magistrali 'golubogo toplivo' " [Trunk lines of blue fuel]. *Sotsialisticheskaia industriia*, April 14, p. 2.

Part III
Perspectives on
Western Policy

5

The Potential Role of Western Policy toward Eastern Europe in East-West Trade

John P. Hardt and Kate S. Tomlinson

CMEA Growth Prospects: Policy Variables

Low Growth Prospects

Economic development in the Council for Mutual Economic Assistance (CMEA) Six and Soviet Union is likely to be modest in the 1980s. (See table 5-1.) Economic growth, modernization of industry, agriculture, and other sectors, and improvement in the consumer's lot are not only likely to be slower but are also likely to fall short of plans and expectations. These three aims of economic growth, modernization, and consumerism are likely to be affected by domestic policy within the CMEA, Soviet energy trade (especially with the CMEA Six), and Western trade and credit policy toward CMEA. Our emphasis is on the last variable, the role of Western economic policies in CMEA performance.

On the whole, Western policies and trade-facilitation measures encouraged the expansion of East-West trade during the 1970s, but since 1980 Western trade restrictions have held down commercial intercourse. Western trade restrictions have had some negative impact on CMEA economic performance. Western controls on strategic exports and applications of embargoes and sanctions have been differentiated in two ways: among Western countries and with respect to individual CMEA members. For example, the Soviet invasion of Afghanistan and the Polish declaration of martial law elicited divergent responses by the United States and the other Western countries. The Western countries, particularly the United States, apply less strict export controls to Poland, Rumania, and Hungary than to the Soviet Union and the remaining East European countries. Similarly, the Federal Republic of Germany has a preferential trade and credit policy for the German Democratic Republic (GDR).

The views expressed in this chapter are those of the authors and not necessarily those of the Congressional Research Service or of the Library of Congress. The authors would like to thank the Trilateral Commission for earlier substantive contributions to the preparation of this chapter.

79

Table 5-1
Economic Performance, USSR and CMEA Six, 1976, 1980, 1981-1985
(annual increase percentage)

	1976	1980	1981-1985
Gross domestic product			
USSR	4.7	2.0	2.6
CMEA Six	3.4	0.8	1.9
Investment			
USSR	6.6	3.6	2.0
CMEA Six	4.7	1.6	1.9
Labor force			
USSR	0.8	0.9	0.4
CMEA Six	0.9	0.4	0.6
Industrial growth			
USSR	4.2	3.1	2.7
CMEA Six	4.0	1.5	2.2
Consumption			
USSR	3.7	0.5	1.0
CMEA Six	5.5	1.5	2.1

Source: Daniel L. Bond, "CMEA Growth Projections for 1981-85 and the Implications of Restricted Western Credits" (paper prepared for the NATO Economic Colloquium, March 31-April 2, 1982, Brussels), p. 21. Reprinted with permission.

Western credit policies have also encouraged the expansion of East-West trade. If trade is to continue to expand, credit from Western governments and commercial banks will be needed. Western credit policy is also characterized by differentiation and divergence in policy.

Throughout Eastern Europe domestic factors will tend to retard economic growth in the 1980s. Two observations flow from this conclusion. First, since Eastern Europe will not be able to rely on domestic sources of capital, labor, and other inputs for growth, modernization, and consumerism, it will continue to need energy supplies from the Soviet Union and trade with the West. But for political and economic reasons, these factors, which were the engines of economic growth in the 1960s and 1970s, will not necessarily be available. Even if they are available, they may cost Eastern Europe more than in the past. Second, low or zero growth may endanger labor incentives and political stability in Eastern Europe. During the 1970s there appeared to be an effective, if tacit, social contract between East European regimes and citizens, in which the latter accepted the leading role of local communist parties; rigid, centralized regimes; and their adherence to Moscow's dictates in domestic and foreign policies in return for steady improvements in consumer welfare. Thus, unless the governments of Eastern Europe are able to modify the social contract, stagnant or declining standards of living may vitiate incentives for hard work and political acquiescence.

Soviet Energy Policy and Western Trade and
Credit Policies as Engines of Growth

During the 1960s and 1970s expanding imports of Soviet oil and gas
fostered economic growth, modernization, and consumerism in Eastern
Europe. Believing that they were assured of abundant, low-cost supplies of
energy, the East Europeans emphasized energy-intensive industries. In the
late 1960s and 1970s, the East European countries increasingly turned to the
West for industrial and agricultural products and adopted import-
substitution policies. Western trade and credit, which was often extended
on favorable terms, also fueled economic growth, modernization, and consumerism in Eastern Europe. But as imports expanded to meet the goal of
modernization—the ability to produce goods salable on Western markets—
exports did not keep pace, in part because recession and inflation in the
West reduced demand for Eastern goods during the mid- to late 1970s. Thus
the external debt of most of the East European countries expanded more
rapidly than anticipated.

While the energy-intensive development and import-substitution
policies that the availability of inexpensive energy supplies from the Soviet
Union and of trade and credit from the West engendered caused problems
for the East European economies, the continuation of East European
economic growth, modernization, and consumerism may depend on the
continuation of favorable Soviet and Western policies. In the near future,
however, the East Europeans may not be able to count on the past engines
of growth. For purely economic reasons, both the Soviet Union and the
West may not be willing or able to continue their past policies toward
Eastern Europe. Severe energy rationing by the Soviet Union and restrictions on trade and credit by the West are possible. Yet for a variety of
political and some economic reasons, the continuation of past favorable
Soviet energy policies and preferential West trade policies, albeit in a
modified form, is more likely.

If the goals of the Soviet Eleventh and Twelfth Five-year plans are not
met, the Soviet Union may have to lower the energy-supply commitments
made to Eastern Europe at the June 1980 CMEA meeting. Even if it meets
its energy targets, the Soviet Union may find that continued energy supplies
to Eastern Europe may mean forgoing opportunities for hard currency sales
to Western Europe and for energy diplomacy in the Third World.

Because energy is a key lever of Soviet control over Eastern Europe, the
Soviet Union may find it politically necessary to maintain its preferential
supply policies for Eastern Europe even if they are perceived as burden-
some. The increase in Poland's allocation in 1981, which was offset by cuts
in allocations for other East European countries, reveals the political and
economic uses of Soviet energy policy. In addition to the vital goal of main-

taining control over Eastern Europe, the Soviet Union also seeks to foster economic growth and political stability in the region. With strong, expanding economies, Eastern Europe's substantial contributions to the Soviet Union could be maintained. Stability in East European politics not only aids in the maintenance of Soviet control and adherence to Moscow's policy guidelines but also helps maintain the economic incentives that affect productivity.

While supplies of Soviet energy are critical to attaining these goals, the economic and political criteria for energy policy may conflict. On the one hand, a reduction of energy deliveries, necessitated by slow Soviet energy supply growth and expanding demand at home and abroad, may lead to slower growth in national and personal incomes in Eastern Europe and perhaps political instability. It might also slow the modernization of East European industry and agriculture, which is significant for raising the quality of East European exports to the USSR and thus to Soviet economic performance. Higher quality exports and increased output of hard goods could reduce the subsidy the Soviets perceive they pay to East Europe. On the other hand, flexible energy rationing by the Soviet Union in a tight supply market may greatly increase its leverage and expand its policy options for dealing with the variety of problems in Eastern Europe. Conformance to Soviet internal and foreign-policy preferences may be orchestrated with each East European country as the price for favorable energy supply agreements.

Austerity and slow growth in Eastern Europe might result in pressures to move away from Soviet-approved economic systems and CMEA integration and toward the West. For Eastern Europe a turn to the West would require preferential Western treatment on trade and credit issues. In the longer term, Eastern Europe may be able to increase exports to the West through modernization, especially if Western economies recover and if Western governments do not apply antidumping policies that discriminate against imports from communist countries. In the shorter term, however, Western credits are the key to expanding East European imports. At present, the possibility of default by Poland and Rumania and the potential for repayment problems in other East European countries make Western governments and banks unwilling to extend further credits to most of them. But if East European debts can be rescheduled and then repaid, Western commercial bank credits, as well as government credits, may again be available.

A test of whether the West will return to preferential credit policies toward the East European countries will be the rescheduling of the Polish debt and the conditions applied. The application of stringent International Monetary Fund-type conditionality would be painful for Poland in the short run but in the long run would increase economic recovery. It would also increase the influence of Western banks and governments on Polish economic policy. Thus it would probably require at least tacit Soviet consent. This form of preferential Western policy and increased influence may be extended to other East European countries through the same route, rescheduling and conditionality. Rumania and Yugoslavia are likely candidates to suffer the Polish foreign-debt malady.

Preferential treatment by the West might be supplemented by similar treatment by some of the OPEC nations—for example, an extension of barter or other favorable energy terms by Kuwait, Iran, Libya, Iraq, and Saudia Arabia.

Policy Variables and the Social Contract

Soviet energy and Western trade and credit fostered the substantial improvement in living standards throughout Eastern Europe during the 1970s. One measure of rising living standards was the increase in per-capita net material product. (See table 5-2.)

Another measure was the increase in per-capita meat consumption, in many cases made possible by rising imports of Western grain. (See table 5-3.)

Nominal wages increased at an annual average growth rate ranging from 1.8 percent in Bulgaria to 10.3 percent in Poland between 1970 and 1977. As food—the largest item in family budgets—was subsidized, the increases in real income were generally proportionate, especially in Poland. Although domestic output of consumer-durables output, including cars and housing, did not expand at the same rate as disposable income, some expansion in imports of high quality foreign consumer durables furthered the perception that living conditions were improving.

Table 5-2
East European Growth in Per-Capita Net Material Product, 1970-1977

Rumania	6.2%	to	9.9%
Poland	4.7	to	7.7
Bulgaria	3.2	to	6.8
Hungary	2.8	to	5.6
German Democratic Republic	3.5	to	5.3
Czechoslovakia	2.6	to	4.5

Source: Range in estimates is derived largely from higher official and lower Western estimates of performance. Paul Marer, "Economic Performance and Prospects in Eastern Europe: Analytical Summary and Interpretation of Findings," in U.S. Congress, Joint Economic Committee, *East European Economic Assessment* (1981), 2:33.

Note: Data are range of estimates of annual growth.

Table 5-3
East European Meat Consumption per Capita, 1970-1978
(kilograms)

	1970	1978
German Democratic Republic	66.0	86.2
Czechoslovakia	71.3	83.4
Hungary	58.0	71.2
Poland	52.6	70.6
Bulgaria	41.4	61.6
Rumania	30.0	51.9[a]

Source: Allen A. Terhaar and Thomas A. Vankai, "The East European Feed-Livestock Economy, 1966-85: Performance and Prospects," in U.S. Congress, Joint Economic Committee, *East European Economic Assessment* (1981), 2:563.
[a]1977.

Increased provision of food, consumer durables, transportation, and housing seems to have facilitated a tacit social contract between citizens and regimes in Eastern Europe. Never spelled out by rulers or ruled, the social contract was and remains a tacit and ill-defined understanding. In return for increased material benefits and in some countries greater professionalism in planning and management, East Europeans tolerated low participation in economic and political decision making, rigid and highly centralized political and economic systems, and the denial of many basic civil rights. As it existed in the 1970s, the social contract was somewhat akin to the consumerist policies advocated by Malenkov in the Soviet Union during the late 1950s and derided by Khrushchev as "goulash communism." In other words, more sausage or goulash was offered instead of political freedoms and participation.

The social contract of the 1970s was most evident in Gierek's Poland, but it was shattered by the economic collapse and sixteen months of direct challenge to the system by the "renewal" forces. Poland might succeed in creating a new social contract more in line with economic realities if the government is willing to rescind martial law and work with Solidarity and the Catholic Church. Although less dramatic in other countries, prospective default on the consumerist aspect of the social contract threatens domestic support in the other CMEA countries.

The degree of flexibility and technical professionalism injected into planning and management in the GDR and the New Economic Mechanism (NEM) in Hungary supplemented the consumerist basis of the social contract. In anticipation of the slowdown in economic growth and hence stagnant or falling standards of living expected during the 1980s, Hungary and the German Democratic Republic (GDR) appear to have managed to modify the social contract. In Hungary new mechanisms of planning and management, which allow a greater degree of pluralism in economic organization, have been introduced. In the GDR, planning and management have been made more flexible and technically professional.

A modified social contract is important to output and quality of goods and services because of the relationship between societal interests and incentive systems. Acquiescence to the system may range from apathy to participation. Control systems, including martial law, may reduce the prospects of work interruptions or violence, but they do not provide a climate of productivity. A flexible system, such as the Hungarian NEM, may effectively relate private, cooperative, even second-economy activity to the official sector. More professional systems of planning and management, like the Hungarian NEM or GDR technocratic system, marshal decision making and administrative talent at the planning and enterprise levels more effectively.

Pressed by a myriad of growth-retarding factors, Eastern Europe must look to both favorable Soviet energy policy and preferential Western trade in technology, credit, and food. Hence the centripetal and centrifugal forces of integration with the East and interdependence with the Western markets may be offset. Also systemic changes by the CMEA Six such as the adoption of a more flexible, professional, even pluralistic system like Hungary's NEM may provide the basis for a new social contract and improved domestic performance. Thus the goals of economic growth, modernization, and consumerism in Eastern Europe may be served if Soviet energy policy is preferential, Western credit policy continues to stimulate trade, and a new, more flexible social contract is worked out within the countries of the CMEA Six.

Prospects for Western Economic Relations with CMEA

Availability of Western Imports to CMEA Six and USSR

Economic growth, modernization, and consumerism in the USSR and the CMEA Six have been tied to imports of specific Western products:

1. Western machinery and equipment have been important in investment expenditures, especially for large projects designed to produce for export.
2. Nonagricultural materials have been related to increasing industrial production.
3. Industrial consumer goods have been important for expanding consumption.
4. Grain, especially feed grain for livestock, has been important for expanding the quantity and quality of food available.

In each case the Western imports had a comparative advantage over CMEA alternatives. In most cases CMEA substitutes could have been found in time with some reduction in quality but at the cost of slowed growth, modernization, and consumer improvement that could have been significant.

In the first half of the 1980s imports by the Soviet Union are expected to expand, while imports by the CMEA Six contract. (See table 5-4.)

It is difficult to generalize about the importance of the projected slowdown of Western imports by the CMEA Six between 1981 and 1985. But the Polish experience from 1979 to 1982, when shortages of key imports forced production slowdowns, suggests the bottleneck impact may be greater than anticipated. Shortages of unique equipment, spare parts, and materials not available in CMEA may mean that a slowdown in Western imports will cause a greater than proportionate slowdown in economic growth. To the extent that imports for industrial cooperation projects are reduced, the Polish experience indicates that slowdowns due to bottlenecks could become common.

In the CMEA Six per-capita meat consumption increased by 50 to 90 percent in the 1970s. This buildup in livestock herds represented an investment based on an expectation of continued large imports of Western feed grain. Even with average weather years, net grain imports by the CMEA Six and the USSR are expected to be substantial through 1985. (See table 5-5.)

As table 5-6 indicates, the value of imports from the West in current dollars is expected to rise, despite the contraction in volume.

Table 5-4
Western Imports by the Soviet Union and CMEA Six, 1976-1980, 1981-1985

	1981-1985 Ratios Relative to 1976-1980 Ratios	
	Soviet Union	*CMEA Six*
Ratio of imports from the West of:		
Machinery and equipment to investment expenditures	1.15	0.73
Nonagricultural materials to industrial output	1.13	.70
Industrial consumer goods to consumption	1.00	.72

Source: Daniel L. Bond, "CMEA Growth Projections for 1981-85 and the Implications of Restricted Western Credits" (paper prepared for the NATO Economic Colloquium, March 31-April 2, 1982, Brussels), p. 16. Reprinted with permission.

Table 5-5
Soviet and CMEA Six Grain Balances, 1976, 1980, 1981-1985
(millions of metric tons)

	1976	1980	1981-1985[a]
Soviet grain balance			
Grain production	223.8	189.0	208
Domestic grain use	231.0	221.8	232
Net grain imports	7.2	32.8	24
CMEA Six grain balances			
Grain production	78.5	80.5	85
Domestic grain use	89.5	93.9	96
Net grain imports	11.0	13.4	11

Source: Daniel L. Bond, "CMEA Growth Projections for 1981-85 and the Implications of Restricted Western Credits" (paper prepared for the NATO Economic Colloquium, March 31-April 2, 1982, Brussels), p. 23. Reprinted with permission.
[a]Annual average projected.

Availability of Western Credit to CMEA Six and USSR

The potential for default by Poland and Rumania and serious problems with international solvency in other East European countries have effectively dried up Western sources of credits, both official and private, for most East European countries. Were Poland or Rumania to go into default, this shutoff of credit might become a determining factor in the supply of Western credit to CMEA in 1980s. If rescheduling rather than formal default is the norm, the East European hard-currency debt may continue to increase, albeit unevenly, as Wharton Econometric Forecasting Associates predicts. (See table 5-7.)

Table 5-6
CMEA Six Imports from the West
(billions of current dollars)

	1976	1980	1985
Fuels	1.7	6.2	8.0
Agricultural products and food	3.5	5.3	10.6
Machinery and equipment	6.0	7.3	9.3
Nonfood materials	10.2	14.4	15.9
Industrial consumer goods	.9	1.6	1.3
Total	22.4	34.8	45.1

Source: Daniel L. Bond, "CMEA Growth Projections for 1981-85 and the Implications of Restricted Western Credits" (paper prepared for the NATO Economic Colloquium, March 31-April 2, 1982, Brussels), p. 26. Reprinted with permission.

Table 5-7
Net Hard-Currency Debt to the West, 1980-1985
(billions of current dollars)

	1980 (Actual)	1985 (Projected)
Poland	22.3	23.9
Rumania	9.4	13.5
German Democratic Republic	11.7	16.1
Hungary	6.7	7.7
Czechoslovakia	3.4	4.6
Bulgaria	2.6	1.8
CMEA Six	56.1	67.6
USSR	9.4	20.0

Source: Daniel L. Bond, "CMEA Growth Projections for 1981-85 and the Implications of Restricted Western Credits" (paper prepared for the NATO Economic Colloquium, March 31-April 2, 1982, Brussels), pp. 13, 24. Reprinted with permission.

The nominal increase in Soviet debt from an estimated $9.4 billion to $20 billion represents an approximately 40 percent increase in real terms. The nominal increase in CMEA Six debt from $56.1 billion to $67.6 billion represents a decline of approximately 20 percent in real terms.[1]

Estimates of future debt as long as five years in advance are subject to question. It is worth noting that the Wharton estimates of December 1981 were substantially higher.[2]

Western Policy toward Eastern Trade: Prospects for Unity

Trade and Diplomacy in the 1980s: Carter and Reagan Administration Policy Post-Afghanistan

The Carter administration used sanctions and embargoes after the Soviet invasion of Afghanistan and the Reagan administration used them after the Polish declaration of martial law. Although the sanctions imposed by the two administrations differed in important respects, both were attempts to use the leverage of trade in diplomatic relations with the USSR. The Reagan administration also sought stricter limits on the sale of strategic goods that might benefit the military capability of the USSR.

The Carter use of trade leverage may be assessed in the context of the actions taken after the Soviet invasion of Afghanistan: the partial grain embargo; the restrictions on exchange of phosphates for ammonia; the restrictions on the licensing of high-technology exports; the Olympic boycott; and restraints on fishing and landing rights and government-to-government exchange programs.[3]

During its first year in office the Reagan administration focused on several issues related to trade and diplomacy: removal of the embargoes on grain and phosphates and extension of the U.S.-Soviet Long-Term Grain Supply Agreement for one year; discussions with Western governments on the dangers of financing the West Siberian natural-gas export pipeline; the Polish debt issue; efforts to define an appropriate policy on technology exports to Eastern Europe and to respond effectively to the Polish declaration of martial law in December 1981; and efforts to redefine critical technologies and limit exports of strategic technology through COCOM.

Both the Carter and Reagan administrations' approaches to trade and diplomacy raise questions of effectiveness and appropriateness. Divergencies in the Western countries' policies on East-West trade undermine the potentialities for unified Western action.

Carter Administration's Use of Trade and Diplomacy: The Afghanistan Sanctions

The year 1981 was a time for assessing the sanctions declared by President Carter in the wake of the Soviet invasion of Afghanistan in December 1979. On December 31, 1980, Secretary Philip Klutznick wrote identical letters to House Speaker Thomas O'Neill and president of the Senate Walter Mondale to justify the administration's use of export controls, as required by the Export Administration Act of 1979. This appraisal, similar to President Carter's communication of December 31, 1979, established the administration's policy on the use of foreign trade as an instrument of diplomacy. Moreover, it extended the export controls imposed in response to the Soviet invasion of Afghanistan for another year.[4] In general, the report found that the sanctions were necessary and successful in the past and required in the future. Thus had Carter been reelected, the assessment could have been a blueprint for subsequent action.

Even those who view the Carter sanctions as a short-term political success would not necessarily consider them a detailed prototype for future action in American relations with the USSR or for the general purposes of effectively relating our foreign commerce to the conduct of our diplomacy. The sanctions may alternatively be viewed as having been necessary regardless of whether the economic impact on the Soviet economy was as severe as expected or whether the domestic costs to American farmers and businesses were considered to have been shared equitably. The long-term policy lessons of this reappraisal may be critical factors in delineating policy bases for greater Western unity in Eastern policy.

Rationale for the Carter Sanctions: The United States acted to punish the Soviet Union economically and thereby deter Soviet leaders from using the

Afghanistan invasion as a prototype for other such extensions of power. The administration clearly doubted that the sanctions would compel a Soviet withdrawal. For the Soviet Union the test of the success of the Afghan adventure was not a prolonged occupation but the establishment of an indigenous, effective bureaucracy responsive to its guidance. If the Afghan rebels are able, largely on their own, to frustrate the Soviet attempts to build an Afghan Communist apparatus, the primary Soviet objective would be frustrated, independent of U.S. economic actions. Notwithstanding the success or failure of the Afghan venture, the cost inflicted by the U.S. sanctions might deter Soviet policymakers from engaging in other such uses of direct Soviet military force against sovereign nations. This deterrence conceivably might even apply in cases where the prospects for success, at least in the short run, are more promising than was the case in December 1979 in Afghanistan. The sanctions were a clear signal of the importance the United States and other countries attached to the Soviet action. The political message of the largely economic sanctions was probably as effective as available political-military action and far less risky.

Impact of the Sanctions on the Soviet Union: All of the sanctions had some negative impact on the Soviet economy, although the severity of the punishment inflicted fell short of the Carter administration's initial estimates. In assessing the impact of the individual sanctions on the Soviet Union, the critical question is the difference between likely performance without the sanctions and actual performance with the sanctions.

Partial Grain Embargo: Although the Soviets received 8 million metric tons of U.S. wheat and corn, 17 million additional tons that were contracted for or agreed to were not shipped. During a speech on August 29, 1980, Soviet leader Brezhnev claimed that the Soviet Union had met its import needs for all commodities, including grain.[5] Soviet grain importers claimed to have arranged lower prices for soybeans, which largely offset higher grain prices. Whether these claims are true, the cost of importing grain from other sources probably was greater, perhaps by as much as $1 billion, as U.S. intelligence suggests. On the basis of the available information, it is difficult to document a figure of this magnitude, however.

Absent the embargo, the Soviets might have produced more meat and expanded their herds and grain reserves toward desired levels. Still, the shortfalls in meat production appeared to be largely the result of poor weather and systemic problems in Soviet agriculture rather than simply a consequence of the embargo. In fact, the embargo is probably a poor third as a causal factor.

Phosphates and Ammonia: Despite President Carter's decision to embargo shipments of superphosphates by Armand Hammer's Occidental Petroleum

Company to the Soviet Union, the Soviet Union did not stop shipping ammonia or abrogate the contract. This contract, which calls for the exchange of $20 billion worth of American superphosphates and Soviet anhydrous ammonia over twenty years, is the largest current U.S.-Soviet bilateral agreement. The U.S. supply of superphosphates is of unique importance to Soviet plans to bring new nonblack soil lands into production to augment production of dairy products and vegetables. Although the ban on phosphate exports came too late to affect 1980 crops, it might have had a critical impact on Soviet agricultural production during the Eleventh Five-year Plan (1981-1985) had it been continued.

Licensing of High-Technology Exports: The criteria for licensing exports of products and processes, including spare parts, to the USSR were more rigorously applied and a few items were added to the U.S. list of controlled goods as a result of the embargo policy. Important as high technology from the West may be to Soviet economic modernization, the largely unilateral U.S. embargo on high technology seems to have limited current impact. While no large Soviet project for which contracts were concluded was halted or seriously affected, there has been some shift away from the United States and Japan to West European contractors. Most of the Soviet projects under discussion with American and Japanese suppliers in December 1979 have been taken over by other Western contractors. Thus the short-term impact on the Soviet industrial economy appears to have been negligible.

Olympic Boycott: The absence of the United States and many other nations made the Olympics nonrepresentative and less than the political triumph anticipated by Soviet leaders. To the extent that the absence of many nations depreciated the value of the Moscow Olympics to Soviet leaders and populace, a cost or punishment was meted out by the U.S.-led boycott. The withdrawal of many American contractors supporting the Olympics may have further reduced the benefits the Soviets hoped to extract from hosting the games. Nonetheless, the games were held, were widely publicized, and seventy-nine nations participated.

Restraints on Fishing and Landing Rights and Exchanges: Allocations for catches in U.S. waters were reduced, and some air landing rights were limited. The loss in anticipated catch and inconvenience from landing restrictions entailed minimal economic and political costs for the USSR. The scaling down of all official bilateral exchanges had a symbolic value, but the net effect is debatable.

Impact of the Sanctions on the United States: At the same time most of the measures taken were costly to U.S. farm and business groups and to the federal budget. In the longer run, they may also have the effect of closing

U.S. exporters of agricultural and industrial products out of the Soviet market. In addition, the economic costs to the United States were unevenly shared. Yet the political benefits accruing to the United States may have been more positive. Generally the reaction of Western and developing, especially Islamic, nations was negative to the Soviet invasion and positive to the U.S. political-economic response. Many favoring the U.S. response were especially relieved that it took an economic rather than a military form. In the short run, however, the sanctions had the negative political consequence of straining U.S. relations with its allies in Western Europe and Japan. While many nations supported the Olympic boycott, no other nation followed fully the U.S. embargo and restrictions. This illustrated the difference between the United States and other Western allies, which generally supported the political aspects of the sanctions but not the principle of economic punishment adopted by the Carter administration.

Reagan Administration's Use of Trade and Diplomacy: Change and Continuity

There was some continuity and some change in the Reagan administration's actions on the Carter sanctions policy.[6]

Removal of Grain-Phosphate Embargo and Extension of LTA: Within a few months of taking office, the Reagan administration returned U.S.-Soviet trade in grain and phosphates to its normal basis. On April 24, 1981, President Reagan lifted the embargo on agricultural commodities, including phosphates. In August the administration announced that the two sides had agreed to extend the grain agreement for an additional year and to hold negotiations on a new long-term agreement (LTA) in the fall. After it became apparent that the 1981 corn harvest would probably be the second largest in U.S. history and that the wheat harvest would also set a record, the Reagan administration decided to offer the Soviets 15 million metric tons (MMT) more grain than the 6 to 8 MMT called for in the agreement during its sixth year.

Western Financing of Export Natural-Gas Pipeline: The Reagan administration made concerted efforts to dissuade the West European countries, especially the Federal Republic, the key participant, from going ahead with the pipeline. The president raised the issue at the head-of-state level on several occasions—in April 1981 and January 1982 with German Chancellor Helmut Schmidt in Washington and in July 1981 at the Economic Summit at Ottawa with French President Mitterrand as well as the chancellor. The administration's chief argument was that the additional gas deliveries would make major NATO allies dependent on Soviet gas, and hence vulnerable to Soviet threats to cut off the gas during a political crisis. The administration also argued against the pipeline on the ground that it would provide the Soviets with large amounts of hard currency, perhaps as much as $11.1 billion annually by the mid-1980s, according to an estimate by the Defense Intelligence Agency, which could be used to pay for major purchases of high technology from the West. The administration proposed U.S. coal and revival of plans for development of nuclear electric power as substitutes for Soviet gas. As a minimum precaution if they decided to go ahead with the pipeline, the U.S. urged the West Europeans to arrange standby facilities (for example, Dutch or Norwegian gas).

For much the same reasons some members of Congress—notably Senator Jake Garn and Congressmen John LeBoutillier and James Nelligan—actively opposed the pipeline and urged the president to take a stronger position against West European involvement and to oppose any U.S. participation. Other members, such as Congressmen Gillis Long and Henry Reuss, called for a clarification of U.S. policy with appropriate concern for differing European perspectives.

Two schools of thought are identifiable in the debate on U.S. policy toward the pipeline. One proposes strenuous efforts to stop Western equipment sales and credit to the Soviets for the pipeline; the other counsels acceptance of the West European commitment to the pipeline and urges concentrating on a "safety net" to avoid vulnerability and on obtaining good terms of trade and credit to minimize the prospects of Soviet windfalls.

The stop-the-pipeline school, led by Defense Secretary Caspar Weinberger in the administration, argues that Europe may become hostage to the USSR or Finlandized if the pipeline deal goes through. In their view, the Soviets may spend all or most of the over $10 billion in hard currency that the large new gas sales are expected to generate on Western high technology. They warn that large-scale imports of the sophisticated technologies the Soviets seek in the West would be of significant value to Soviet military power.

Taking this argument one step further, some members of the stop-the-pipeline school argue that the United States may be forced to devote even more resources to countering Soviet military power than at present. In the same vein, the benefits to the Soviet military may be even greater if one believes, as many members of this school do, that the indirect mechanisms of technology transfer that accompany East-West commercial relations (such as training and technical documentation) exceed direct transfers in importance.

U.S. efforts to dissuade the West Europeans from going ahead with the pipeline failed, although the Italian government did agree to a pause to reconsider the Soviet offer after the Polish declaration of martial law. Their intensity also further strained U.S. relations with the West European allies.

The West European perception that increased imports of natural gas and oil from the Soviet Union and sales of energy equipment are desirable is another example of the divergence in the West. It rebuts U.S. arguments against the pipeline on the following grounds. First, any increment of energy in the world market tends to assure reliable supply through a diversity of sources and holds prices down. As energy independence is not the option for Europe and Japan that it is perceived to be for the United States, energy security is the product of diversity in sources of supply. Second, large equipment orders are especially beneficial to stagnant European and Japanese metallurgy and machinery sectors and provide substantial job and production prospects for many years ahead. Third, economic interdependence with the East may stabilize political relations and provide useful tools for Western diplomacy.

The Polish Debt Issue: When Poland proved unable to repay some of its obligations on private bank loans guaranteed by the Commodity Credit Corporation, the Reagan administration had to decide whether to declare Poland in default and accelerate Poland's payment requirements or to reimburse a group of private U.S. banks holding Polish debt guaranteed by the U.S. government. Some administration officials argued that the United States should precipitate a Polish default because the Soviet Union would then be forced to expend its scarce hard currency on Poland. Other administration officials, notably from the Departments of State and Treasury, argued against this course for several reasons. First, a Polish default under accelerated payments would have serious financial repercussions in European and American financial markets as debt holders scrambled for Poland's few attachable assets. Second, Poland would have no incentive to repay its debts if it were forced into default. Third, in the case of default, Poland would have no access to Western credit markets and would be tied even more closely to the Soviet Union. Thus far President Reagan has come down on the side of those opposing a declaration of default, although the issue will remain on the administration's agenda for the foreseeable future.

Technology Export Policy toward Eastern Europe and
Response to the Polish Declaration of Martial Law

In its public statements the Reagan administration has tentatively endorsed the independent-country approach to licensing exports to East European countries.[7] Under this approach, previous administrations, including Carter's, followed a slightly more liberal licensing policy for exports to Poland, Rumania, and Hungary than for the Soviet Union or the remaining members of the CMEA Six. However, the Reagan administration's concerns about the possibility of diversion to the Soviet Union may lead it to modify its position.

Reagan Administration's Sanctions against Poland: After the Jaruzelski government declared martial law on December 13, 1981, the Reagan administration reversed its preferential trade policy toward Poland. On December 23 the president announced the following sanctions against Poland: suspension of Polish fishing rights in U.S. waters; nonrenewal of Poland's line of credit insurance from the Export-Import Bank for short-term trade financing by private banks; a halt to official U.S. food aid; suspension of Polish landing rights in the United States; and a proposal for tighter COCOM restrictions on exports of high technology to Poland. (See appendix 5-B for details.)

Impact of the Reagan Sanctions on Poland: In responding to the Polish declaration of martial law, the Reagan administration faced a dilemma. It wanted to punish the Jaruzelski government for its restrictions on civil liberties but not the Polish people. Given the weakness of Poland's economy, however, the sanctions are likely to inflict severe harm on the economy. For example, the expiration of the credit guarantees will effectively cut off Poland's access to credits to finance imports from the United States. Polish officials claim that the sanctions will dramatically reduce chicken production. Such statements undoubtedly are in part an attempt on the part of the government to blame the United States for food shortages, but the sanctions may well have a serious impact on the availability of meat and fish.

Reagan Administration's Sanctions against the Soviet Union: On December 29, the administration imposed sanctions on the Soviet Union that the president said bore a "heavy and direct responsibility" for martial law in Poland. The sanctions consisted of the following restrictions on U.S.-Soviet commercial and scientific relations: expanded controls on exports of oil and gas equipment; a halt on the issuance of validated licenses for high-technology exports; postponement of negotiations on a new long-term grain agreement; suspension of negotiations for a new U.S.-Soviet maritime agreement; nonrenewal of several bilateral scientific exchange agreements; suspension of Aeroflot's landing rights in the United States; and termination of the Soviet Purchasing Commission. (See appendix 5-B for more details.)

Impact of the Reagan Administration's Sanctions against the Soviet Union: *Expansion of Export Controls on Oil and Gas Equipment:* The Reagan administration expanded controls on exports of oil and gas equipment, which were imposed by the Carter administration in 1978, to cover equipment and technical data for the transmission and refinement of natural gas and oil. The chief effect of this sanction was the revocation of the Caterpillar Tractor Company's license to export pipelayers for use on projects other than the export pipeline and a ban on the General Electric Company's export of rotors and other parts for the compressors that three West European companies are to build for the export pipeline. The Reagan administration considered, but reportedly rejected, an effort to extend the embargo on technical data such as the GE patents to non-U.S. licensees, particularly a French firm, Alsthom-Atlantique, which is licensed by GE to produce rotors.[8] An alternative source for the pipelayers is Komatsu, a Japanese firm, which has already received Soviet orders for comparable equipment.

Halt on the Issuance of Validated Licenses for High Technology: Due to the slowdown in U.S. exports of industrial products, especially those embodying high technology, that resulted from the Carter sanctions, the moratorium on the issuance of licenses is not expected to have much impact on the Soviet Union. Some American firms may lose orders they might otherwise have received. In the long run, this measure is likely to increase the Soviet Union's already apparent tendency to treat U.S. firms as suppliers of last resort.

Postponement of Negotiations on a New Long-Term Grain Agreement: While the Reagan administration decided to postpone negotiations on a new grain agreement, it did not restrict sales of wheat and corn during the sixth year of the agreement, which ended on September 30, 1982. The Soviets could still buy up to 23 MMT of U.S. wheat and corn. Thus, the U.S.-Soviet grain trade will not be affected by the actions of the Reagan administration in the short run. In the longer run, however, the Reagan administration may find that 1981 was a propitious time for renegotiating the grain agreement, as it was the third bad year for Soviet grain production.

Suspension of Negotiations on a New U.S.-Soviet Maritime Agreement: With the expiration of the second bilateral maritime agreement on December 31, 1981, Soviet ships will have to request permission to enter U.S. ports ten days in advance rather than four days in advance. This measure will cause the Soviet Union some inconvenience and possibly some hard-currency losses as the administration plans a restrictive approach to authorizing Soviet port calls.[9] The immediate effect of this measure is not expected to be major since Soviet port calls have been declining since the Carter sanctions and the longshoremen's eighteen-month boycott of Soviet ships at East and Gulf Coast ports. Some observers believe that in the longer run the absence of a maritime agreement might preclude a new grain agreement.

Nonrenewal of Several Bilateral Scientific Exchange Agreements: While the decision not to renew three of the bilateral scientific agreements (space, energy, and science and technology) will further reduce the amount of official scientific interchange between the two countries, which has been limited since the Carter sanctions, the net and long-term effects of this measure are difficult to predict.

Suspension of Aeroflot's Landing Rights in the United States: This measure will inconvenience those traveling between the two countries and may cause the Soviet Union some hard-currency losses, but it is not expected to have a major impact on either country.

Termination of the Soviet Purchasing Commission: Due to the depressed level of U.S. sales of industrial products to the Soviet Union, this measure is not expected to have much impact.

Critical Technologies and Strategic Goods Exports

The long-awaited Office of Technology Assessment Critical Technology Study was completed in October 1980. The emphasis of the study was more on technology transfers than product sales. The Reagan administration adopted the concept of emphasizing technology and added a heightened concern about controlling industrial espionage by foreign countries in the United States.

    If a COCOM member wishes to authorize the export of an item appearing on the lists of controlled goods, it must request an exception. In general, the United States has attempted to broaden and lengthen the lists of strategic items and to apply a no-exceptions policy. Some members, such as France and the Netherlands, have strongly resisted the more restrictive U.S. approach. The Reagan administration plans a major effort to increase this case and no-exceptions approach, thus sharply restricting trade in critical technology with the East.

Appeals by the Carter and Reagan Administrations for a Unified Western Policy

Both the Carter and Reagan administrations realized that U.S. export controls and economic sanctions would not be effective without the support of the other Western industrialized nations. Therefore the Carter administration sought the allies' agreement not to undercut the U.S. restrictions on sales of grain and high technology to the Soviet Union following the invasion of Afghanistan. Similarly the Reagan administration has placed emphasis on pursuading the Western European countries not to go ahead with the pipeline and on inducing the Western European countries and Japan to impose sanctions on Poland and the Soviet Union. It has had little success with either goal, although the Common Market countries have agreed to restrict some imports from the Soviet Union.

In reviewing U.S. policies on East-West trade, the Reagan administration concluded that it would have to seek the support of the fourteen other members of COCOM, Japan, and the NATO countries except Iceland, for stricter controls on exports to the Soviet Union and Poland and for the inclusion of the critical-technology approach in COCOM's guidelines for granting exceptions to them. The administration's assessment of COCOM's effectiveness as an informal mechanism for controlling exports to the Soviet Union was offered by Robert D. Hormats in November 1981:

> The COCOM multilateral embargo, coordinated with our major allies over the years, has been reasonably effective in controlling items on the embargo lists. However, there have been significant exports of controlled items in circumvention of regulations, as well as some exports of items not now under control, which have helped the Soviet Union strengthen its military-industrial base.[10]

Toward the High-Level COCOM Meeting

At the Ottawa Economic Summit in July 1981, the leaders of the United States, the United Kingdom, the Federal Republic of Germany, Japan, France, Canada, and Italy signed a declaration stating that their economic relations with the Eastern countries would continue to be compatible with their political and security objectives. At the time they did not reveal how they intended to maintain the desired compatibility. The generality of the wording, in fact, concealed divergent views on how trade and diplomacy ought to be related. The heads of state further agreed to hold a high-level meeting to discuss controls on exports to the Soviet Union. In the U.S. view, the high-level COCOM meeting was to be "the first broad reconsideration of our technology control system in nearly thirty years."[11]

In addition to the frictions that COCOM's day-to-day operations cause, there are serious areas of disagreement between the United States and the other members of COCOM stemming from divergent views on East-West trade. (For a description of COCOM's operating procedures and an assessment of its effectiveness in controlling Western exports to the East, see appendix 5-A.) The United States has traditionally favored a more restrictive approach toward East-West trade and more definition of what constitutes a strategic export than the other members. The United States tends to link political and commercial relations with the communist countries, whereas the West European countries and Japan tend to view them as separate.

When they do use linkage, it tends to be positive, as opposed to the negative linkage used by the United States. The United States uses export controls for foreign-policy purposes as well as national-security purposes; the others base their controls strictly on national security. Under British, French, Japanese, and German law, there is a presumption of approval for exports unless they would be detrimental to national security. In fact, a German firm may sue the government if it feels that there is not a legitimate national security reason for the denial of its license. Concomitantly the American process of making decisions about East-West trade differs from those of the West European countries and Japan. Those of the latter are less public, involve fewer officials, allow business a greater role, and emphasize the roles of foreign trade ministries over those of defense ministries.[12]

The chief sources of the differing views of the U.S. and other COCOM members on trade with the East are differing perspectives on how overall relations with the communist countries ought to be handled and the differing importance of trade with the East. The West European and Japanese economies are more dependent on trade than is the American economy. Trade with the East is more important for their economies than it is for the American economy.[13] It is especially important for employment in certain sectors of a number of their economies—such as German steel and French medium-machine building—while it is only important for one sector of the U.S. economy—agriculture.

The differing perspectives of its members and decision-making processes result in disputes and frictions within COCOM. Commercial rivalries are an additional source of division, sometimes leading members to accuse others of seeking commercial advantage.

All of this is not to say that there are no areas of consensus or unifying factors. There are. All members agree that some controls on exports to the East are needed to preserve Western security. All agree that COCOM is an appropriate mechanism for coordinating the necessary controls. All agree that consensus should be COCOM's guiding principle.

The Afghanistan sanctions that President Carter imposed in January 1980 without fully consulting the other COCOM members in advance, and, it will probably turn out, the Reagan administration's new approach have placed COCOM at a crossroad. While COCOM did respond with a virtual halt on granting members' requests for exceptions to COCOM controls for exports to the Soviet Union, Japan was the only country to follow the U.S. lead in restricting commercial relations with the Soviet Union. (For a description of the exceptions process, see appendix 5-A.) France, the FRG, and even the Conservative government of British Prime Minister Margaret Thatcher essentially maintained normal commercial relations with the Soviet Union. But Japanese businessmen, who fear Soviet commercial retaliation, are now challenging the policy. The election of French President

François Mitterrand may have the effect of moving French policy closer to that of the United States, but France is unlikely to abandon its policy of promoting trade with the East, especially given its increasing unemployment.

Results of the High-Level COCOM Meeting

At the meeting, which was held on January 19 and 20, 1982, in Paris, the United States proposed the adoption of the critical-technology approach that would focus on controlling the transfer of modern technologies and active technology-transfer mechanisms. This would amount to a fundamental change in COCOM's guidelines. Specifically, the United States proposed tighter controls on advanced computers, other electronics, fiber optics, semiconductors, and several metallurgical processes.[14] It probably also sought restrictions on the construction of turn-key plants in militarily relevant industries and Western agreements to train Easterners in militarily relevant technologies. In the same vein, the United States was reported to have proposed that all contracts worth $100 million or more be subject to COCOM's approval to make sure that they did not transfer any critical technologies.

According to at least one account in the press, the United States also sought agreement to stop granting exceptions for exports to the Soviet bloc.[15] While a moratorium on exceptions involving the Soviet Union was instituted after the invasion of Afghanistan, a no-exceptions policy for the entire Soviet bloc would be a major change in COCOM's operations. This report is probably accurate since it squares with statements by the administration before the meeting that it intended to propose tighter controls on exports to certain communist countries—first for the Soviet Union and, after General Jaruzelski's declaration of martial law, to Poland as well. Probably the United States also continued its push for better enforcement of the controls at the meeting.

From comments to the press by administration officials and the statement released after the meeting, it seems that the Reagan administration met with some success.[16] The other members apparently agreed to redefine COCOM's guidelines and procedures, to include modern technologies on the lists, and not to make exceptions requests until the 1982 list review is finished. An anonymous U.S. official explained that many differences still remained, not surprising given the radical nature of the U.S. proposals.

Thus, for the time being at least, COCOM appears likely to move in the direction proposed by the Reagan administration. But it remains to be seen whether COCOM will soon substitute a case approach for the list approach—the goal of the critical technologies identification process—and agree to dramatically tighter controls on exports and transfers to the Soviet bloc. The other members' greater stakes in trade with the East and their philosophic differences on the management of East-West trade all but ensure that there will continue to be conflict as well as cooperation within COCOM.

Such conflicts are not likely to cause COCOM's demise. There is too much agreement, even by countries that have been critical about COCOM's record, that the organization is a useful mechanism for coordinating export controls and that some controls on exports to communist countries are essential for Western security.[17] In addition, members might view formal dissolution of COCOM as the wrong signal to send the Eastern countries.

The Reagan administration's policy on East-West trade represents both a continuation or further development of that set by the Carter administration following the Soviet invasion of Afghanistan and a departure from it.

Both administrations sought to use the leverage of trade in relations with the East. Thus, both presidents responded to Soviet challenges with economic sanctions and other restrictions on bilateral relationships. Both sought to limit the foreign availability of embargoed products by enlisting the support of the West Europeans and Japanese. The Reagan administration retained and enlarged its predecessor's restrictions on high-technology exports to the Soviet Union. It also maintained the foreign-policy controls on equipment for the Kama River truck plant and on oil and gas equipment. The Reagan administration broadened the latter after the Polish declaration of martial law to include equipment and technical data for transmission and refinement, as well as exploration and production. Other elements of continuity include the slowdown in activity in official scientific exchanges and a preferential export-licensing policy for China.

Elements of change include the Reagan administration's decision to lift the embargo on grain and phosphates. Although shared by previous administrations, including Carter's, the Reagan administration's concern about industrial espionage and evasion of U.S. and multilateral export controls by communist countries appears to represent a qualitative change. In addition, the impending expiration of the grain and maritime agreements and several of the scientific exchanges presented the Reagan administration with new issues. Other issues emerged with the Polish debt crisis and the progress made by West European countries and the Soviet Union in the pipeline negotiations. While the Reagan administration endorsed the policy of differentiation in export licensing for Eastern Europe, its heightened concern about the possibility of diversion of U.S. exports from Eastern Europe to the Soviet Union and the view prevalent among some officials that the CMEA countries may be viewed as a Soviet bloc may augur a departure from this policy.

Agenda of Variables in Unified Western Policy

Toward More Government Intervention or
Reliance on Market Mechanisms?

Western policies on trade and credit during the 1980s are potentially significant for economic outcomes in the Soviet Union and the CMEA Six.[18]
Western policy may follow three courses: (1) preferential, encouraging
growth, modernization, and consumerism through government credit and
business facilitation; (2) discriminatory, encouraging renewed Eastern isolation from the West and world markets by stricter licensing criteria, credit
restrictions and market-denial policies such as quotas, antidumping pro-
ceedings, and restrictive tariffs; or (3) withdrawal, relying on market forces
to set commercial and credit terms.

A preferential policy might involve extensive government loans and
guarantees more favorable in terms of size, interest rates, grace periods,
dates of maturity, and conditions of repayment, including possibilities for
rescheduling, than those available on international capital markets.
Government facilitation of commercial relations, exchanges, and availability of statistics would tend to ease and expand commerce. Expanded Commodity Credit Corporation (CCC) credits for agricultural purchases might
even be sought for Eastern countries not currently eligible for most-
favored-nation (MFN) and credit benefits. Without such a favorable policy,
East-West trade is likely to decline from the trends of the 1970s. This trade-
promoting option may be considered the Helsinki option because it would
be in compliance with the economic provisions of the Helsinki Final Act.[19]
This policy presumably would find support among agricultural and certain
industrial interests in the United States.[20]

A discriminatory policy would involve negative government interven-
tions in the conduct of East-West commerce such as more restrictive licensing by the United States and its COCOM partners and discouraging the extension of private credit. The latter could be accomplished directly by
halting government credits and guarantees to Eastern Europe or indirectly
by letting commercial banks know that using loanable funds in the Eastern
market would not be in keeping with U.S. policy. With congressional approval, trade might be restricted not only on strategic but also on economic
grounds—a return to the spirit and letter of the Export Control Act of 1949,
which was applied in such a manner as to prevent the export of goods that
would augment the economic as well as military capacities of the communist
countries. Foreign-policy controls—embargoes and sanctions—might be
used extensively in response to foreign or domestic actions of the Eastern
countries, although with limited economic relations there would be less
leverage available. This variant could also be called mercantilistic in the

traditional sense of the word in that *raison d'état* rather than *raison d'affairs* would dictate commercial exchange. It finds support in the current policy of the Reagan administration.[21]

Reliance on market forces would entail limitations on government action to either encourage (credits, market facilitation) or discourage (trade restrictions, antidumping actions) commerce. This might be called a laissez-faire or free trade policy. As applied to the USSR and the CMEA Six, a laissez-faire policy would be likely to retain some export controls for strategic reasons. It is largely supported by segments of U.S. business, agricultural, and banking interests.

Toward a Differentiated or Unified Western Commercial Policy?

Western policy may be doubly differentiated—with respect to the CMEA Six as opposed to the Soviet Union or among the Western countries. For example, the West may apply preferential policies toward the smaller members of CMEA but discriminatory policies toward the Soviet Union. Due to the larger size and lower trade dependence of the Soviet economy, the impact of this differential would be less for the Soviet Union than for Eastern Europe.

Although the United States and other Western countries have tended to apply differential credit and licensing policies to the USSR and the CMEA Six in recent years, a more unified policy is possible and may be likely. When Poland and Rumania encountered debt-servicing problems, some governments and banks shut off their facilities to most other Eastern countries, regardless of their individual credit worthiness. This may be considered the reverse side of the umbrella theory that holds the USSR to be the Eastern debtor of last resort. This unified credit perspective might hold that if one country is not credit worthy, then all must be ineligible for Western loans. On licensing one might hold that all the CMEA Six are direct conduits to the USSR so that restrictions on technology trade with any one of them should be based on the Soviet case. Similarly all technical information obtained in any way by any CMEA country would be assumed to flow automatically from the Eastern recipient to Moscow.

Among the Western countries, commercial policy is differentiated to a significant degree, with U.S. policy diverging from West European and Japanese policies. If the United States and the other Western countries follow different policies toward the CMEA countries—for example, a discriminatory American policy and preferential European policy—the outcomes may not only be different but also deepen Western political disunity. Western assessments of the use of trade in diplomacy, exports of strategic goods, credits and conditionality, differentiation or unity within CMEA, and interdependence are marked by unity and diversity.

Trade Policy: Embargoes or Negotiations? For the most part, the West Europeans are opposed to economic sanctions or warfare against the CMEA countries.[22] They argue that past embargoes have not been very effective in changing the target country's policies. Moreover, they argue, embargoes represent an inflexible use of trade leverage in diplomatic relations and reduce the number of levers available to the Western countries for influencing Eastern policy. They reject the notion prevalent in some U.S. quarters that relations with the East are a zero-sum game, in which benefits to the East are costs to the West. They stress the belief that continuing the process of negotiation and economic relations with the East is crucial, especially when political tensions are high.

These perceptions, which diverge substantially from those of many in the United States, have an economic as well as a philosophic basis. Trade with the East is much more important for Western Europe than for the United States. Thus Western Europe is more vulnerable to contractions in it. Beside economic impacts, West Europeans fear that tensions aroused by U.S. sanctions have a greater political impact in Europe than in the United States.

Like the United States, the West Europeans differentiate among the CMEA countries in trade relations. This differential is strongest in the case of the Federal Republic's trade with the GDR, but the other West European countries also apply differentiated policies. The American policy remains differentiated in law, the Export Administration Act of 1981, but in certain cases it is more unified in practice than the legislation would suggest.

Strategic Goods: A Changed COCOM? Western Europe, Japan, and the United States agree on the general principles of COCOM—the need for controlling exports of strategic goods to the East and for a multilateral mechanism for coordinating members' controls—but disagree on the specifics. Changes in the lists and tighter controls on certain items are acceptable to all members of COCOM, but the West Europeans and Japanese would not be likely to approve wholesale changes in the lists or a dramatic tightening of the controls. Although COCOM has agreed to U.S. proposals to work elements of the critical technology approach into COCOM's guidelines (see appendix 5-A), many West Europeans appear unconvinced that the critical technology approach is workable. Europeans and Japanese also seem unwilling to accept the broader definition of technology transfer inherent in the new U.S. approach.

Credit Policy: Default and Restrictions or Rescheduling and Conditionality? Few in Europe are in favor of precipitating a formal Polish default.

Part of the reason is that West European governments and banks, which have a larger exposure than their U.S. counterparts, stand to lose more in the event of a Polish default. But they also fear that if a formal declaration of default were made, Poland would no longer have any incentive to repay its debts and would have no other option than a closer Soviet orientation in economic and political policy.

U.S. commercial banks and some private citizens have proposed conditionality as a means of avoiding defaults, assuring repayment, and maximizing benefits to the West. Economic conditionality is familiar from its use by the International Monetary Fund. As applied to Poland and, in the future, possibly to other East European countries on the verge of formal default, economic conditionality might include the following elements: provision of adequate and verifiable information, the establishment of a consistent long-range stabilization program by the indigenous government, and progress with the two preceding elements as a condition for rescheduling old loans. U.S. commercial banks have taken the lead in arguing for applying economic conditionality to the rescheduling of the Polish debt despite the lack of enthusiasm on the part of the West European banks.

Political conditionality is a more delicate issue with less clear precedent. But it is certainly not unknown for a country in debt to another or dependent on another for a key import to be responsive on a variety of political and economic issues. Political conditionality is the key to new loans to many Eastern countries. Political conditionality therefore is an issue primarily for Western political leaders, not for bankers. The West European governments appear even more reluctant to apply political than specific economic conditionality. The Reagan administration has not raised the issue, but political conditionality would appear to be compatible with its use of economic leverage in diplomacy, although the emphasis would be more on sticks than carrots. The possibility of applying political conditionality may come up in the future; it was not included in the ten Western governments' agreement to reschedule official Polish 1981 debts in July 1981. They did, however, apply their leverage by agreeing not to reschedule official Polish debts falling due in 1982 until martial law is lifted.

Western Perceptions: Differentiation or Uniformity within CMEA? In the United States the perception of a Soviet bloc has come back into currency in a number of ways. Increasingly exports to any East European country, including Hungary, are assumed to be readily available to the Soviet Union. Also industrial espionage and illegal purchases of high-technology items by communist countries increasingly are thought to be part of a unified CMEA operation. These three mechanisms are considered a major means of technology transfer to the Soviet Union.

Europeans, however, still accept an independent-country approach similar to that of the Export Administration Act and apply differentiated policies in trade, credit, and licensing, especially toward the CMEA Six.

Without changing the basic legislation, the United States has applied a more restrictive trade and credit policy toward the Soviet Union and the CMEA Six. The opposite has been true in regard to the People's Republic of China. Since the extension of MFN status, government credits, liberalized licensing, and trade-facilitation measures in the 1979 normalization, the tilt toward China continues. The Japanese may be said to share this policy toward China. In this period of differential policy practices under a continuing legislative framework, Yugoslavia appears to be in the grey area: sometimes a China-like tilt but more often a CMEA-like restriction.

Isolation or Interdependence? The Europeans do not consider interdependence with Eastern Europe as an option. Instead they view it an established fact and as a necessity. By contrast, many in the United States view interdependence as both avoidable and to be discouraged, except in the grain trade. Differences in philosophy and levels of trade with the East account for these divergent perceptions on either side of the Atlantic.

In their weakened economic conditions, the CMEA Six may view any Western policy short of preference as discrimination. Such a perception could lead to a return to isolation. A return to isolation would deny the CMEA Six Western credit, technology, and grain and restrain politically necessary modernization and consumer improvement. Professional reform would likely be set back as well.

A Resolution of Western Commercial Policy

The three basic commercial policy options available to the United States—a preferential or Helsinki policy, a discriminatory or mercantilistic policy, or a market or laissez-faire policy—would have quite different effects on the U.S. effort to forge a common Western policy.

A Helsinki-option U.S. trade and credit policy could form the basis for a unified Western policy. As Western preference is critical to economic growth, modernization, and consumerism in Eastern Europe, it would have a beneficial effect on the economies of the CMEA Six. A preferential policy orientation would offer more benefits to the East European members of CMEA than to the Soviet Union and would serve as a counterweight to Soviet influence on the smaller members of CMEA.

A preferential Western credit policy to East Europe might not necessarily involve any new loans to any CMEA Six at this time or in the 1980s, especially from commercial banks. Even with strict conditionality for payment of interest and rescheduled principal, new resources from Western banks normally would not be available for Poland, Rumania, or the other CMEA countries. Yet some Western governments may be willing to make credit and credit guarantees available to the economically stronger East European countries under certain political conditions, including some forms of economic reform. In that case, Western commercial banks might reevaluate their lending policies based on prospects of improved East European planning and management. Reform, in turn, might facilitate economic conditionality on rescheduling and repayment.

A mercantilist U.S. trade and credit policy would be divisive in the West, especially if it included embargoes, economic sanctions, or a marked tightening of export controls. It would have a detrimental effect on economic growth, modernization, and consumerism in Eastern Europe. East European leaders could then blame their economic failures on the United States. A discriminatory policy would have a greater impact on the economically weaker East European countries than on the Soviet Union and might strengthen the latter's inclination to use force and tighten controls in Eastern Europe.

The West Europeans would not be likely to join the United States in adopting a discriminatory policy. If they did, a unified Western policy of discrimination would lead in the direction of mutual isolation. Such a policy might well make slow economic growth inevitable for Eastern Europe and exacerbate East-West tensions.

A laissez-faire or market U.S. trade and credit policy toward Eastern Europe probably would be viewed as discriminatory by East and West Europeans. Without the Western governmental umbrella, commercial relations between Eastern Europe and the West probably could not continue as in the past, given current economic woes in Eastern Europe. For their part, U.S. banks and firms, which generally lack the long experience in dealing with the CMEA countries that some banks and firms in Western Europe have, might conclude that absent the U.S. governmental umbrella, they could not deal profitably with communist countries due to their dominance of domestic markets and foreign trade monopolies. As European and Japanese governments are heavily involved in East-West and North-South trade, a laissez-faire orientation would not likely develop in their East-West trade.

Whether Western trade and credit policies are preferential or discriminatory might also indirectly influence Soviet policy toward Eastern Europe. Western analysts generally consider Soviet energy policy toward Eastern Europe preferential because the Soviets supply oil and gas to East European countries at less than the OPEC or world market price and accept a mixture of hard and soft currencies as payment. They conclude that Soviet terms for energy sales confer an implicit subsidy on Eastern Europe.

(While some note that the exchange rates used to estimate the subsidy—Soviet purchases of East European foods at less than world market
prices—and political benefits to the Soviet Union from trade with Eastern
Europe can influence the size of the implicit subsidy, it is generally assumed
to be positive and in favor of the CMEA Six.) A preferential Western policy
would tend to strengthen Eastern Europe's position regarding the Soviet
Union and might thereby encourage a similar preferential Soviet policy
toward Eastern Europe: continued preferential energy supplies and for-
bearance on rising East European debts to the USSR.

At the same time perceptions on preference or discrimination are not
universal. Most CMEA countries, for example, view current Soviet energy
and Western credit-rationing policy as discriminatory. In addition to factors that may offset the perceived Soviet energy subsidy, the East Europeans feel that past discrimination during the Stalinist period needs to be
rectified. Moreover, many countries such as the GDR and Hungary feel that
it would be unfair, unwise, and discriminatory for the West to treat them as
a uniform part of an Eastern bloc. Indeed the GDR feels the absence of
Western credit results from an American administration policy to use credit
as a weapon in East-West confrontation. Hungary feels that the quotas, antidumping actions, and restrictions on credit and licensing, which the West
applies to Rumania or other CMEA countries, are discriminatory in its
case.

If Western policy is to be effective in influencing the CMEA Six, it must
be unified. Due to the widespread availability of goods, services, and
loanable funds in Western Europe and Japan, the United States cannot take
unilateral action. A laissez-faire or mercantilistic U.S. policy is unlikely to
be the basis for a unified Western policy. The Reagan administration is
seeking to put credit on a government-controlled basis and is unlikely to
adopt a free-market approach to East-West trade. In addition, the governments of Western Europe and Japan are unlikely to endorse a policy that
would deny them the ability to influence commercial relations with the East.
Nor would a mercantilistic policy be likely to serve as a basis for a common
policy, even though the West European countries and Japan might be willing to accept some new restrictions on exports for strategic reasons.

Both policies would be perceived as discriminatory in Eastern and
Western Europe—the mercantilistic policy on its face and the laissez-faire
policy because of its likely effects. These policies would also tend toward
mutual isolation of East and West and might also worsen the tensions between them. In Eastern Europe, the goals of economic growth, modernization, and consumerism might be set back. In the absence of a preferential
Soviet policy, the results might well be political instability.

A Helsinki-type U.S. policy with appropriate and well-enforced controls on strategic exports could serve as the basis for a unified Western

policy because it is compatible with the general outlines of West European and Japanese policies. Moreover, such a policy is based on the only formal accord on East-West commercial and political relations. Through the astute application of political and economic conditionality, a Helsinki-type policy toward the CMEA Six could encourage political and economic change in Eastern Europe.

Notes

1. Daniel L. Bond, "CMEA Growth Projections for 1981-85 and the Implications of Restricted Western Credits" (paper prepared for the NATO Economic Colloquium, Brussels, March 31-April 2, 1982), p. 21.

2. Wharton Econometric Forecasting Associates, *Current Analysis*, December 7, 1981.

3. The discussion of the Carter administration record is drawn largely from *An Assessment of the Afghanistan Sanctions and Embargoes: Implications for Trade and Diplomacy in the 1980's*, by John P. Hardt and Kate S. Tomlinson, released by the House Foreign Affairs Committee in April 1981.

4. Reprinted in U.S. Department of Commerce, International Trade Administration, Office of Export Administration, *Export Administration Annual Report, FY 1980* (Washington, D.C.: U.S. Government Printing Office, February 1981), appendix D (hereinafter cited as Carter Administration Report).

5. Translated in *Current Digest of the Soviet Press*, October 1, 1980, p. 4.

6. On December 31, 1981, Secretary of Commerce Malcolm Baldridge submitted to Congress the Reagan administration's first annual report on export administration, in U.S. Congress, Joint Economic Committee, *1982 Report of the President* (Washington, D.C.: U.S. Government Printing Office, 1982) 2:241.

7. See, for example, U.S. Congress, Joint Economic Committee, *East-West Commercial Policy: A Dialogue with the Reagan Administration* (Washington, D.C.: U.S. Government Printing Office, 1982), pp. 22, 24, 29, 33.

8. Clyde H. Farnsworth, "U.S. Shifts on Soviet Gas Line," *New York Times*, April 16, 1982, pp. D1, D10.

9. U.S. Department of Commerce, "President Imposes Economic Sanctions on the U.S.S.R. and Poland," in *East-West Commercial Policy: A Congressional Dialogue with the Reagan Administration*, p. 68. (Reprinted as appendix 5-B).

10. Testimony of Robert D. Hormats, Assistant Secretary of State for Economic and Business Affairs before the House Committee on Foreign

Affairs, Subcommittee on International Economic Policy and Trade, November 12, 1981, in *Export Controls on Oil and Gas Equipment* (Washington, D.C.: U.S. Government Printing Office, 1983).

11. Caspar W. Weinberger, "Technology Transfers to the Soviet Union," *Wall Street Journal*, January 12, 1982, p. 32.

12. John R. McIntyre and Richard T. Cupitt, "East-West Strategic Trade Controls: Crumbling Consensus?" *Survey* 25 (Spring 1980):93-94.

13. For some statistics, see U.S. Congress, Office of Technology Assessment, *Technology and East-West Trade* (Washington, D.C.: U.S. Government Printing Office, 1980), p. 38.

14. Paul Lewis, "Allies Discuss More Curbs on Sales to Soviet Bloc," *New York Times*, January 20, 1982, p. A8.

15. Ibid.

16. Ibid. Paul Lewis, "Soviet Pipeline Called Vulnerable," *New York Times*, January 21, p. A4; "U.S., Allies Agree to Redefine Rules on Sales to Soviets," *Wall Street Journal*, January 21, 1982, p. 31.

17. The authors of the Office of Technology Assessment's study reached the same conclusion.

18. We would like to express our appreciation to Lawrence Brainard and Donald Green for useful insights for this section.

19. For the text of the final act, see U.S. Department of State, *Department of State Bulletin*, September 1, 1975, pp. 323-350.

20. *East-West Commercial Policy*, pp. 6, 13, 44; Carter Administration Report, Enclosure 3.

21. *East-West Commercial Policy*, pp. 20-33.

22. See, for example, Angela Stent, *Embargo to Ostpolitik: The Political Economy of West German-Soviet Relations, 1955-1980* (Cambridge: Cambridge University Press, 1981), pp. 215-219, 233-243.

Appendix 5A: COCOM's Operating Procedures and an Assessment of Its Effectiveness

COCOM's Procedures

Membership

Japan and all of the NATO countries except Iceland are members of COCOM. Thus, several important sources of technology, among them Sweden and Switzerland, are not members.

Target Countries

COCOM controls apply to the USSR, the People's Republic of China (PRC), Eastern Europe except Yugoslavia, and Asian communist countries. Cuba is not subject to COCOM controls.

Operating Principles

Informal Basis: COCOM is based not on international treaty or law but on agreement. This has several important consequences for the organization's operations and effectiveness. First, decisions are not legally binding on its members. Rather, they are recommendations, which the members must then implement through their own national laws. In the United States, participation is effectuated through the Export Administration Act of 1979 as amended in 1981, which supersedes and incorporates the relevant provisions of the Battle Act. Second, COCOM has no enforcement mechanism or sanctions that can be brought to bear on a member that disregards its recommendations. Nonetheless, members seem to regard COCOM decisions as obligations to be met.

Unanimity: As befits an informal organization, unanimity or, in some cases, unanimity of all members present is the decision-making rule. This has several important consequences for COCOM's operations. First, no one member can impose its will on the others, but, paradoxically, each member has an effective veto. Second, this method of decision making may therefore be characterized as consensual or, in the view of some, as a search for the least common denominator.

Secrecy: Deliberations within COCOM and most of the details about its operations are not publicized. The high degree of discretion with which COCOM operates is not surprising considering its hazy status in law, but there are other reasons for it. For some countries participation may be incompatible with domestic law or may arouse criticisms from nongovernmental leftist political parties. As a result, it is difficult to study COCOM and assess its effectiveness. Fortunately, much is reliably known about COCOM's operations from executive communications to Congress and other open sources.

The Lists

Description: Officially, the three lists of embargoed commodities, which are the basis for the control system, are classified, but it is possible to get a fair idea of what they contain. For example, it is well known and officially acknowledged that the items on the COCOM lists are on the U.S. Commodity Control List (CCL). Despite the fact that the COCOM lists can be partially reconstructed from the U.S. list and those of some of the other members, a commonly advanced rationale for keeping the COCOM lists secret is that publication could show the Soviet Union where to focus its R&D efforts.

The three lists are the following: a munitions list; an atomic-energy list including all sources of fissionable materials, nuclear reactors, and reactor components; and an industrial-commercial list, which includes dual-use items with both civilian and military uses. Understandings about COCOM procedures and operations are appended to the lists as footnotes. Since it is fairly clear what items belong on the munitions and atomic-energy lists and because of the obvious security implications of exporting these kinds of commodities, the first two lists cause few disagreements within COCOM. As might be expected from the nature of the commodities on it, the industrial-commercial list gives rise to most of the controversy within COCOM and accounts for most of its work. It is divided into a number of categories, according to product.[1]

According to some sources, the industrial-commercial list is divided into three sublists, depending on the degree of control: International List I (export prohibited unless an exception is granted), International List II (exports permitted but limited either by sales volume or number of items unless an exception is granted), and International List III (export permitted but exporting nation must provide information).[2] According to at least one source, however, International Lists II and III were abolished in 1958 and a new list (International List IV) of items to be considered for possible inclusion on International List I was established.[3]

Number and Scope of Items on Lists: Over time the number of items on the lists has varied. From a variety of public and private sources, John R. McIntyre and Richard T. Cupitt have compiled a table showing the changes in the length of the lists. (See table 5A-1.) The number of items on the list increased until mid-1954 and then decreased, with some exceptions, during the 1960s. Since then the number of items on the list has levelled off. The number of items on the lists is one measure of the severity of the controls, but the scope of individual items must also be considered. Another important factor is the number and value of exceptions approved.

Reasons for Inclusion of Items on Lists: The reasons for the inclusion of an item on the list(s) are classified. Nonetheless various administrations have informed Congress of at least some of the criteria. COCOM apparently uses the same criterion embodied in the Export Administration Act of 1979: "significant contribution to the military potential" of the communist nations.[4] In the case of the munitions and the atomic-energy lists, this criterion is relatively easy to apply. But as U.S. experience attests, it is often difficult to apply this criterion to dual-use items. Significance must be defined and specific criteria established. A report on multilateral export controls prepared by the Carter administration enumerated some of the more-specific criteria in COCOM's listing decisions: (1) whether an item is "prin-

Table 5A-1
Number of Items on the COCOM Lists

List Dated	Number of Items	Added	Deleted	Strengthened	Relaxed
November 1949	86				
November 1951	270				
January 1952	285				
March 1954	266				
August 1954	170				
March 1958	181	(elimination of the China differential, 1957)			
April 1961		3	6		
July 1962		5	5	17	22
June 1964	150	8	4	5	
August 1965	161			25[a]	36
March 1967				2	8
September 1969	156			37	67
September 1972	151				
March 1976	149	2	4		
June 1980		7	7		

Source: Adapted from John R. McIntyre and Richard R. Cupitt, "East-West Strategic Trade Control: Crumbling Consensus?" *Survey* 25 (Spring 1980):98; "CoCom: East-West Trade Relations: The List Review Process," cited by Samuel M. Rosenblatt, "East-West Trade in Technology: A Purpose in Search of a Policy," *Contemporary Issues* (International Economic Studies Institute), no. 4 (April 1980):41.

[a]Sixteen of these items were also relaxed.

cipally used in peacetime for the development, production, or use of arms'';
(2) whether technology "of military significance" could be extracted from
the item; and (3) whether items represent "items of military significance in
which the proscribed countries have a deficiency."[5] Another factor known
to be considered is availability from non-COCOM sources, although the
United States apparently tries to restrict outside availability through
negotiations with non-COCOM suppliers.[6]

Not surprisingly, COCOM members disagree on specific applications of
the agreed-on criteria. The other members tend to believe that the U.S. interpretation is too restrictive and that some of the items listed are outmoded
in the sense that the Eastern countries can produce identical or comparable
items. Conversely, U.S. officials are thought to find the other members' interpretations too lenient.

List Reviews

The lists are reviewed at intervals of about three years to take into account
changes in the technological levels of the Eastern countries and technological advances in the West.[7] Items may be added or deleted, and the
degree of control on individual items may be strengthened or relaxed. U.S.
officials have admitted that it is difficult to keep the list up to date given the
rapid pace of technological progress. List reviews have occurred in 1954,
1958, 1961, 1964, 1965-1966, 1971, 1974-1976, and 1978-1979. The next list
review is scheduled to begin in fall 1982. To provide flexibility and to
facilitate updating the lists, definitional discussions may be held on specific
items between list reviews. Changes in individual items on the lists may be
proposed at any time.

Before a list review begins, member countries may submit any number
of original proposals to add, delete, or change the degree of control on an
item. The other members may then submit counterproposals, also before
the review begins. At any time during the review, a member may submit a
revised proposal if at least two members agree that such a proposal would
help COCOM achieve agreement. An individual member may also submit a
proposal for consistency at any time if a change in one item would require a
change in another to maintain technical consistency. Each of the two
rounds in a list review is supposed to be finished within ten months, but extensions apparently are possible. Changes in the list generally go into effect
sixty days after a draft document describing them is circulated. But original
proposals to decontrol items that have been in commercial use in the West
for more than five years take effect within thirty days unless a member ob-
jects by filing a counterproposal. Members are then expected to modify
their national lists as necessary. Changes made during the last list review,

which was begun on October 2, 1978, and finished on December 14, 1979, became effective on April 1, 1980. To take account of these changes, the United States issued a new CCL on June 25, 1980.

U.S. procedures for preparing proposals and counterproposals for a list review have the advantage of ensuring that all of the interested agencies and technical experts in the government and private sector have an opportunity to contribute but the disadvantage of being cumbersome and time-consuming. During the 1978-1979 review the General Accounting Office (GAO) issued a report highly critical of U.S. licensing of exports to the Eastern countries and of U.S. performance in compiling list proposals. On the latter, GAO's main conclusions were the following:

> The development of timely and comprehensive U.S. proposals was handicapped by the lack of high priority and the inability of some participating agencies to prepare complete technical positions. The authority to mediate conflicting foreign availability claims was widely diffused and this important issue did not receive sufficient attention. . . .
>
> As a result of indecision and tardiness, the number and completeness of U.S. proposals was limited.[8]

Since the procedures the United States will use for the next list review may be modified to take into account the GAO recommendations and the provisions of the Export Administration Act of 1979, as amended in 1981, the procedures used during the 1978-1979 list review and problems encountered will not be described in any great detail. Under that act, as under the Battle Act and the Export Administration Act of 1969, the secretary of state is responsible for developing a U.S. list review position and for negotiating it with COCOM. In practice, authority is delegated to the assistant secretary of state for economic and business affairs. The key coordinator of the process is working group 1 of the Economic Defense Advisory Committee (EDAC), especially its executive committee, which is chaired by the State Department's Office of East-West Trade. The members of working group 1 are senior staff members of the EDAC agencies: State, Defense, Commerce, Energy, and Treasury. Working group 1 receives and evaluates proposals from the technical task groups (TTGs) on whether to propose additions, deletions, or amendments of items on the lists and whether to file counterproposals in response to proposals by other members. TTGs are composed of representatives from the EDAC agencies. The following are among the factors the TTGs consider: production capabilities and availability in the United States, and in COCOM, non-COCOM, and communist countries; potential civilian and military uses and the significance of the latter; the feasibility of controlling items, including the possibility that target countries could substitute other items for controlled items; changes in use parameters caused by technological advances and the rate of change; the feasibility of reverse engineering; and critical technologies and keystone equipment.[9] TTGs are assisted in some cases by technical advisory committees (TACs) of business and government experts on particular technologies.

During the most recent list review, the United States submitted original proposals on seventy-nine items, including sixteen new items and an undisclosed number of deletions, including thermal detecting cells and ion microscopes. Some of the proposals were for liberalizing controls on such items as numerically controlled machine tools and semiconductors. Others were for strengthening or expanding coverage in certain items such as jet-engine manufacturing equipment and underwater-location apparatus. Several proposals were for clarifying existing coverage without inceasing or decreasing it such as a proposal to revise completely the atomic-energy list. According to a preliminary U.S. evaluation, most of the other members' proposals were for liberalization, but some were for clarification.[10]

According to an official interviewed by McIntyre and Cupitt, the review did not result in "a significant increase or decrease of coverage either in scope or item number."[11] Proposals on computers by the United States and other members were set aside for discussion in fall 1980. The overall result cited is in line with the results of other recent list reviews. In its report, the Carter administration noted that the lists have stabilized in recent years and offered the following explanation:

> The process of considering which items meet the strategic criteria has been repeated many times over the years. As a result, changes during list reviews are now seldom dramatic. A few items are deleted and a few new ones are added. But most of the changes consist of modernizing the technical descriptions to reflect technological progress.[12]

The results of the 1978-1979 general review or the 1980 computer review were not publicized in detail, but a number of recent proposals by the United States are known to have been adopted. Among them are the following: the addition of specific references to technology as well as products to the COCOM strategic criteria (1978); the inclusion of controls on technology in the COCOM lists themselves instead of in an "administrative principle," as was previously the case (1978); and tighter controls on semiconductor manufacturing equipment, polycrystalline silicon, and fiber optics (1980).[13]

Exceptions

With a few exceptions a COCOM member that plans to authorize a company to export an embargoed item must submit an exception request.[14] If, however, the item is a spare part or servicing, is of small value, or is a temporary export (such as a display for an exhibit), the exporting country may approve the export but must notify COCOM. A more important case in which a unilateral decision to export a prohibited item is permitted is administrative exceptions for lower-performance items. Administrative exceptions have averaged $100 million in recent years.

Once a week representatives to COCOM, at least those from the five key members, meet in Paris to consider exceptions requests. Their work load is fairly heavy—about 1,000 cases annually in recent years. Typically they recommend disapproval in about 2 to 4 percent of the cases and partial approval (with recommendations that would make the export acceptable) in a larger percentage of the cases. About 3 to 5 percent of the cases are withdrawn. The remainder are approved. As table 5A-2 shows, the value of exceptions approved has risen dramatically in the past ten years. Although growing, the value of COCOM exceptions cases averages less than 1 percent of the value of exports to target countries by members. About half of the cases involve computers, as table 5A-3 shows. Many of the remaining items are also electronics related.

Since 1976 exceptions for computers have been approved subject to the conditions of the safeguard program. Under this program the importing country is required to permit inspections by representatives of the exporting company. They are required to visit the facility where the computer is installed at regular intervals to make sure that it is in its stated location and being used for the specified civilian purpose.

In recent years, U.S. exceptions requests have grown to account for about one-half of all requests. This may be due to the U.S. lead in computers,

Table 5A-2
Value of Exceptions Requests Approved by COCOM, 1967-1977
(millions of current U.S. dollars)

1967	11
1968	8
1969	19
1970	62
1971	56
1972	124
1973	106
1974	119
1975	185
1976	162
1977	214

Source: *Special Report on Multilateral Export Controls, Submitted by the President Pursuant to Section 117 of the Export Administration Amendments of 1977*, reprinted in *Export Administration Act: Agenda for Reform*, Hearings, 95th Cong., 2d sess., October 4, 1978, p. 52.

Table 5A-3
Computer Cases Approved as a Percentage of Total Cases Approved, 1971-1977

	Value in Millions of U.S. Dollars	Percentage of Total
1971	21	23
1972	66	39
1973	80	50[a]
1974	120	66[a]
1975	147	64[a]
1976	123	52
1977	168	63

Source: Ibid.

[a]Omitting two high-value cases in 1973, one in 1974 and one in 1975 that the administration felt would distort the figures. In none of the four cases did the export actually occur.

which account for a large share of total approvals, or because the United States is more diligent in submitting requests than other members, as some analysts suspect. Nonetheless, the U.S. position as the largest requester of exceptions causes friction within COCOM, especially because the United States tends to be stricter than other members concerning exceptions requests. For example, the United States objected in thirty of the thirty-one cases COCOM disapproved in 1977. The combination of these two factors leads some COCOM members to question whether Western security or commercial advantage motivates the United States. In addition, some members are said to view the exceptions procedure as a form of intra-Western commercial espionage.

Some members are said to complain that the United States is not sufficiently responsive to their economic and political circumstances. Some Americans would argue that internal factors such as employment or political pressures in a member country should be considered irrelevant in COCOM's decisions on exceptions requests. Leaving aside the question of whether such factors should be considered, it seems that the Carter administration interpreted the agreed-on criteria as including economic and political factors in the exporting country if they were relevant to security. In the Carter administration's interpretation, the primary factor to be considered was the risk of diversion to significant military use, but it was willing to consider international political factors in the importing country as well.

Another factor that causes friction is the length of time required for a U.S. decision on an exception case. The process, similar to that used in a decision whether to approve a validated license application by a U.S. firm, is lengthy. Up to the time of the GAO report, and perhaps even today, it took the United States longer to process requests than any other member. The GAO report noted a particularly striking detail: of all the delegates, only the American and one other had not been authorized to approve routine cases with clear precedents. Especially in the past, other COCOM members tended to believe that American commercial motivations accounted for the delays. It is now thought they have come to the conclusion that the cumbersome nature of U.S. procedures is responsible. Conversely U.S. officials complain that other COCOM members rely on the United States for detailed analyses of exceptions cases.

The U.S. requirement for the licensing of reexports is another source of friction within COCOM. The United States is the only COCOM member with this requirement. Since many of the other members' exceptions requests include U.S.-origin components (about one-quarter in 1977), this requirement slows down the processing of their requests. The other members also feel that the U.S. requirement betrays a lack of trust in COCOM.

Given the realities of the exceptions process, politics is known to intrude into the consideration of technical factors from time to time. For example, France reportedly once threatened to withdraw from COCOM if one of its requests was denied. In the Serpukhov computer case, the United States objected to a British request on the grounds that the proposed export was strategic but reversed its decision using a different definition of strategic in the face of high-level British pressure. In other, more prevalent examples of hard bargaining, the other members are thought to hold U.S. exceptions requests hostage to favorable U.S. treatment of their own.[15] Similarly the Carter administration report noted that the United States takes care that its decisions on cases submitted by other members are in conformity with decisions made on previous U.S. cases.

Since the Soviet invasion of Afghanistan, COCOM's treatment of exceptions cases has changed significantly. At the urging of the United States, COCOM virtually stopped approving exceptions for exports to the Soviet Union. According to official estimates, the no-exceptions policy and the addition of a few items to the list around the same time reduced exports by COCOM members to the Soviet Union and other communist countries by approximately $50 million.[16]

Under the appropriately named national-interest exception, a member may disregard a denial of an exception request if it deems the export to be in its national interest.

Enforcement

As a voluntary organization, COCOM has no mechanism for forcing members to accept its recommendations. It does conduct periodic consultations on the other kind of enforcement—preventing unauthorized exports—which is the responsibility of individual members.

There is, however, a voluntary mechanism for preventing the diversion of exports between COCOM countries to target countries. Under the imported certificate-delivery verification system, a government may require an exporter to present an import certificate before it approves the license. The import certificate is filled out by the importer and certified by his government. In it the importer states an intention to import the goods specified and that they will not be reexported unless approved by the government. After the export is shipped, the exporting country may require a delivery-verification certificate from the exporter. This certificate, which states that the goods actually were received in the importing country, is filled out by officials there.[17] Transit authorization certificates (TACs) are issued to show that shipments made via third countries are actually licensed for delivery to a communist country.

The Reagan administration plans special efforts to improve the U.S. enforcement system and to encourage the other members to do so also.[18] When the government believes that an illegal diversion may be attempted overseas, it starts an investigation. If the diversion is thought to be of a U.S.-origin good, the case is referred to the Compliance Division of the Department of Commerce or to the Customs Service. In such cases the United States relies primarily on the country of jurisdiction to stop the shipment and/or prosecute those responsible, although the Export Administration Act of 1979 contains authority for investigating suspects and denying them permission to import goods from the United States.

If the goods in question are not alleged to be of U.S. origin but are subject to COCOM controls, the case is referred to working group II of the EDAC. Working group II considers the case and has it referred to the appropriate foreign government, if warranted. If immediate action is required and if the export is clearly embargoed, the Department of State may act immediately and later refer the case to working group II, which meets regularly. Economic defense officers (EDOs) stationed at U.S. embassies and consulates overseas aid in the enforcement process by performing the following tasks: prelicensing and postshipment checks, reporting of potential diversions, participation in field investigations, the serving of legal papers where permitted by local law, maintenance of contacts with law authorities, and informing American and local businesses about U.S. export regulations. Some countries have complained that direct questioning of firms and the serving of judicial or quasi-judicial papers on their nationals by EDOs violate their judicial sovereignty.

Toward an Evaluation of COCOM's Effectiveness

COCOM's effectiveness may be assessed from the narrow perspective of how well it can potentially and how well it actually administers the controls to which its members have agreed. For example, Congressman Jonathan B. Bingham and Victor C. Johnson concluded that "COCOM seems almost designed for evasion" and that it "has not worked very well."[19] By contrast, others believe that COCOM is fairly effective in both senses. But more important, it may be assessed from the broader perspective of the correctness of the controls it establishes and how well it functions as a mechanism for coordinating its members' policies. If COCOM functions well from this perspective, it could serve as a useful forum for achieving a unified Western policy.

The Narrow Perspective

In the narrow perspective two issues are important: how faithfully members abide by COCOM procedures and how tightly they enforce national export controls. Due to the usual reticence of COCOM members in publicizing noncompliance by other members and to the obvious secrecy on the part of violators of export controls, definite conclusions are impossible.

An obvious source of inefficiency is cases in which a member fails to bring up an export that COCOM should consider as an exception case. Such cases do occur. A Reagan administration official acknowledged that the United States occasionally approves exports that other members feel should have been brought up in COCOM but asserted that the opposite case was more common.[20]

Willful intent to circumvent COCOM need not be involved. The lists, which contain complex technical definitions and perhaps some faulty translations, can be difficult to interpret. But in other cases, willful intent to circumvent COCOM controls or a desire to consult at a higher political level may be involved.

Well-known cases in which a member has reportedly not brought up an export for COCOM consideration include the British sale of the Harrier jet and advanced Rolls Royce jet-engine manufacturing equipment (Spey engines) to the PRC and a French case involving metal-forming presses.[21]

In the third case, which is less certain than the other two, the French government is thought to have neglected to submit an exception request for stretch-forming presses that ACB-Loire sold the Soviets.[22] The case came to light when an American firm, the Cyril Bath Company, applied for a license to export one such press. The Carter administration denied the application on national-security grounds. In his capacity as chairman of the House Subcommittee on International Economics and Trade, Congressman Bingham held hearings on the license denial. At the hearing an official from the Cyril Bath Company testified that Avtopromimport, a Soviet purchasing agency, had requested bids for ten stretch-forming presses. The U.S. firm bid on all ten presses but was told that the Soviets would purchase one press from it and the other nine from ACB-Loire. The reason given to the American firm was that the Soviet agency had previously brought ACB-Loire presses, which were working well. Later the French company confirmed this information. Although the Soviets did not tell the American company, the technical specifications led the latter to conclude that the Soviets intended to use the presses for forming aircraft bodies instead of their alternative use in automobile production. After reviewing the case, the Carter administration reversed itself and granted the license on the grounds of foreign availability. When the United States submitted the necessary request for an exception, the French government reportedly denied that French companies were manufacturing such presses but then acknowledged it stating that the presses were for use in the automotive industry. Since France apparently did not admit that the machines it was supplying were comparable to the one the Cyril Bath Company sought to export, COCOM had not acted on the U.S. request as late as 1979, according to Bingham.

It may be that these three cases are inaccurate or atypical. Using an innovative approach, McIntyre and Cupitt conclude that they may be fairly common. They argue:

> If the United States has only a 15 percent share of the socialist country imports of high-technology products and if the United States represents only some 50 percent of COCOM exceptions requests, obviously the other 85 percent of the business is being done in some simple manner, but not through COCOM.[23]

Their argument may be questioned, however. Since about half of the exceptions cases are for computers, in which the United States has a lead, a higher percentage of U.S. exports may well require COCOM's consideration.

There may be some cases in which high-level political intervention results in the export of an item that should be embargoed, according to others members' interpretations of the lists. Possible examples include the British request in the Serpukhov computer case and the French threat to withdraw from COCOM if one of its requests was not approved.

A built-in means of circumvention is the national-interest exception, which allows a member to proceed with an export despite a COCOM denial if the government deems the export to be in its national interest. This clause, however, has rarely been invoked—only about a dozen times in COCOM's thirty years of operations—according to an official interviewed by McIntyre and Cupitt.[24]

In theory, there are factors that would reduce the likelihood of members' deliberately circumventing the controls. First, at least a majority of the items on the lists must be there because members agree that exporting them would threaten Western Security. Second, members could join together to apply pressure on a member that consistently flouted procedures. But one of the criticisms of the U.S. government's approach is that it does not respond strongly enough to evasions by members for fear that strong pressure would cause COCOM's demise.[25]

Availability of technology from nonmembers is another built-in and probably irremediable factor reducing COCOM's potential for controlling the flow of technology to the East. Countries like Sweden and Switzerland have not shown an inclination to become members. In practice, however, they are said to cooperate informally with COCOM since antagonizing its members is not in their interest.[26] In addition, U.S. licensing requirements apply to some of their exports—those made by subsidiaries of U.S. companies based in their countries and products incorporating U.S.-origin components subject to licensing requirements.

It is difficult to assess how greatly violations of members' export controls reduce COCOM's effectiveness since some obviously go undetected and not all known cases are publicized. While the United States has long been concerned about transshipments and diversions, the level of concern has been increasing in recent years, and a number of cases have been publicized. The Reagan administration is especially concerned about industrial espionage and illegal exports of items like microprocessors that are easy to carry but hard to detect.

Other efforts by communist countries to evade COCOM controls reduce their effectiveness. Of these, the most likely are diversions of exports approved for civilian use to military use. According to the testimony of a State Department official in 1979, the United States had "no unequivocal evidence" of diversion of any item approved by COCOM but did have evidence of five possible cases.[27] Similarly the Carter administration report concluded that the safeguard system for computers appeared to be "working well," although there had been one case in which the inspection visit was not permitted.[28]

The report argued that importing countries have an interest in abiding by end-use provisions to avoid being denied further exports. The GAO Report, however, noted some problems U.S. officials encountered in administering the system.[29] Diversions to the Soviet Union from countries for which less stringent controls are applied (for example, Poland and Rumania) and, after COCOM stopped approving exceptions for exports to the Soviet Union, the East European countries as a group, are a potential problem. Reasoning similar to that of the Carter administration in the case of diversion to military use may be relevant to this case as well. Thus the United States has not proved any diversion of agricultural or industrial commodities from Eastern Europe to the Soviet Union, following the January 1980 sanctions against the latter.

The Broader Perspective

Lacking complete information on COCOM's operations, it is difficult to assess how well COCOM administers the controls to which it has agreed. It is even more difficult to assess how well COCOM members have identified strategic goods to be controlled and what COCOM has accomplished in its thirty years of operations. These two aspects are difficult to assess due to the inherent subjectivity of the concepts involved.

To answer them, one must first decide what makes a good "strategic," and what constitutes a significant contribution to military capability. There are some goods such as weapons and fissionable material that everybody can agree are clearly strategic, but they are few in number. For a far larger group of dual-use items, drawing the line between strategic and nonstrategic is far more difficult and produces disagreement. Equally subjective is the significance of the contribution that a given item could make to communist military capabilities.

The Kama River Truck Factory case illustrates some of the problems.[30] In 1971 the Nixon administration approved the initial licenses for U.S. firms to equip a factory for constructing general-purpose trucks. The Ford administration approved additional licenses, notably one for an IBM computer. In December 1979 trucks produced at Kama were used in support of the Soviet invasion of Afghanistan. Consequently the Carter administration, which had been investigating reports of diversion to military use before the invasion, rescinded IBM's license to export spare parts for the computer. The truck-manufacturing equipment and the computer exported were dual-use items, which by definition may be put to military as well as civilian uses. Depending on their technical specifications, truck-manufacturing equipment and computers may be used in the production of military as well as civilian goods—for example, engines for armored personnel carriers as opposed to engines for general-purpose trucks. If the Soviets had used the trucks produced at Kama exclusively for civilian purposes such as transporting grain, most would conclude that they were not contributing to Soviet military capabilities. Some experts, however, would reach the opposite conclusion: that the trucks from Kama were permitting the Soviets to divert trucks that would otherwise be required for civilian transport to military uses. The Soviets did put the trucks to military use. Some would argue that any military use would represent a significant contribution, while others would argue that this particular use did not represent a significant contribution. To resolve this issue, detailed information on Soviet truck-producing capacity, truck inventories, and specific uses would be helpful, but it would not remove the need to make subjective judgments.

This case illustrates the subjectivity of the factors that need to be considered in determining how well COCOM has succeeded in achieving its goal of denying the communist countries goods that would make a significant contribution to their military capabilities. As some assert, efforts by the Eastern countries to evade the controls indicate that the controls, if properly enforced, would prevent their access to some to the goods they seek.[31]

Then there is the problem of how one might test this proposition for all exports, not just a particular export. A recent article argues that the differences of opinion on COCOM's effectiveness stem from differing perspectives on what COCOM controls can accomplish. The authors contrast the " 'economic warfare' type of embargo with its aim to deny outright as much trade as can conceivably be of any help to a potential adversary from the policy of delaying the communist acquisition of strategic technology, where a technology gap can be ascertained."[32] Thus, in their view, a test of COCOM's effectiveness is the "maintenance of an evolving technology gap between East and West as determined for each specific commodity or commodity line." After reviewing the available studies, they conclude that evidence of technological gaps "may be indicative of the effectiveness of the West's control policy, of inadequate Soviet technological absorption, utilization, and diffusion, or both." In addition to the problem of gathering all the information needed for a full-scale application of such an approach, there are the problems of comparing technological levels in two countries organized differently. As John W. Kiser suggests, different requirements, not gaps in technological abilities, may account for apparent gaps in some areas.[33]

Notes

1. The precise number of categories is not certain. According to some sources, there are ten; according to others, eight. Because of this information gap and the somewhat arbitrary nature of categorization, the following list should be viewed simply as an illustration of the kinds of goods and materials subject to control: metalworking machinery; chemical and petroleum equipment; electrical and power-generating equipment; general industrial equipment; transportation equipment; electronic and precision instruments; metals, minerals, and their products; chemicals and metalloids; petroleum products; and rubber products. Cf. U.S. Congress, Office of Technology Assessment, *Technology and East-West Trade* (Washington, D.C.: U.S. Government Printing Office, 1980), pp. 155-156, and John R. McIntyre and Richard T. Cupitt, "East-West Strategic Trade Control: A Crumbling Consensus?" *Survey* 25 (Spring 1980):90. A possible explanation for the discrepancy in number is that categories 9 and 10 were merged into other categories or deleted around 1976.

2. Samuel M. Rosenblatt, "East-West Trade in Technology: A Purpose in Search of a Policy," *International Economic Studies Institute, Contemporary Issues*, no. 4 (April 1980):38-39.

3. Jeffrey W. Golan, "U.S. Technology Transfers to the Soviet Union and the Protection of National Security," *Law and Policy in International Business* 11 (1979):1041.

4. *Special Report on Multilateral Export Controls, Submitted by the President Pursuant to Section 117 of the Export Administration Amendments of 1977*, reprinted in U.S. Congress, House Committee on International Relations, Subcommittee on International Economic Policy and Trade, *Export Administration Act: Agenda for Reform*, Hearings, 95th Cong., 2d sess., October 4, 1978, p. 52 (hereinafter cited as Special Report on Multilateral Export Controls).

5. Ibid., p. 52.

6. U.S. Congress, House, Committee on Foreign Affairs, Subcommittee on International Economic Policy and Trade, *Export Administration Amendments Act of 1981*, Hearings, 97th Cong., 1st sess., March 26, April 14, 1981, p. 105 (hereinafter cited as *Export Administration Amendments Act of 1981*).

7. Sources for this section include: ibid., p. 104; Special Report on Multilateral Export Controls, pp. 52-53; McIntyre and Cupitt, "East-West Strategic Trade Control," pp. 94-95; and U.S. Congress, House Committee on International Relations, Subcommittee on International Economic Policy and Trade, *Export Licensing: COCOM List Review Proposals of the United States*, Hearings, 95th Cong., 2d sess., June 14, 26, 1978, pp. 84-86 (hereinafter cited as Export Licensing).

8. U.S. General Accounting Office, *Export Controls: Need to Clarify Policy and Simplify Administration* (Washington, D.C.: March 1, 1979), pp. iii, 23 (hereinafter cited as GAO Report).

9. U.S. Congress, *Technology and East-West Trade*, p. 157.

10. *Export Licensing*, pp. 86-87, 92-93. This source provides an unusually detailed description of U.S. proposals for the most recent review. For additional details, see pp. 94-97.

11. McIntyre and Cupitt, "East-West Strategic Trade Controls," p. 99.

12. Special Report on Multilateral Export Controls, p. 53.

13. *Export Licensing*, pp. 86-87, and *Export Administration Amendments Act of 1981*, p. 103.

14. Unless specified, this section is based on the following sources: GAO Report, pp. 9-11, 13-16; Special Report on Multilateral Export Controls, pp. 53-54, 56-58; McIntyre and Cupitt, "East-West Strategic Trade Controls," pp. 99-100; and *Export Administration Amendments Act of 1981*, pp. 103, 105.

15. McIntyre and Cupitt, "East-West Strategic Trade Controls," pp. 86, 101.

16. Paul Lewis, "Allies Discuss More Curbs on Sales to the Soviet Bloc," *New York Times*, January 20, 1982, p. A8.

17. Golan, "U.S. Technology Transfers," pp. 1041-1042.

18. *Export Administration Act Amendments of 1981*, pp. 36-40.

19. Jonathan B. Bingham and Victor C. Johnson, "A Rational Approach to Export Controls," *Foreign Affairs* 57, no. 4 (Spring 1979):906.

20. *Export Administration Amendments Act of 1981*, p. 82.

21. McIntyre and Cupitt, "East-West Strategic Trade Control," p. 102.

22. Bingham and Johnson, "Rational Approach," p. 905, and U.S. Congress, House Committee on International Relations, Subcommittee on International Economic Policy and Trade, *Export Licensing: Foreign Availability of Stretch Forming Presses*, Hearings, 95th Cong., 1st sess., November 4, 1977.

23. McIntyre and Cupitt, "East-West Strategic Trade Control," p. 102.

24. Ibid., p. 101.

25. Bingham and Johnson, "Rational Approach," p. 906.

26. *Technology and East-West Trade*, pp. 153-154.

27. Quoted in Rosenblatt, "East-West Trade," p. 46.

28. Special Report on Multilateral Export Controls, p. 55.

29. GAO Report, pp. 155-156.

30. Drawn from John P. Hardt and Kate S. Tomlinson, *An Assessment of the Afghanistan Sanctions: Implications for Trade and Diplomacy in the 1980's*, Report prepared for the House Foreign Affairs Committee, April 1981, pp. 68-70.

31. This point was recently made by Harry Kopp, deputy assistant secretary of state for business affairs, in *Export Administration Amendments Act of 1981*, p. 82.

32. Gary Bertsch, Richard T. Cupitt, John R. McIntyre, and Miriam Steiner, "Technology Transfer and CoCom," *Osteuropa Wirtschaft* (June 1981):126-127.

33. "What Gap? Which Gap?" *Foreign Policy* 32 (Fall 1978):93-94.

Appendix 5B: Department of Commerce Article on the Reagan Administration's Sanctions against Poland and the Soviet Union

President Reagan, citing heavy and direct Soviet responsibility for the repression in Poland, on Dec. 29 imposed a number of sanctions affecting U.S.-Soviet economic relations. . . . This action followed suspension on Dec. 23 of major elements of the United States economic relationship with the Polish Government to underscore opposition to the imposition of martial law in Poland and the ensuing suppression of human rights. The sanctions on U.S.-Soviet economic relations consist of the following steps:

Suspension of Aeroflot service to the United States;

Closing of the Soviet Purchasing Commission;

Postponement of negotiations on a new U.S.-Soviet long-term Grains Agreement (LTA);

Suspension of negotiations on a new U.S.-Soviet Maritime Agreement;

Suspension of issuance or renewal of validated export licenses to the U.S.S.R. for electronic equipment, computers and other "high-technology materials";

Expansion of the list of oil and gas equipment requiring validated export licenses and suspension of the issuance of such licenses; and

Non-renewal of some exchange agreements on energy and technology.

Underlining U.S. desire for a constructive and mutually beneficial relationship with the Soviet Union, the President stressed that: "We are prepared to proceed in whatever direction the Soviet Union decides upon—towards greater mutual restraint and cooperation, or further down a harsh and less rewarding path."

This article originally appeared in *Business America*, January 11, 1982. It was reprinted in U.S. Congress, Joint Economic Committee, *East-West Commercial Policy: A Congressional Dialogue with the Reagan Administration* (Washington, D.C.: U.S. Government Printing Office, 1982), pp. 67-68.

As a direct result of the Dec. 29 sanctions, U.S. exports to the Soviet Union in 1982 will probably be about $200 million less than previously projected. Exports will reach perhaps $3.5 billion, including $2.5 billion in agricultural commodities and $1 billion in non-agricultural goods. Imports may total as much as $800 million, partly contingent on projected increases in U.S. purchases of ammonia.

The projected totals compare with U.S. exports to the U.S.S.R. of about $2.5 billion and imports of $350 million in 1981.

Following is a brief description of the sanctions imposed on the U.S.S.R.:

1. Aeroflot Service Suspension. The Department of State, in cooperation with other federal agencies concerned, is taking the steps necessary to suspend Aeroflot service to this country after Jan. 3, until further notice. Under the U.S.-Soviet Civil Air Agreement of 1967, which remains in effect, the United States is no longer obligated to permit any specific number of flights by the Soviet airline because the U.S. carrier, Pan American, ceased its service between the United States and the Soviet Union in October 1978. Since early 1980, Aeroflot had operated two weekly flights from Moscow to Washington. In 1980 it carried approximately 6,000 round-trip passengers.

2. Termination of the Soviet Purchasing Commission (SPC). The Soviet Purchasing Commission has been notified that it will have to close by Jan. 13, 1982. The SPC (formerly Kama Purchasing Commission) has operated in New York since 1973 as an arm of the U.S.S.R. Ministry of Foreign Trade, placing orders for U.S. products, originally for the Kama River Truck Plant. Permission for establishment of the Commission was extended in 1972 by the Secretary of Commerce simultaneously with an undertaking by the Soviet Foreign Trade Ministry to accredit offices of U.S. companies in Moscow, of which there are now 28. U.S. operating authority for the Purchasing Commission in the United States was renewed periodically, most recently until April 1982. The Purchasing Commission was responsible for about $1.5 billion in exports of U.S. equipment and services for various Soviet projects, including an industrial tractor plant, an ammonia production complex, and the Moscow World Trade Center. These purchases represented about one-third of Soviet orders for U.S. non-agricultural goods. Purchasing activity by the Commission has been at a low level since imposition of U.S. trade sanctions in response to the Soviet invasion of Afghanistan. Other Soviet commercial organizations in the United States are not affected by this measure.

3. Suspension of Issuance of Validated Export Licenses. The Commerce Department has published formal regulations that suspend processing of applications for validated licenses to export to the U.S.S.R., effective Dec. 30, 1981. Under the Export Administration Act, the Department maintains lists of specific items—products, technical data, and services—which require validated licenses before being exported to the Soviet Union.

As a result of the current steps, no new licenses will be issued for export or reexport of high technology or of oil and gas equipment subject to export controls (see point 6). About 240 license applications worth about $130 million were pending to the U.S.S.R. Western sales of high technology have excluded equipment that would contribute significantly to Soviet military potential. Sales of other kinds of "high technology" have continued and include items such as machine tools, pumps, centrifuges, certain measuring and control instruments, and various types of electrical machinery. Industrialized Western countries exported about $2.3 billion of "high technology" products to the U.S.S.R. in 1980. The United States exported about $85 million of these products, or about 4 percent of the Western total.

4. Postponement of Negotiations on a New Long-term Grains Agreement. U.S.-Soviet grain trade is currently being conducted under the terms of a one-year extension of the 1975 U.S.-Soviet Grains Agreement, valid until Sept. 30, 1982. Under the existing agreement, the Soviet Union is committed to buy 6 million metric tons of wheat and corn annually, and the United States is obligated to permit shipments to the Soviet Union of up to 8 million tons. In October the United States had informed the Soviet side that it may buy up to 15 million tons in addition to the 8 million tons during the 12-month period ending Sept. 30, 1982. Up to now the U.S.S.R. has purchased about 11 million tons. Postponement of negotiations on a new long-term agreement will not affect current U.S.-Soviet arrangements on sales or shipments of grains nor should it have any immediate effect on this trade.

5. Suspension of Negotiations on a new U.S.-Soviet Maritime Agreement. The United States has been engaged in negotiations toward a new Maritime Agreement, with the most recent meeting ending inconclusively in early December. These negotiations are now being suspended. Under the 1975 Long-term Maritime Agreement, merchant vessels of the Soviet Union had access to 40 U.S. ports on the basis of four days' advance notice. That agreement expired on Dec. 31, 1981. The Soviets now will be required to request permission for one of their ships to call at a U.S. port at least 14 days in advance. Decisions on Soviet requests will be made on a case-by-case basis. The United States will take a restrictive approach toward requests for ships engaged in traffic, including passenger service, between the United States and third countries. In the first 11 months of 1981 there were 337 port calls by Soviet ships, compared with 406 in 1980 and 1,383 in 1979. These figures reflect the decline in U.S.-Soviet trade in 1980 following the post-Afghanistan sanctions and the International Longshoreman Association's boycott affecting most non-grain shipments from east coast and Gulf ports from January 1980 to June 1981.

6. Oil and Gas Equipment Controls Broadened. The Commerce Department is expanding controls governing the export of oil and gas technology to the Soviet Union. Under new regulations effective Dec. 30, 1981,

a variety of products, equipment and technical data for the transmission or refining of petroleum or natural gas will require validated export licenses. (Examples of equipment affected by this expansion of controls are air and gas compressors, gas turbine engines for compressors, sensors, meters and mixing equipment, and pipeline cleaning equipment.) Equipment and technology in the petroleum exploration and production areas have required validated licenses for export to the U.S.S.R. since 1978. Until 1981 applications for export of equipment covered by the 1978 controls were generally approved. The Department is now suspending action on all applications for export of oil and gas equipment and technology. Oil and gas equipment has been a major non-agicultural U.S. export to the U.S.S.R. during the last ten years. In 1980 direct exports of such equipment to the Soviets totaled about $50 million; in 1979, $141 million was exported.

7. Non-renewal of U.S.-Soviet Exchange Agreements. The United States does not intend to renew the U.S.-Soviet Agreements on Space, Energy, and on Science and Technology which come up for renewal in May, June and July, 1982, respectively. Eleven bilateral exchange and cooperation agreements are currently in effect with the Soviet Union, including agreements covering agriculture, environmental protection, housing, health and transportation. The agreements provide for visits in both directions and cooperative research projects in designated fields by U.S. and Soviet scientists. Following the Soviet invasion of Afghanistan the United States severely curtailed activities under these programs, continuing only low-level exchanges. There will be a complete review of all these agreements.

The sanctions imposed on Poland on Dec. 23 are:

Suspension of Polish civil aviation privileges in the United States;

A halt in the renewal of the Export-Import Bank's line of credit insurance to the Polish Government;

Suspension of the right of Poland's fishing fleet to operate in American waters; and

Proposal to our Allies for the futher restriction of high-technology exports to Poland.

Under the sanctions,
1. LOT, the Polish airline, will no longer have landing privileges in the United States for its regular or chartered flights. A bilateral agreement governing civil aviation in the two countries will be allowed to expire on March 31, 1982. No U.S. airline currently services Poland.

2. The U.S. Export-Import Bank will not renew a $25 million line of credit insurance to support short-term (180 day) loans to Poland for suppliers and banks to pay for imports from the United States. Without such

insurance, private lending to Poland to finance imports is unlikely because of Poland's financial condition. The line of credit expired Nov. 30, 1981.

3. Poland will not be granted a portion of surplus U.S. fishery resources in the 200-mile fishing conservation zone in 1982. Poland's allocation for 1981 was 231,326 metric tons. The U.S. decision will have a substantial impact on Poland's overall fisheries, namely, a decline in the availability of fish in Poland and a hard-currency loss to the Polish Government from lost sales to traditional purchasers, among them, the United States.

4. We will discuss with our Allies and Japan tightening the way controls are applied to the export to Poland of advanced technology with strategic implications.

Polish-U.S. trade totaled $942.2 million through the first three-quarters of 1981; U.S. exports of agricultural commodities represented about two-thirds of this figure.

6 A European View of East–West Trade in the 1980s

Jean-Marie Guillaume

The area of East-West trade is one among several where American and West European views are expected to differ. Whether these differences are the consequence of conflicting economic interests or whether they illustrate a gap in political strategies remains unclear. Equally unclear are the perspectives of East-West trade in the 1980s.

While some analysts see the Soviet gas pipeline as the confirmation of a trend toward stronger East-West links in Europe, others visualize the collapse of the East European economy, as exemplified by the catastrophe of Poland, as a signal that the heyday of East-West trade is past and that Western Europe cannot avoid a general contraction of commercial relations between East and West. These perceptions in turn raise a question of policymaking: do we have the means to exert real influence on these evolutions, and, if so, in what directions should we try to exercise our influence? This chapter analyzes two issues: Europe in East-West trade and the future of East-West trade.

Europe and East-West Trade: The Politics of Ambiguity

The transatlantic debate on East-West trade is heavily politicized, offering two conflicting views of what a fair burden sharing would be. Washington emphasizes the impact of East-West trade on the Soviet bloc and suggests that trade helps the Soviet bloc to resolve the dilemma of a military buildup in a stagnating economy. According to this view, European countries not only do not bear a fair share of the miltary burden of the West but undermine the U.S. effort by making the Soviet military buildup less costly. On the other side of the Atlantic, European countries emphasize the impact of East-West trade on their own economies, suggesting that the damage would be greater for them than for the East. The ultimate result would be a weakened Western alliance rather than a weaker Warsaw Pact.

The interests of Western Europe and the United States with regard to East-West trade are therefore assumed to be very different, and politicians often draw conclusions from those assumed differences. While some U.S. circles link an alleged European complacency toward Soviet policies to selfish European commercial interests, West European politicians contend that their countries cannot restrict East-West trade without jeopardizing important sectors of their domestic economies.

A closer look at the figures is necessary to clarify this debate so as to make a fair assessment of East-West trade and of its impact on Western and Eastern economies. Where should we actually put the emphasis? Whose interest should predominate? How do politics and trade policies interplay?

The Economic Perspective

Impact on West European Economies: A Comparative Analysis: Trade with Eastern countries is more important for Western Europe than for the United States. Nevertheless this statement must be qualified: East-West trade represents but a minor share of the global economic activity of European countries.

The difference in volume of East-West trade between the United States and other Western countries is significant in absolute terms; in percentages of trade, it is much less so. Table 6-1 shows that if the involvement of West Germany is greater than that of other countries, owing to intra-German trade (which amounts to one-quarter of total West German trade with the East), this involvement remains globally very limited compared with total West German foreign trade. This modest picture of the impact of East-West trade on West European economies is confirmed by labor statistics of persons whose jobs depend directly on East-West trade. In West Germany, where the impact is the greatest among European Community members, the percentage of active labor force dependent on East-West trade is estimated to be no more than 1.23 percent; or 275,000 workers.[1]

These very low figures are significant, but they must be qualified by an analysis of the internal structure of East-West trade, which varies greatly

Table 6-1
East-West Trade in 1980

	United States	European Economic Community	Federal Republic of Germany[a]	France
Volume (billions of dollars	5.28	56.8	23.8	10.21
Share of foreign trade (%)	1.14	4.14	6.2	4.2
Share of GNP (%)	0.2	2.0	2.9	1.58

Source: Organization for Economic Cooperation and Development (OECD) Statistics, complemented by United Nations Commission for Europe, for intra-German trade figures.
[a]Includes intra-German trade ($5.9 billion).

between the United States and Western Europe and among West European countries themselves.

Structure of Exports: The major difference lies in the share of food exports in total exports to the East (table 6-2). While food makes up the major part of U.S. exports, it represents only a minor share of European exports to the East, except for those of France, which nonetheless can hardly be compared in terms of volume exported with the United States, except in 1980.

But when one looks at specific agricultural products exported by France, the picture is a little different. In 1980, 50.9 percent of French exports of veal, 30.6 percent of butter, 15.7 percent of sugar, and 11.9 percent of grain were exported to the East. So were 30 percent of German exports of flour, 26.3 percent of grain, 21 percent of sugar, 13.2 percent of butter, and 6.9 percent of meat. The clear conclusion is that if European food exports cannot substitute for American exports, the East bloc provides a welcome opportunity to deplete the always too large stocks of the European Community.

The counterpart point is that capital goods are a major part of European exports to the East, particularly to the Soviet Union, where they represent between 20 and 30 percent of West European exports.

The figures in table 6-3 explain why East-West trade, in spite of its limited impact in terms of global weight, can become a sensitive issue in West European countries. Capital-goods trade usually develops through large contracts involving a limited number of major European companies that engage in so-called turnkey sales. The most significant case is West Germany. The COMECON countries buy 20 percent of Mannesmann exports and 33 percent of Salzgitter exports. In France, such companies as

Table 6-2
Food Exports to the East in 1979 and 1980

	United States		European Economic Community		Federal Republic of Germany		France	
	1979	1980	1979	1980	1979	1980	1979	1980
Volume (billions of dollars)								
USSR	3.5	2.4	1.4	2.8	0.3	0.7	0.4	1.0
CMEA Six	2.2	1.0	0.5	1.4	0.06	0.4	0.2	0.6
Share of exports to the East (%)	62	65	7	12	4	7	10	24
Share of exports to the Soviet Union (%)	63	64	6	14	2	8	10	21

Source: OECD statistics.
Note: Intra-German trade is excluded.

Table 6-3
Capital-Goods Exports to the East in 1979 and 1980

	United States		European Economic Community		Federal Republic of Germany		France	
	1979	1980	1979	1980	1979	1980	1979	1980
Volume (billions of dollars)								
East	0.5	0.4	6.6	6.4	3.0	3.1	1.5	0.8
USSR	0.3	0.2	3.0	2.9	1.4	1.5	0.8	0.6
Share of exports to the East (%)	8	9	32	28	34	33	36	17
Share of exports to the Soviet Union (%)	9	14	36	28	38	34	41	24

Source: OECD statistics, Standard International Trade Classification categories 691 and 7, except 78 and 79.

Note: Intra-German trade is excluded.

Pechiney, ETPM, and Thomson receive a not-insignificant share of their export earnings from Eastern countries.

This development of capital-goods sales in European trade with the Soviet Union has many consequences. Among them, it increases the visibility of East-West trade and therefore creates political pressure for its development. Lobbying is also made easier by the concentration of decision making in a few people and by the frequent involvement of government at various levels (technology-transfer controls, subsidized credits, political impact of major contracts). From a financial viewpoint, the greater share of capital goods in West European trade with the East leads to the greater financial involvement of West European countries in commercial and often subsidized credits because other categories of goods are normally sold on a cash-and-carry basis, or with short-term loans, without government intervention. The development of medium- and long-term loans parallels the development of capital-goods sales by European countries.

Structure of Imports and Balance of Trade: The second major difference between American and European trade with the East lies in the contrast between the large surpluses of American trade and the growing deficits of European trade (table 6-4). This situation is the consequence of the large European imports of Soviet energy and the very small American imports from COMECON countries (table 6-5).

This factor explains why the European Economic Community (EEC), in spite of a trade volume that in 1980 was more than ten times that of the United States, accumulated in the 1970s only half of the surplus of the United

Table 6-4
Trade Balance with COMECON
(billions of dollars)

	1979	*1980*	*Total Trade Balance, 1970-1980*
United States	+ 3.81	+ 2.44	+ 17.8
European Economic Community[a]	− 1.00	− 4.56	+ 9.8
Federal Republic of Germany[a]	+ 0.78	+ 0.9	+ 17.97
France	− 0.6	− 0.53	+ 3.85

Source: OECD Statistics, complemented by the United Nations Commission for Europe (for intra-German trade).

[a]Trade with the German Democratic Republic is included.

States. Moreover, the European surplus of the 1970s was a contraction of wide deficits of the United Kingdom and the Netherlands, compensated for by a large German surplus. The European surplus may now turn into a deficit because of the stagnation of East European imports and of the steady expansion—in value if not in volume—of Soviet energy exports. Exports to debt-ridden Eastern Europe can no longer compensate for imports from the Soviet Union.

This situation is all the more detrimental to European interests in that the accumulated surplus of the United States has materialized in cash payments, or short-term loans already paid, while the dwindling European

Table 6-5
Percentage Share of Energy in Imports from the USSR and COMECON

	1979		*1980*		*Volume in 1980[a]*	
	USSR	*CMEA*	*USSR*	*CMEA*	*USSR*	*CMEA*
United States	4.75	6.9	4.1	5.2	0.01	0.10
European Economic Community	66.9	43.3	74.4	50.8	10.6	13.3
Federal Republic of Germany	68.9	42.8	75.7	44.8	3.0	3.8
France	60.1	42.6	76.5	58.9	2.7	3.1

Source: OECD Statistics.

Note: Intra-German trade excluded.

[a]Billions of U.S. dollars.

commercial surplus is, to a significant amount, covered by long-term loans that have yet to be reimbursed.

Geographical Structure of Trade: The last major difference between the United States and Western Europe in the past has been the geographical structure of trade (table 6-6).

Except in 1980 when trade flows were disrupted by the embargo, West European exports have been much less Soviet oriented than has been American trade. This situation is quickly changing, however, with the rapid growth of energy imports and the impending crisis of Eastern countries. European exports, which were sent primarily to Central Europe, may now be reoriented toward the Soviet market, and the structure of West European trade with the East may become more similar to the structure of U.S. trade, except that the pattern of European trade now seems to be import driven, while U.S. trade has clearly been export driven.

These various elements together make up a specifically European picture of trade with the East European countries. East-West trade may not be so much more important to West European economies, but its specific structure accounts for some of the transatlantic differences that have arisen since 1979:

> The centrality of the food trade for the United States has no equivalent on the other side of the Atlantic, a fact that partly explains why European governments have resisted American pressures for more restricted trade, often recalling President Ronald Reagan's decision to lift the grain embargo. Any American trade policy that leaves the grain trade unaffected has no credibility in Western Europe or the Soviet Union.

> West European trade has less flexibility than U.S. trade because of the nature of the goods being exchanged. On the demand side, capital-goods exports are related to Eastern countries' multiyear investment policies;

Table 6-6
Share of the Soviet Union in Western Trade with COMECON, 1979 and 1980

	United States, 1979-1980	European Economic Community, 1979-1980[a]	Federal Republic of Germany, 1979-1980[a]	France, 1979-1980
Exports	63.6-39.3	36.7-40.3	32.1-34.5	49.7-53.1
Imports	31.0-32.1	44.3-50.2	37.0-34.6	54.4-68.0
Total trade	58.5-37.3	40.6-45.8	34.5-34.6	51.9-61.0

Source: OECD Statistics, complemented by the United Nations Commission for Europe (for intra-German trade).

[a]Includes intra-German trade.

the typical cycle is a five-year one. On the supply side, capital-goods exports imply long-term investment decisions on the part of exporting industries. Food exports, in spite of attempts to bring continuity through multiyear agreements, are related to annual crops and therefore vary greatly from year to year. This difference is illustrated by the trends of trade: American trade shows ups and downs unknown to European trade.

The West European trading position with the Soviet Union is vulnerable. The payment of present exports is tied to future West European imports, while the deficit created by the growing value of Soviet imports helps build pressure to develop West European exports. But one cannot infer from this weaker trading position that Europeans are politically more vulnerable to trade pressures from the East.

The question of whether the Soviet Union uses its strong trading position to reap political or economic advantages over its West European partners cannot be answered without questioning the Soviet system itself. Economic analysis alone can substantiate neither European self-righteous claims about the economic necessity of trade nor American fears of European complacency resulting from Soviet pressures. Western Europe is not in a good position to exert pressures through trade, but it does not necessarily follow that the Soviet Union is in a better position to exert political pressures on Western Europe through trade. The issue is a political one: What was the commitment? What were the expectations of West European nations when they engaged in trade with the East? And what is the view from Moscow?

The Political Perspective

The Political Trap: Trade with the East did not develop as the result of a carefully planned, long-term strategy of the Western countries. It grew in a period when bankers had plenty of cash and were searching for places where they could recycle the surpluses made available by oil-price increases. Business was looking for markets to sell capital goods. The East—taken as a whole because at the time the Soviet Union was perceived as the ultimate guarantor of other Eastern countries—seemed to be the perfect place. It had energy exports to guarantee the payment of imports. It had industrial workers and discipline to make investments cost-effective. And it had the willingness to invest and to take the full benefit of the credits extended by the West.

This approach was not specifically European, but it was widely shared by the business community. It had little to do with politics except that the development of détente had lifted the obstacles that could have constrained what was deemed to be a natural outcome of well-understood Western economic interests.

Yet political implications were quick to surface, not only in the United States with the debate on the most-favored-nation clause but also in Western Europe. Both sides of the Iron Curtain linked the political and economic issues. Bilateral commissions were set up at government levels, and credit facilities were extended at government-subsidized rates. The extreme case was the 850 million deutsche mark swing facility extended to the GDR by the FRG. While West European governments were asking for more contracts on the grounds of their détente-oriented policy, Eastern governments were asking their Western partners to give substance to their political posture with concrete gestures in terms of credits and technology. And when Western partners became less complacent about Eastern demands, Eastern governments contended that letting economic negotiations come to an end would bring the most damaging consequences because it would be taken as a political signal and would trigger a cumulative, hardly controllable process: politics was being used to reap economic advantages. The process also worked the other way: Eastern countries (more than West European countries) did try to extract political advantage from economic relations, a point that is obvious from the way bilateral economic meetings are conducted in the East. The Eastern press coverage, which is always extensive, emphasizes the political meaning of economic meetings. But economic leverage was also used to achieve political ends in less conspicuous ways. A high-level Soviet official would stress that bilateral economic relations with country X has always had a political dimension and that a deterioration in the quality of the political climate inevitably would have negative commercial consequences; he would seldom suggest that an improvement in the political climate would generate more trade.

This kind of bargaining, which is now not unusual in international trade, cannot be ascribed solely to East-West trade; relations with the Organization of Petroleum Exporting Countries have similar traits. But the particular nature of Soviet bloc countries gives increased credibility to the linkage between economic and political issues. Totalitarian states are expected to unify the economic and the political perspective, and the fact that economic relations may be but one aspect of a more global strategy, including politico-military aspects, reinforces the economic leverage. Contrary to the case with Saudi Arabia or any other Gulf state, the Soviet Union does not have to rely on economic relations to bring pressure to bear on the Western world. It has other means of showing its power, and it may be all the more willing to use the economic card as it has other cards in its hand; the partner is also less inclined to call the bluff. The pressure can then become a signal, one that is reinterpreted in a broader, noneconomic context. This is a clear case of reverse leverage, where the threat of diminishing trade with the Soviet Union in the case of a deteriorating political climate can create the fear of losing profitable contracts; but this fear would be reinforced by the further fear that diminishing trade in turn would provoke further deterioration of the political climate. The combination of potential economic and political leverages is a special trait of East-West trade that distinguishes it from other types of international trade.

The permanent use of political-economic linkage in East-West trade does not say anything about the efficiency of the linkage. One can argue that it has all been a bluff and that economic relations and political relations have followed two independent courses, even if both partners tried to reap windfall benefits from their artificial linkage.

But the mere fact that West European policies toward the Soviet Union may be interpreted as a result of economic pressures is in itself a windfall profit for the Soviet Union. It inserts the wedge of suspicion in transatlantic relations at just the right moment. Moreover, considering the political mood now dominant in the United States, any European move in the direction of more (or less) East-West trade inevitably would be interpreted as a political gesture, even if it was motivated by purely economic reasons, and this consideration can be enough to deter any such move.

European countries can therefore be paralyzed by the weight of economic and political issues resting on their shoulders. Their statements are not taken at face value when they pretend that they can prevent economic relations from spilling over into the field of politics, but they are not strong enough economically to argue convincingly that they are immune to commercial blackmail. East-West trade works as a trap easily fallen into but difficult to escape from later.

Policies of Ambivalence: Limited Impact of East-West Trade on Eastern Countries: The weaker commercial and political position of European countries makes it more difficult for them to resist the politicization of trade while at the same time creating greater reluctance to such a politicization. The best way to avoid this political trap may be for European countries to minimize the role of trade as a weapon, or an instrument, in their relations with the East. Ambivalence has been preferred to a declared strategy.

Trade can foster change in Eastern countries. It can help to develop a network of interests that would constrain Soviet international behavior. But if trade ever brings such results, they would be received as windfall benefits, not as the expected outcome of a chosen policy. The present American disappointment with East-West trade and the alleged U.S. overreaction are thus considered in Europe as a by-product of former overexpectations. Europeans pretend to be too realistic to put such hopes at the center of their policy; they can therefore hardly be disappointed.

This policy of ambivalence, which accepts the idea that East-West trade cannot avoid politics but does not expect major political breakthroughs of trade relations, could rightly be rejected for its absence of strategic vision if it were not based on a specific assessment of the impact of East-West trade on Eastern countries. In the case of France, this policy would be more accurately described as a policy of ambiguity than ambivalence. French authorities have no illusions on the political windfall benefits of trade and have made clear that peace is secured by a sound balance of forces, not by the development of trade. But the collapse of trade could have a negative political impact.

European countries do not reject the idea that East-West trade has an impact on the East, but this impact is not so large as statistics show, and it can hardly be transformed into policy-influencing forces that would change the present course of Eastern countries.

Statistics show indeed that East-West trade is much more important for the East than it is for the West (table 6-7). This asymmetry, which is particularly obvious in the case of the Council for Mutual Economic Assistance (CMEA) Six, is even more pronounced for investment figures; some specialists argue that 10 to 15 percent of Soviet investment comes from imported goods. But this very high figure must not lead to false conclusions. Let us take the example of a fertilizer plant imported from the West. At the statistical level, the increase in output of fertilizer may look impressive, but the economic impact may be less so. The fertilizer may not be appropriate, it may not be delivered at the right place or at the right moment, and it may not be properly used. The net result may then fall short of the expectations raised by statistics.

The real impact of East-West trade is cushioned by the many inefficiencies and bottlenecks of a centrally planned economy. A change in the volume of East-West trade does not have the impact that statistics suggest.

This analysis explains why it is so difficult to transform the impact of trade into political influence. The American argument that severe cuts in East-West trade would force the Soviet leadership to reconsider the priority that it has given to military spending can be rejected on the ground of eco-

Table 6-7
East-West Trade and Soviet Bloc GNP, 1980

	USSR	CMEA Six	CMEA Europe
Volume of trade with OECD (billions of dollars)	46.4	39.1	85.5
Share of GNP (%)	3.4	6.2	4.2

Source: OECD Statistics and unclassified CIA data (for GNP).

nomic analysis. The problem of Soviet agriculture is not so much a problem of resources—many resources have been allocated to agriculture in the past ten years—as one of how resources are being used.

In short, Western capital goods are worth little in an environment of economic inefficiency. The impact of trade policies could be greatly cushioned if Soviet authorities were to decide to change their present allocation of resources.

This last proposition is indeed not true in the case of high technology, which can have a direct military use. There, the systematic involvement of KGB agents in trade with the West enables the Soviet military industry to make quick and efficient use of Western technological discoveries. But constraining the Soviet military potential is a qualitative problem—one that must be addressed through qualitative measures—and not a quantitative issue—one that would be addressed through an overall limitation on the volume of trade—since there is no direct relation between Soviet economic potential and the volume of East-West trade.

This assumption is the bedrock of European attitudes toward East-West trade. In the 1970s, Western Europe chose a policy of ambivalence, the consensus being that it could afford such a policy without taking too many economic and political risks. European countries have been sitting around the political trap that détente had opened for them, in a game that was never innocent but was deemed acceptable so long as it remained limited.

Choices of the 1980s

In retrospect, the decade of the 1970s might appear to be a period when everybody was trying to buy time and to avoid facing hard choices. But in the 1980s, economic constraints in both the East and the West are bound to increase, and the long-term trend of East-West trade will be shaped by economics rather than by politics.

The flow of Western goods and credits in the 1970s has failed to bring the qualitative changes that could have been expected in the Eastern bloc. Imports from the West have not brought the short cut toward progress that the leaders of the Soviet bloc had anticipated. This failure is most obvious in Poland, but it affects all East European countries to a lesser degree.

Maximizing Imports of Capital Goods: The
Failure of the Soviet Strategy of the 1970s

Trade relations with the Soviet Union in the 1970s could be characterized as a losing race; East European countries tried to catch up with increases in the price of energy imported from the Soviet Union by boosting their exports of capital goods to that nation. West European countries and Japan have had the same sort of relationship with members of OPEC, but two major points differentiate these otherwise comparable situations. First, Japan has been able to win the race, and second, the relationship between West European countries and OPEC is not a closed, bilateral one but part of a broader framework of trade in which surplus oil revenue has been recycled, propping up exports in industrialized countries. The same cannot be said of the Soviet bloc trade relationship, which is for the greater part isolated from the rest of the world and must therefore be balanced on a bilateral basis.

Notwithstanding the flow of Western capital goods, Central European countries have failed to achieve the technological breakthroughs that would have enabled them to compensate for the natural advantage of the USSR. According to figures compiled by Jan Vaňous for Wharton Econometric Forecasting Associates and expressed in special drawing rights (SDRs) so as to eliminate exchange distortions in the ruble area, European CMEA countries multiplied their exports of machinery and equipment to the USSR by a factor of three between 1970 and 1979, while the USSR was multiplying its own exports of energy to the East European area by a factor of seven (table 6-8).[2]

Eastern Europe has achieved a high degree of specialization in its exports of machinery and equipment to the Soviet Union (53 percent of Soviet imports) but not enough to compensate for the sharp decline in terms of trade with the USSR. The cumulative surplus of Soviet trade with European CMEA countries for the period 1970 through 1979 is probably about 2,900

Table 6-8
Soviet Trade with European CMEA Countries:
Machinery, Equipment, and Energy
(millions of SDR)

	1970	1979
Energy exports (share in exports to Eastern Europe, %)	1,015 (15)	7,722 (37.5)
Machinery and equipment imports (share in imports from Eastern Europe, %)	2,926 (44)	10,320 (53)
Balance of trade		
Machinery and equipment	−1,510	−5,750
Energy	+856	+7,199
Machinery, equipment, and energy	−654	+1,449

Source: Adapted from Jan Vaňous, "Soviet and East European Foreign Trade in the 1970s: A Quantitative Assessment," in U.S. Congress, Joint Economic Committee, *East European Economic Assessment* (Washington, D.C.: U.S. Government Printing Office, 1981), 2:688.

million SDR. The race with the Soviet Union has definitely been a losing one. But if it is a symptom of a general failure, the real issue is elsewhere and the economic failure is a failure of the whole bloc.

The Soviet surplus, which is in rubles, cannot be used to finance deficits with market economies. (OECD figures put the cumulative deficit of the Soviet Union with OECD for the period 1970 through 1979 at $12.262 billion. Wharton Econometric's estimate of Soviet deficit with the industrialized countries for the same period is 14.478 billion SDR.) If one isolates those elements, it is clear that it would have been in the Soviet Union's best economic interest to eliminate this surplus, which partly amounted to a subsidy (not to mention the lower oil price charged to CMEA partners). The USSR theoretically could have done so, either by increasing its imports—probably impossible for technical reasons, both in Central European countries (limited export capacities) and in the Soviet Union itself (rate of investment)—or by limiting its oil exports to CMEA and increasing its oil exports to the market economies. The interesting fact is that it did not follow that second course; there may have been a harmonized policy of capital-goods imports throughout the Eastern bloc, with the USSR and the CMEA Six both accumulating deficits with OECD (table 6-9).

This fact confirms the point that accepting the surplus with CMEA countries was probably a deliberate policy of the Soviet Union. The purpose was to encourage CMEA partners to develop their imports of capital goods from the West (a declared orientation of CMEA countries in the early 1970s). Moreover, if the Soviet Union had wanted to limit Western capital-goods imports by Eastern countries, it could have easily done so by limiting its own exports of energy to Eastern Europe. This decision would have squeezed Eastern economies' import capacities, thus provoking an earlier decline in their overall trade position. The trade surplus of the USSR with respect to European CMEA members can therefore be considered as a way to facilitate CMEA imports of capital goods while limiting CMEA imports of energy. The alleged Soviet surplus with respect to Eastern partners (a direct consequence of its oil exports), which does not make sense if one analyzes Eastern trade relations in national terms, becomes logical when the analysis is made at a more global level. At the Soviet bloc level, the best way

Table 6-9
Trade Deficits of the East with OECD
(millions of dollars)

	USSR	European Six	Total CMEA Europe
Cumulative deficit, 1970-1980	− 9,071	− 25,615	− 34,686

Source: OECD statistics.

to maximize imports of capital goods from the West was to obtain the participation of the whole bloc rather than to concentrate imports on the Soviet Union, whose import capacities were already technically stretched thin and which does not always make the best use of those imports. On the other hand, the USSR is now limiting its capital-goods imports, while it could expand them to compensate for the reduction of capital-goods imports in other CMEA countries; this may be one more confirmation of the uniformity of policy decisions in the CMEA bloc at the macroeconomic level.

The analysis of East-East trade then leads to an important conclusion for the future of East-West trade: the development of East-West trade by East European countries was probably a deliberate and global policy of the Soviet Union, and Central European countries have played the role of an intermediary between Western industrialized countries and the Soviet Union, with large imports of machinery and equipment from the industrialized countries and still larger exports to the Soviet Union, the developing world, and the other centrally planned economies. The fact that these exports were not enough to compensate for Soviet energy imports confirms that Soviet priority was given to maximizing at the bloc level the amount of capital goods imported from the West rather than to reaching a balance in East-East trade. (See table 6-10.)

This policy did not bring the expected qualitative improvements for the Soviet bloc. The rate of growth declined, and Central European countries were unable to improve their economies to the point where Soviet subsidies would have become superfluous. The Soviet strategy would have made sense if it had provided a bridge to self-sufficiency and if this group of countries had been able to develop an autonomous export capacity. The

Table 6-10
Machinery and Equipment Trade of European CMEA Members
(millions of SDR)

	Volume, 1977	Balance of Trade, 1977
Imports from West[a]	5,287	− 3,909
Exports to USSR	7,482	+ 3,342
Exports to developing countries	2,010	+ 1,993
Exports to other centrally planned economies	974	+ 653
Total		+ 2,079

Source: Adapted from Various, "Soviet and East European Foreign Trade," pp. 695-696.
Note: USSR excluded.

[a]This same year, Soviet imports of machinery and equipment from the West were 4967 million SDR.

Soviet Union would then have been freed from the burden of supporting those countries through energy supply because they would have managed to earn enough hard currency to buy both energy and capital goods outside the ruble area. But instead of becoming economically self-sufficient, Central European countries have become more vulnerable at the very moment when the Soviet Union's own economic problems make subsidies to Eastern Europe costlier for Moscow.

The most striking characteristic of Central European countries' foreign trade is indeed their growing dependence on imports of Western nonfood raw materials (table 6-11). Industrialized countries, which have taken the place left vacant by the Soviet Union, represented in 1977 approximately the same share in total nonfood raw-material imports that the Soviet Union represented in 1970 (47 percent instead of 47.2 percent). This reversal of roles between the Soviet Union and the industrialized countries is worrisome for Central European economies because they cannot limit their dependency without reducing overall economic activity, considering the Soviet inability to meet their needs in nonfood raw materials. If one combines the growing pinch of energy imports (due to limitation of Soviet deliveries), the necessity for nonfood raw-materials imports, and the incapacity to develop a real export capacity toward market economies, the picture is grim for the European satellites of the Soviet Union.

Table 6-12 shows that the surplus in manufactured goods ($3,797 million) achieved by Soviet satellites in their trade with NATO countries is almost totally eaten up by the deficit in food, chemical products, and crude

Table 6-11
Imports of Nonfood Raw Materials by European CMEA Members, Showing Origin of Imports and Share in Total Nonfood Raw-Material Imports
(millions of SDR)

	1970	1977
USSR	2,926 (47.2%)	5,651 (33.1%)
Other centrally planned economies	275 (4.4%)	725 (4.8%)
Developing countries	594 (9.5%)	1,528 (10.2%)
Industrialized countries	2,402 (38.7%)	7,012 (47%)
Total	6,197	14,916

Source: Ibid., pp. 695-696.
Note: USSR excluded.

Table 6-12
Trade Balance of CMEA Members with NATO Countries in 1980
(millions of dollars)

	CMEA Six	USSR	European CMEA
Food	−1,581	−3,534	−5,115
Crude materials and chemical products	−1,844	+353	−1,491
Manufactured goods	+3,797	−2,778	+1,019

Source: NATO unclassified.

materials ($3,425 million). That does not leave much maneuvering space for imports of equipment and energy. It means that even if the financial problems created by high debt-service ratios did not exist, the bad structure of the balance of trade by itself would be sufficient to provoke a major reappraisal of East-West trade in Eastern countries. The financial squeeze makes this reappraisal all the more necessary.

The Reappraisal of the 1980s: Counting on
One's Own Strength

The Soviet bloc has several ways of reacting to this new situation, but it cannot afford, and its creditors would not accept, the mere extrapolation of the trends of the 1980s. The Soviet Union plans to boost its production of gas and thus make up for the stagnation and decline of its oil production.

It is assumed that in terms of all CMEA countries, there will be an approximate balance throughout the 1980s, with a diminishing Soviet surplus and a deficit among the satellites.

The new important factor is the limitation of Soviet energy exports to CMEA satellites and a greater reliance of satellites on dollar area imports. One could then suggest that the Soviet Union from now on will increase its share of capital-goods imports paid in hard currency, while Soviet satellites will reduce their own imports of capital goods. But this policy is formally contradicted by official plans for the next years, which put very tight limits on the level of investment in the USSR. Whether this policy will be reversed later and whether Soviet imports of capital goods will rebound in the second half of the 1980s are doubtful. By 1985, bottlenecks are likely to multiply in the Soviet Union, and increased imports of food, chemical products, and consumer goods may be more immediately necessary than capital-goods imports and may use up the diminishing amount of hard currency available. Whether the Soviet Union will have the capacity to maintain some oil exports to the West while increasing its gas exports will make the difference between a severe crisis and protracted difficulties. The latter hypothesis is more likely.

We can therefore assume that energy exports will not provide the bounty that would be necessary to pursue the same course as in the 1970s. The opportunity costs of sustained capital-goods imports inevitably will increase for the Soviet Union itself, making the case more pressing for an overall reappraisal of the Soviet trade strategy with the West.

There are actually many signs that this reappraisal has already started in the Soviet Union and that the changes we are witnessing in satellite states— which can be attributed to obvious financial constraints—take place in a more global reassessment of East-West trade. The contrast is striking between official speeches of the 1970s, when Kosygin and Brezhnev were acknowledging the advantages of international cooperation and technology transfers, and more recent statements—such as the Brezhnev report at the Twenty-sixth Party Congress—where the emphasis is on self-reliance and better use of one's own capacities. The same philosophy appears in Soviet magazine articles dealing with the Polish situation. The dangers of trading with the West and the ineffectiveness of technology imports from the West are underscored, suggesting a very cautious Soviet attitude on this issue in the future. It is thus most likely that the deliberate policy of the Soviet Union will become more selective and will accompany a general decline of East-West trade. Moscow will find some virtue in a trend that is borne out of necessity.

The constraints are indeed much more stringent in the satellite states. I have suggested that the development of their trade must be analyzed as part of a bloc effort to maximize capital goods from the West. A change of policy in Moscow will thus directly affect the trade orientations of Central Europe. The key question is whether the incoming crisis will bring together the Eastern bloc or, on the contrary, will accelerate an already existing differentiation between the USSR and its satellite states and among the satellite states themselves.

There are signs that the satellite states are trying different ways out of the present impasse. Countries where the crisis is more acute—Poland and Rumania—have no choice but to recentralize and allocate scarce resources on an authoritarian basis. Trade is actually going back to clearing agreements, and public statements about economic reforms have more to do with disinformation of the West and self-deception than with actual policies. Political control of the country, not productivity, claims priority, and economic reforms will be limited to price increases.

Hungary is trying the opposite tack. Instead of isolating the internal economy from foreign constraints, it aims at using the foreign constraint as a tool to force the economy to be more competitive. Convertibility of the forint, wider use of international prices, and macroeconomic planning based on a realistic assessment of export capacities are supposed to achieve that ambitious goal. But the obstacles are formidable. The coexistence of two trades, one of which often uses arbitrary pricing methods, creates distortions that are difficult to neutralize without returning to administrative methods. Global demand is hard to control in socialist countries, and there is always a risk that price increases will shift excess demand from the consumer level to the enterprise level. This is precisely what happened in Hungary, and the government is now imposing new regulators so as to pump the excess revenue of enterprises. This decision raises another problem: many firms are only marginally competitive, and the combination of more international competition, tax pressures, and fixed employment is not acceptable to them. They cannot balance their accounts without heavy subsidies from the state. Yet Hungarian authorities have pledged to reduce the amount of subsidies given to enterprises. But the evolution of the budget runs directly against that unrealistic orientation; the deficit has tripled between 1981 and 1982, and subsidies cannot be easily eliminated. The main reason for this failure lies in the rejection of unemployment in communist countries. Virtual unemployment—people who are actually employed but who would not be in a competitive environment—is indeed very high in Eastern countries, probably higher than actual unemployment in market economies, considering the irrationality of many investment decisions in the East and the energy-intensive character of Eastern economies. Economic reform in those societies actually means that they would have to experience the immediate disadvantages of a market economy facing a recession, while the benefits of market competition would have to wait for the medium term.

It is therefore likely that a combination of political wisdom on the part of the leadership (unemployment is not good for political stability) and a sense of self-interest on the part of the working force (why accept the drawbacks of market economies if not to derive the benefits that distinguish it from nineteenth-century capitalism) will progressively constrain effective reforms, supposing that the financial squeeze has not done them in already. Rather than differentiation, difficulties are likely to bring homogenization in the management of the economy. That does not mean that all Soviet bloc countries will look alike. The reaction of the population to hardships may vary from one country to another, and it is not impossible that the countries that have, up to now, been most successful will face the greatest difficulties, perhaps with a certain time lag. From the standpoint of East-West trade, this means that no matter what the Soviet policy will be, no matter what Western policy will be, the dominant element of the 1980s will be a significant reduction in real terms of East-West trade because Eastern countries are more likely to limit their imports through authoritarian planning than to boost exports through a real improvement in their economies. Economic logic will take care of East-West trade in the 1980s and sharply restrain it.

Conclusion: Options for European Policymakers

The context in which European policymakers will have to reassess their trade policy toward the East does not lead to any clear-cut decision. The impact of East-West trade on West European economies is not so big that it can determine that policy. Yet the structure of this trade, as opposed to the structure of U.S. trade, puts the Europeans in a weaker position, whether they want to improve their commercial position or use trade as a political instrument. East-West trade is a political trap rather than an effective tool of East-West policy for West European countries.

The impact of East-West trade on the East is much greater than that on the West. It represents between 30 and 50 percent of CMEA countries' foreign trade and approximately 6 percent of the GNP of the satellite states. Yet the experience of the 1970s shows that if East-West trade may destabilize Eastern countries, it is not enough to promote the economic and political changes that one would expect. In the 1980s, the most likely outcome of the East-West trade of the 1970s may be a recentralization of economies and a return to neo-Stalinist methods. West European countries, even assuming that they could persuade the United States to follow the same course, cannot reverse that trend because it would mean doubling or tripling the amount of credits already extended to the East. It is doubtful that Western governments would have the capacity or the will to take such a risky bet. They can try to impose conditionality and pressures through various means (as the International Monetary Fund has done with Hungary), and it may not be politically insignificant to try this generous orientation, as it was not politically insignificant that Marshall Plan aid was offered to the East. These efforts may fail. Western countries would then have to organize an orderly withdrawal so as to limit their losses. Crisis management would therefore be more necessary than fine-tuning in the 1980s. Yet in the context of a world economic recovery, a differentiated policy of the West toward Eastern countries could make the difference between global re-Stalinization and limited progress. Assuming the inevitability of a reduction of trade and the difficulty of promoting the subtle differentiations, the real policy question is whether West European countries should give political significance to this trend or merely follow it in a low-key way.

The American debate is now focusing on subsidized credits and export guarantees. These factors indeed play a role at the microeconomic level, they are one more example of the weaker position of European exports, compared with American food exports, and they perpetuate this weak posture. But their impact on Eastern countries should not be exaggerated. Subsidies amounted to less than half a billion dollars in 1980. If the American goal is to bring East-West trade back to market conditions, the goal is only $500 million away and not worth a tough fight in the alliance.

On the other hand, if some American policymakers want to stop East-West trade through economic decisions, it may not be in the European interest to follow such a course. One could argue the extreme case that either capital-goods trade with the West is absolutely necessary for Eastern Europe, and nothing will be stopped, or it is superfluous, and West European interests will be hurt more than those of Eastern Europe. My analysis suggests that this trade, while important, has never been an absolute necessity for the East and that it will become less so. Preserving a certain degree of ambiguity while having no doubt about the real orientation of the trend may then be in the Europeans' best interest.

While no credits should be extended to bankrupt countries that expect the West to make the way to neo-Stalinism smoother and while no high technology should be sold to countries that participate in a major military buildup directed against the West, a differentiated policy, with realistic and therefore limited expectations, is still in the interest of the West. We do not have the capacity to shape the history of the Soviet bloc, either to trigger the final crisis or to develop the convergence of systems. But we may help bring about small changes and may, by our own ambivalence, make the position of Eastern countries themselves more ambivalent and therefore more likely to change.

Notes

1. According to estimates made by the *German Institute for Economic Research* (D.I.W.) in West Berlin.

2. Jan Vaňous, "Soviet and East European Foreign Trade in the 1970s: A Quantitative Assessment," in U.S. Congress, Joint Economic Committee, *East European Economic Assessment* (Washington, D.C.: U.S. Government Printing Office, 1981) 2:685.

7

The Evolution and Possible Direction of U.S. Policy in East–West Trade

Marshall I. Goldman

Trading with the Soviet Union is a bit like playing with a yo-yo. If you are lucky, trade is both up and down. If you are unlucky, it is just down. This shows up clearly in the U.S.-Soviet trade statistics since 1918. For extended periods of time, trade was virtually nonexistent. There was almost no U.S.-Soviet trade from 1932 to 1935 and from 1949 to 1959. At other times, trade has tended to expand and contract from year to year.

The reason for the fluctuating nature of U.S.-Soviet trade is politics. It, rather than economics, is the primary determinant of American trade volume when dealing with all communist countries, and since the Soviet Union is viewed as the leader of the bloc, political vagaries have had an especially important impact. Admittedly U.S. trade with Germany and Japan, one-time enemies, has not been devoid of political considerations, but this has not been of major importance in over thirty years. In contrast, since World War II, U.S. trade with the Soviet Union was initially high, then virtually nonexistent from 1949 to 1959, and then occasionally high in 1964 and from 1969 to 1972, and then very high in 1973-1974, and then reduced in 1980 and 1981. Poor Soviet harvests account for some of these peaks, but politics has affected most of the rest.

The aim of this analysis is to show how politics and economics interact and what impact U.S.-Soviet trade has had in facilitating or complicating better U.S.-Soviet political relations.

Trade Leads the Way

Given the underlying suspicion Americans have had about the Soviet Union since its revolution, it is remarkable that U.S.-Soviet relations are sometimes good. In almost all such instances, political improvement has brought with it the flourishing of trade. But there have also been times when trade, not politics, seems to have led the way. That seemed to be the case in the late 1920s and also in the early 1970s. Which comes first, trade or détente, is not always clear. There was mutual interest in working out a strategic arms limitation agreement (SALT) as well as a mutual quest for a general relaxation of tensions. But the simultaneous desire on the part of some Soviets and some Americans for an increase in trade was most striking.

What makes the economic interest in the early 1970s so noteworthy is that it came when the political climate between the two countries seemed to be degenerating. That is not to say that political relations have ever been close. But at least since World War II, trade seemed to follow, not lead, an improvement in political relations. Once Hitler invaded and thereby abrogated the Nazi-Soviet Pact, the Soviets looked for help elsewhere. After the U.S. entry into the war a few months later, the United States and the Soviet Union joined together in a common front against the Germans. With the end of the war, however, what little warmth there had been evaporated quickly as the Cold War took hold. With Stalin's death there was a temporary political improvement. This reached a peak when Khrushchev and Eisenhower began to meet, but that venture too collapsed when the Soviets shot down a U.S. U-2 over Sverdlovsk. This was hardly a climate to foster trade. Any company that traded with the Soviet Union or Eastern Europe ran the risk of consumer boycott and at the least unfavorable publicity. Passions were intensified even more as U.S. involvement in Vietnam increased and as the Soviet Union moved more openly to support their North Vietnamese allies. Selling American products to a country that was the biggest source of support for an enemy or machinery that would threaten American security interests was a common attitude epitomized by the reaction of Secretary of Defense Melvin Laird, who in the spring of 1970 bitterly attacked Henry Ford II for even contemplating a Soviet request to build a diesel truck assembly plant. In effect, Laird ended all thought of Ford's participation when he opposed the export of American technology to the Soviet Union while North Vietnam was receiving Soviet trucks.

Nevertheless some favored trade with the Soviet Union, for several reasons. Some proponents have persistently argued that the United States should trade with all nations because peace comes from trade. Another more practical group was interested primarily because they saw their foreign competitors winning contracts they themselves might have won in a more friendly political climate. At an earlier time, such contracts with the Soviet Union were not particularly important. There were enough opportunities elsewhere in the world, and in addition, the Soviets did not have much to offer. Total West German exports to the Soviet Union throughout the mid-1960s seldom reached $200 million a year. By 1969, however, there was a marked change. Exports by Western Europe and Japan to the Soviet Union rose rapidly. For example, German exports exceeded $400 million for the first time in 1969. American competitors were being left behind. Thus in 1968, after American firms refused to build an automobile plant for the Soviet Union, Soviet officials simply turned to Fiat in Italy, offering a $1 billion contract. Nor was this the only lost sale.

The attitude of the American business community began to change and to reflect its determination to share in the opportunities. The turnabout was sharp. Thus in hearings conducted by the Senate Foreign Relations Committee in 1964 about East-West trade, American businessmen indicated their support for trade, but almost every respondent asked that his name not be made public.[1] But four years later when the Senate Committee on Banking and Commerce conducted a similar set of hearings, with similar findings, the respondents were willing to identify themselves.[2] What made this so unusual was that the businessmen were willing to be identified even though by 1968 the American role in Vietnam had gone beyond the stage of sending in a few advisers. Moreover, U.S. concern with Soviet support to Vietnam had become a major issue. Thus, trading with the Soviet Union surely qualified for trading with the enemy. The specter of lost profits apparently more than compensated for the risk of being criticized, however.

There was another reason for trading with the Soviets, and this was linked with more sophisticated political goals. As developed by presidential assistant for national security affairs and later secretary of state, Henry Kissinger, trade was to be used as a carrot to entice the Russians into political concessions desired by the United States. "The Soviet Union should first demonstrate a commitment to restrained international conduct and a willingness to help settle concrete issues, including Vietnam and Berlin. That attitude was dubbed 'linkage.' "[3] If successful, this linkage theory presumably should not only bring about desirable political ends but should lead to an even greater economic involvement.

The Forgotten Soviet Perspective

The debate as to whether to engage in U.S.-Soviet trade was not limited to only the United States. Soviet officials were equally divided. Those who were against such trade were generally opposed to any undue contact with the West. Such interchange was feared for its corrupting as well as its subversive consequences. Such fears were not unique to modern-day Russia; they are a reflection of a well-entrenched historical paranoia, as well as a sense of inferiority, which were particularly pronounced in the mid-nineteenth century. These Slavophiles argued that Russia had its own unique culture, formed in large part by the peasants and the Russian Orthodox Church. Certainly neither the peasant nor the church was a model the Communist Slavophiles could acknowledge, but the sentiment was much the same. In addition to ideologists, those opposed to trade were also well represented in the police and the army. There were also individual managers opposed to trade, both because they feared such contact would expose the country to unacceptable ideas and because they feared that they might not be able to cope with such modern technology. There were also some who genuinely opposed the American role in Vietnam and the bullying way the United States was behaving.

In contrast, many in industry and the institutes and universities, and even in the army, wanted to promote such trade because they believed it would upgrade Soviet industry. The Soviets have had enormous difficulty generating innovation from within their own economy. To compensate for this lack of innovation, it seemed only logical to turn to the rest of the world. According to the proponents of trade, failure to trade would leave the Soviet Union further and further behind the industrial capabilities of the capitalist world. Moreover, without such technology, the Soviet military establishment would find itself at more and more of a disadvantage.

The Soviet shopping list was immense. In fact, it was so large that when by chance I was given a preview of it in 1969, I remembered thinking that it was an imaginary not a real list. The list was put together by an enterprising American businessman in April 1969 after a series of lengthy interviews and negotiating sessions with senior Soviet planners and foreign trade officials. He in turn had come to me to see about helping him obtain licensing permission. Together we spoke with officials in the White House, but they were not ready to start the linkage process, believing that the political conditions were still too unfavorable. The list was impressive in size, totaling more than $5 billion in 1969 prices. Among the items mentioned were a fiberglass plant, a complete cold roll steel mill, a series of computers for department-store, banking, and industry data processing, equipment to manufacture computers, an automatic telephone switching system, a microwave system for pipeline operation, a diesel truck plant to produce 150,000 trucks, an automated radiator factory, as well as a car-buretor and spark plug factory, and a plant to produce 1.5 million color television tubes a year. Almost all of these orders subsequently have been transformed into actual operating units such as the Kama River Diesel Truck Plant and the T.V. Tube Factory in L'vov. That such information should have been provided to an American businessman in April 1969, a time of tension and strain and a year before Henry Ford's invitation to Moscow to talk about some of the same items, does seem to reflect wishful thinking by Soviet planners, but as they put it to this small American businessman at the time, the Soviets "prefer American equipment and contracts." According to this private communication, "The delivery takes a good 2-3 years, and it is hoped that long before the first truck leaves the production line, the international situation will show a remarkable improvement, and the Viet Nam situation will have been solved long before."

The Soviets have also favored American products because they believe that no one else produces on such a large scale and no where else were the needs and size as comparable to the needs and size of the Soviet Union. In addition, German and Japanese technical prowess in 1969 was not as impressive as it became in the ensuing decade.

No doubt some Soviet officials had other motives as well. By dangling such a tempting list of contract offers in front of American businessmen, who were beginning to express their own interests in such trade, these Soviet officials probably hoped that the United States would agree to some political moves that it might not otherwise have been willing to make. Viewed from the White House, this was a form of reverse linkage. There was no doubt that generating and releasing such an immense list represented a major move at the highest level of Soviet policymaking. Finally, there was also a smaller subgroup of these Soviet officials who viewed East-West, and especially U.S.-Soviet, trade not only as a wedge to make the United States more flexible in its relations with the Soviet Union but also as a way to open up the Soviet Union to the influence of Western technology, and, from their perspective perhaps even more important, to Western procedures and ideas. As opposed to the neo-Slavophiles who opposed such contacts because of their corrosive effect, these Russian neo-Westernizers welcomed such interchange as humanizing and modernizing.[4]

Given the scale and scope of the orders that issued from the Soviet Union in such a short period of time, it was clear that the Soviets were serious about their new shift in policy. Obviously the determination had been made that by itself the Soviet Union could not bring its industrial, and by extension its military, technology up to competitive world levels. Therefore the Soviet Union would have to turn to the capitalist world for new technology, and in some cases even old technology.

The change in strategy was clearly signaled by Premier Alexei Kosygin. After displacing Khrushchev, Brezhnev and Kosygin apparently called for a suspension of the import program begun by Khrushchev. Thus from 1964 to 1966, imports from countries like the United Kingdom, France, and Germany fell markedly from what they had been in 1962 and 1963. After a two-year hiatus, Kosygin in a speech at the Twenty-third Communist Party Congress in April 1966 criticized the past practice of reverse engineering and called for the outright purchase of Western licenses and factories. It was wasteful, he argued, to buy finished Western machinery, break it down and then try to recreate the original productive process in the Soviet factory. "It is more profitable for us in many cases to buy foreign licenses than to try to work out this or that problem ourselves."[5] This speech heralded by only a few months the signing of $1 billion contract with Fiat in August 1966 and a substantial surge in imports from Western Europe and Japan in 1967 and thereafter.

Once embarked on such a course, the Soviets were eager to avail themselves of U.S. markets as well. This is reflected by the shopping list they began to circulate in 1969 and by the concessions they agreed to make in the 1972 Soviet-American Trade Agreement. Admittedly the American side made some major concessions as well, the most notable being their willingness to agree to a bilateral trade agreement. The United States normally does not believe in and does not sign such agreements. It did, however, in 1972, but only after the Soviet Union agreed to some extraordinary concessions, including an agreement to pay back part of their post-World War II Lend-Lease debt and to agree to an antidumping clause by which the Soviets promised to halt exports to the United States if someone in the United States claimed that the Soviet Union was dumping. The Lend-Lease concession represented more a concession as to principle than to principal. For years they had refused even to concede that they owed the United States money from the 1940s. However, by agreeing to repay their past-due debts, the Soviets made themselves eligible to borrow money again from American banks. Thus there was no actual financial sacrifice for the Soviets. In contrast, there was no offsetting gain for the Soviet willingness to halt exports if dumping charges should be raised. This was an unprecedented concession for any country, much less a strong country like the Soviet Union, which is so sensitive about its desire to be treated like an economic equal. It indicated just how eager the Soviets were to break into American markets and to avail themselves of American technology and grain.

In retrospect, there was if anything an overeagerness on the part of Soviet officials to obtain Western and Japanese technology. All too often, Soviet executives would insist that the only way they could solve certain technical problems was to import Western technology. In some instances, that may have been true, but in just as many cases, it was not. As several Soviet economists, including Brezhnev, have come to realize, just as often there was domestic technology that could have served as well as the imported technology.[6] Of course, often that so-called Soviet technology had moved no further than the development stage and therefore was not available for actual use. But when foreign technology was purchased, it became even more upsetting when it turned out, as it did so often, that this hard-currency technology had been used improperly. In a number of cases, the import equipment was left outdoors exposed to Russian weather and component cannibals. In a large number of instances, it was not used at all.[7] For example, the Ministry of Ferrous Metallurgy was criticized for having as much as 1.5 billion rubles worth of equipment from hard-currency countries on hand waiting to be installed. For much the same reason, the deputy minister of the petroleum industry was fired because he had imported $50 million worth of sophisticated recovery equipment and apparently had not used any of it.

Given so many failures, some Soviet authorities began to call for more self-reliance. Alexander Alexandrov, the president of the Soviet Academy of Sciences, warned, ''We must actively develop our national technology and technique. We must not create gaps in our technological development by unjustifiably relying too extensively on foreign techniques.''[8] This was not only a question of chauvinism but a recognition that undue reliance on foreign technology may lead to the neglect of research and development within the USSR itself. This criticism also reflects the belated awareness that technology and factory layouts designed for one economic system with a market set of scarcity relationships may not necessarily be equally suited for an economic system with state centralized planning, where the existence of scarcity is seldom acknowledged. When several imported ammonia plants costing hundreds of millions of dollars could not be made to function, Prime Minister Alexei Kosygin ordered that henceforth Soviet officials could not sign any contracts for imported technology unless the suppliers agreed to provide a guarantee of performance. Realistically no Western exporter could afford to give such guarantees, especially when the machinery was to be operated by Soviet personnel in the Soviet Union. Once Kosygin realized that such guarantees would be meaningless and that suppliers might nonetheless use such clauses as an excuse to charge higher prices, he dropped his insistence that they be included. Such criticisms nonetheless seemed to have had an impact, although it is hard to demonstrate cause and effect. For example, in 1979, 1980, and 1981, the Soviets had to divert large sums of money for the purchase of grain imports. But whatever the reason, there does seem to have been a drop in machinery imports from the Soviet Union's six largest hard-currency suppliers. Thus while machinery imports from the United Kingdom, France, Germany, Italy, Japan, and the United States rose from $3.7 billion in 1975 to a peak of $5.3 billion in 1978, they fell back to $3.7 billion in 1981. Such a measure is not inclusive of all machinery exporters and involves a variety of foreign-exchange ratios. Nonetheless the fact that the figures reported reflect current year, not constant, prices makes it appear all the more likely that such a real drop did take place.

A Two-Sided Lever

Against this backdrop, how has American-Soviet trade been used by the two parties? The answer is, with less-than-complete success.

Both sides have attached significant political strings to their trade. After the end of Lend-Lease shipments following World War II, there was very little trade between the two countries. Until 1969, except for some grain exports in 1964, total American exports to the Soviet Union never exceeded $60 million. However, with the beginning of détente in 1972, trade became an important weapon for both sides. Sensing how eager the Soviets were to trade with the United States, an unlikely coalition of liberals, human rightists, trade unionists, Jews, conservatives, and Pentagon supporters joined together to demand human-rights concessions from the Soviet Union. Finding an issue acceptable to such a divergent group proved relatively easy. They agreed to press the Soviet Union to relax the emigration prohibitions. The lever they chose was trade. They demanded that in exchange for improved trade terms, Soviet authorities should allow relatively free emigration from the Soviet Union. Without such emigration, the Soviets would be ineligible for the most-favored-nation (MFN) status, which under the proposed 1972 trade agreement meant that they would be ineligible for Export-Import Bank credits. This stipulation took the form of an amendment offered by Senator Henry Jackson and Congressman Charles Vanik that was attached to the Trade Adjustment Act of late 1974 and early 1975. This amendment was adopted despite the bitter resistance of the Nixon and subsequent Ford administrations, which did not want to restrict trade or impede their negotiating tactics in this way.

Some of the supporters of this amendment joined in because they felt that anything that might impede trade or force the Soviets to do more than they wanted to do was by definition good. The supporters of the Jackson-Vanik Amendment were opposed by those in favor of trade for political reasons—trade helps to develop friendships—such as the Committee for East-West Accord, as well as those who found American-Soviet trade to be a promising source of new and potentially high profits such as the U.S.-USSR Trade and Economic Council. From the perspective of both of the latter two groups, trade was too important to leave to the politicians. With time and trade, they argued, the Soviet Union would soon find itself making the necessary liberalizing changes on its own, the result of increased contact with the West and the United States in particular. Their opposition to the Jackson-Vanik Amendment was supplemented by others both in and out of government. Some were opposed to this use of trade no matter what the cause. Others were opposed not because they did not want to use trade as a weapon but because trade was being used as a weapon for the wrong reasons. As they saw it, instead of using trade for the parochial purpose of promoting the emigration of Soviet Jews, it would have been more appropriate to use trade to pressure the Soviet Union to sign the Strategic Arms Limitation Treaty or the withdrawal of Soviet troops and advisers from countries such as Angola and subsequently Ethiopia, Afghanistan, and Poland. Those who reasoned this way were not necessarily opposed to the emigration of Soviet Jews but felt there were more central issues at dispute between the two countries.

The trade tool was not an exclusive American conception. The Soviets also sought to use trade for their own purposes. Thus they held out the vision of enormous orders in order to generate opposition to impediments to trade like the Jackson-Vanik Amendment and to muster support for more relaxed military and political stances. Responding to the bait, plane loads of chief executive officers from American corporations went to Moscow for negotiations and almost as often became convinced that any deals were a potential breakthrough that would open up not only new trade opportunities but better political relations.

The Jackson-Vanik Amendment

The deft maneuvering that accompanied the passage of the Jackson-Vanik Amendment destroyed more than one myth. It had been an accepted piece of disinformation that the Soviet Union does not yield to political blackmail, but it did. Taking advantage of the Soviet desire for MFN and credits, seventy senators on October 4, 1972, joined together to sponsor legislation that ultimately was to become the Jackson-Vanik Amendment. As anticipated, the Soviets rejected all such interference in their internal affairs, but their protestations to the contrary, they began to allow a remarkably large number of Jews and a few others, such as Armenians and Germans, to emigrate. Between 1976 and 1980, 14,000 Armenians left the Soviet Union, mostly for the United States. The number of Jewish emigrants rose from 229 in 1968 to 13,000 in 1971, 31,681 in 1972, and then 34,733 in 1973.[9]

Although the number of immigrants in 1974 fell to 20,628, nevertheless by the end of the year, the United States and the Soviet Union seem to have reached an agreement over continued emigration. That at least was Senator Jackson's understanding of the compromise that had been reached on October 18, 1974, between himself and Secretary of State Kissinger. This in turn was based on discussions between Kissinger and his counterpart, Andrei Gromyko. According to Jackson, the administration was to "convey assurances to the Congress that the rate of emigration from the Soviet Union would increase and that punitive actions against individuals seeking to emigrate would cease. In exchange I agreed to introduce an Amendment to the trade bill which would enable the President to waive the credit and Most Favored Nation restrictions of the Jackson Amendment for eighteen months with subsequent one year waivers subject to congresssional approval."[10]

This arrangement spared the Soviets the humiliation of having to acknowledge publicly that they were allowing emigrés to leave at a rate acceptable to the U.S. government, but the result was to be the same. The emigrés would leave and the Soviet Union would be granted MFN status.

But the deal fell apart. The exact cause of the collapse is hard to ascertain. Clearly Gromyko was embarrassed when Senator Jackson made too much of a public stir over the October 18, 1974, agreement. Gromyko wanted to keep the arrangement secret in order to prevent his country from being humiliated. In contrast, Jackson had to make the arrangement public in order to prove to his colleagues that the Soviets had conceded. After the Jackson-Vanik Amendment had passed, however, Gromyko released a letter he had written to Kissinger on October 26, 1974, implying that he had never agreed to the arrangement worked out by Kissinger and Jackson. But the letter could be interpreted as either that the Soviets would reject the Kissinger-Jackson understanding or accept it:

> Dear Mr. Secretary of State: I believe it necessary to draw your attention to the question concerning the publication in the United States of materials of which you are aware, and which touch upon the departure from the Soviet Union of a certain category of Soviet citizen. I must say straightforwardly that the above-mentioned materials including the correspondence between you and Senator Jackson created a distorted picture of our position as well as what we told the American side on that matter.

> When clarifying the actual state of affairs in response to your request, we underlined that the question as such is entirely within the internal competence of our state. We warned at the time that in this matter we have acted and shall act in strict conformity with our present legislation on that score.

> But now silence is being kept precisely about this. At the same time, attempts are being made to ascribe to the elucidations that were furnished by us in the nature of some assurances and nearly, obligations on our part regarding the procedure of the departure of Soviet citizens from the Soviet Union. And even some figures are being quoted as to the supposed number of such citizens, and there is talk about an anticipated increase of that number as compared with previous years.

> We resolutely decline such an interpretation. What we said, and you, Mr. Secretary of State, know this well, concerned only and exclusively the real situation of the given question. When we did mention figures—to inform you of the real situation—the point was quite the contrary, namely about the present tendency towards a decrease in the number of persons wishing to leave the Soviet Union and seek permanent residence in other countries.

> We believe it important that in this entire matter, considering its significance, no ambiguities should remain as regards the position of the Soviet Union.

Although there is little doubt that the Soviets resented the way Senator Jackson proceeded to humiliate them, the tone of the Gromyko letter suggests the Soviets were willing to bear it. Gromyko did not flatly reject the U.S.-Soviet Trade Agreement in his letter. Only later, on January 18, 1975, did the Soviets decide that the arrangement was "insulting" and announce that as far as they were concerned, the U.S.-Soviet Trade Agreement had been abrogated. But in retrospect there is good reason to believe that it was not the passage of the Jackson-Vanik Amendment that upset the Soviets but the additional passage three days later of the Stevenson Amendment. The Stevenson Amendment limited the amount of Export-Import Bank credits available to the Soviet Union to $300 million over a four-year period. With special congressional approval, the total could be increased.[11] In addition, only $40 million of those credits could be used for fossil-fuel research in exploration, and none could be used for fossil-fuel production. Based on discussions with Soviet officials, there is good reason to believe that access to credit was more important to the Soviet Union than the granting of MFN status.

Emigration in 1975 did decline after the Jackson-Vanik Amendment was passed, but in the hope that Congress might change its mind, the Soviet Union increased emigration every year thereafter; by 1979, the total for that year exceeded 51,000. Presumably the Soviets hoped that this show of good faith would facilitate the sale of grain that they badly needed in 1979. There were also signs that even in 1979 they still hoped to win MFN status. For a time it indeed looked as if the Congress would vote to extend MFN treatment to the Soviet Union. Although relations between the two countries had deteriorated, the record emigration figures seemed to indicate that the Soviets were meeting the spirit of the Jackson-Vanik Amendment. Moreover, China had also asked for MFN status, and it seemed sensible to argue that if MFN were given to China, it should also be accorded to the Soviet Union. Ultimately the Carter administration decided to act on China alone; in 1979 the United States agreed to give China MFN status effective as of February 1980. (Recognizing that the Soviet Union was being criticized for not allowing people to emigrate, Vice-Premier Deng Xiaoping offered to provide as many immigrants as the United States wanted.) That certainly did nothing to reassure Soviet leaders about America's interest in reviving détente. It almost seemed as if there was nothing to lose. Not surprisingly, relations between the two countries deteriorated even more.

It may be that given the makeup of the coalition opposing MFN status for the Soviet Union, there was in fact nothing the Soviet Union could do to qualify for MFN. When they began to allow 50,000 emigrants a year, they in effect satisfied Senator Jackson's initial requirements. Senator Jackson reportedly agreed that this was an adequate number and asked that President Carter discuss the issue with Brezhnev in Vienna in 1979 and then make an announcement that the Soviet Union was in compliance with the Jackson-Vanik Amendment. President Carter apparently did neither. Not surprisingly, relations between the United States and the Soviet Union began to deteriorate so that there was not much chance of immediately reviving the air of good feeling, a great disappointment to many in the Soviet and American business communities.

At various times Soviet leaders have been led to believe that they would get MFN status. In part this was because Soviet officials had become victims of their own rhetoric. In their view of the United States, the country was controlled by the business community. Since one leading capitalist after another, especially the members of the U.S.-Soviet Trade and Economic Council, had flocked to Moscow with promises that they would fight for and win MFN status for the Soviet Union, the Soviets assumed that it was only a matter of time before Congress and the administration did as they were told.

Although it hardly conforms to Marxist doctrine, it is the farmers who seem to have had the most control over American foreign policy regarding trade with the Soviet Union. As evidence, the 1975 grain embargo was quickly rescinded after pressure from the farmers, as was the Afghanistan grain embargo of 1980. Indeed, Senators Robert Dole and Roger Jepsen, representing farm states, have convinced President Reagan that the United States should actively seek to sell more grain to the Soviets.[12] Their aim is to increase agricultural exports and thus improve economic conditions for their constituents. It should be clear at this point that short of a particularly venal act by the Soviet Union, it is unlikely that any administration in the near future can use agricultural products as a foreign-policy lever. That eliminates one of the most effective nonmilitary instruments in the American arsenal.

The View from Western Europe and Japan

With the farmers unwilling to allow the use of grain as a policy lever and the Jackson-Vanik coalition insisting on some additional limitations of trade after every human-rights violation in the Soviet Union, American policymakers quickly came to realize that they had little leeway in using East-West trade as a bargaining tool. Nor was it only a question of trying to coordinate differing factions within the United States. There were also differences of opinions and goals between the United States and its allies in Western Europe and Japan. More and more, they had come to oppose the use of trade as a political lever. If anything, they came to view East-West trade as a source of raw materials, especially energy materials, and as an outlet for exports.

The general lack of enthusiasm in the United States compared to a much greater eagerness in Western Europe and Japan is due in part to geography. The United States is farther from the Soviet Union than any other country in the northern hemisphere. Thus historically Russian trade with the United States generally has been more modest in scale than it has been with countries like Germany and the United Kingdom. This reduced volume of activity in turn has tended to make Americans less enthusiastic about the market opportunities in the Soviet Union than their counterparts in Western Europe. If American-Soviet trade is curbed, what does the United States have to lose? Since it normally exports more to small Belgium than to the Soviet

Union, limiting sales to the Soviet Union normally does not impose much strain on American companies. Moreover, agricultural products constitute the overwhelming bulk of U.S. trade with the Soviet Union, which means the loss to industry of a cessation in trade is even smaller than it might appear. At the same time, the fact that the Soviet Union is by far the world's largest market for grain imports explains why farmers are so united and so effective in protesting any curtailment of agricultural sales to the Soviet Union.

In contrast to industrial exports from the United States, industrial exports from allies to the Soviet Union are relatively much more important, particularly those from Western Europe. Trade generally constitutes a larger share of their GNP. For that reason, they tend to fight for the right to maintain their trade with the Soviet Union much more than does the United States. First, Soviet raw materials are an important source of supply, particularly for energy. In addition, in a time of recession, exports to the Soviet Union become economically important even if they happen to be subsidized. It is widely reported that several European businesses have been ordered to submit low bids on projects because government officials in their countries have concluded that a government subsidy for low-interest loans or low-price contracts will be cheaper for the governments, both economically and politically, than government expenditures for unemployment compensation.

Allies also recognize that if the United States were to offer MFN and credits for Soviet exporters and at the same time reduce its licensing control over American exports, the United States would pick up a large share of the Soviet contracts that now go to Western Europe and Japan. This realization also leads to a certain amount of distrust by U.S. allies who are never quite sure if the United States is opposing trade with the Soviet Union because it has legitimate concerns or simply because it does not want allies to profit at its own expense. This concern receives support when the West Europeans see the United States abandoning the grain embargo. In addition, those who trade with the Soviet Union are usually aware that such trade is economically smart. It is one of the few countries to which equipment can be exported without a worry that the technology will be used to produce competing products. It may be used militarily, but economically there does not seem to be much to fear.

Many Europeans also have a different political strategy for dealing with the Soviet Union. By no means is there universal agreement, but many feel that rather than restrict trade with the Eastern bloc, they should promote it. To many Americans, particularly those in the Reagan administration, this may appear to be naive, but large numbers of Europeans believe that trade is not only an effective lever but a good way to bring about a reduction in the Soviet Union's insularity and its sense of isolation. They also feel that the more the Soviet Union is involved with Western Europe through peaceful interaction, the smaller the likelihood of hostile interaction. To the Americans who warn that linkage is a two-directional device, the Europeans respond by insisting that trade leads to increased contact and as a consequence better relations. In addition, even if gas imports through the controversial natural-gas pipeline are included, the level of trade is still relatively minor. Therefore the Soviet Union will not be able to exercise the leverage that some fear.

The Soviets Do Wrong Even When They Do Right

In assessing East-West trade policies since World War II and particularly since President Nixon's visit to Moscow in 1972, many Americans tend to concentrate almost entirely on what the West did wrong. They sometimes forget that the Soviets are probably their own worst enemy. They have a knack for doing the wrong thing at just the right time. The arrest of a Shcharansky, the expulsion of a Solzhenitsyn, the exile of a Sakharov are acts that are guaranteed to generate protest from those who oppose dealing with the Soviet Union. The Soviet treatment of refusniks is another source of friction, as is the occasional arrest of American businessmen.

Given the geopolitical rivalry between the United States and the Soviet Union, it is not surprising that in addition to the continuing irritants caused by human-rights abuse, there is also a counterpoint of friction generated by international confrontation. Angola, Chile, Ethiopia, Afghanistan, Nicaragua, Poland, and El Salvador provide enough real issues to absorb those opposed to trade. In addition, there are imagined frictions such as the supposed buildup of Soviet troops in Cuba in 1980 or American support of the rebels in Afghanistan in 1980. Fact or fiction, such disputes strengthen the hands of those opposed to trade in both countries.

Admittedly there is no lack of malevolence in Soviet domestic and foreign policy. Nonetheless it is necessary to recognize that sometimes it almost seems that even when the Soviets do something that might normally be considered to be a positive gesture, it becomes perceived as a hostile act. For example, when the Soviets first entered into negotiations to buy large quantities of grain in 1972, both the American and the Soviet negotiators thought this would be viewed as a helpful effort to reduce U.S. grain supplies and raise farmers' incomes. Instead it was viewed as a raid on American food supplies paid for by the American consumer and taxpayer. The consumer had to pay because the price of grain rose from $1.63 per bushel to $5. The taxpayer had to pay because grain exports were subsidized.

Nor are Soviet exports treated much better. When the Soviets sell a raw material such as oil, as they did in the late 1950s, it is often called dumping. When they sell strategic products like titanium, American producers begin to warn that if Soviet exports are allowed to continue, they will force American producers out of business. Then, the argument goes, the United

States will find itself dependent on the Soviet Union for critical supplies. American ammonia producers have repeated the same complaints.

Can the Trade Lever Be Used Effectively?

Given the rather dismal record so far, what policy guidelines can be recommended for the future? Can trade be used as a mechanism to humanize Soviet behavior and to further American-Soviet relations, or will it continue to be a source of irritation, not only between the United States and the Soviet Union but also between the United States and its allies?

The first question to be answered is whether the fuss about trade is warranted. Is the trade lever misnamed or misguided? Does the denial of American exports or MFN status influence Soviet behavior?

There is considerable debate about the issue, and the arguments partially reflect the vested interests of the debaters and partially the differing sets of assumptions and targets. It is unlikely, for example, that the Soviet Union would ever be forced to make structural changes in communism merely because the entire noncommunist world threatened to withdraw all exports and reject all imports. In other words, it is unlikely that trade can be used to produce an upheaval in the Soviet system, at least in the short run. That does not mean that trade and intercourse with the West will have no impact on Soviet behavior, only that basic changes are unlikely.

But trade can be an effective weapon for more limited objectives. First, there has to be agreement within the United States as to goals and expectations for the trade weapon. If the effect of what the United States hopes to do is to last more than a few months, its allies will also have to cooperate. But so far attaining such agreement or cooperation has been very difficult. Nonetheless, despite the lack of a unified purpose, the trade weapon has proved to be moderately effective. Despite Soviet denials, they have responded to the use of the trade weapon. The remarkable decision to allow the emigration of over a quarter of a million people since 1970 is evidence of that. Such a decision was not due to altruism but made in the hope of gaining access to credits and MFN status. Similarly, there have been times when the Soviets have moderated their behavior because of their need for grain. In particular, after the poor 1975 harvest and the subsequent U.S. decision to embargo grain exports, the Soviets abruptly muted their criticism of American foreign policy in the Middle East and watched as Henry Kissinger negotiated a first-stage Israeli withdrawal from the Sinai. Prior to the bad harvest, the Soviets had insisted that they be included in all such negotiations.

The Soviets nevertheless claim that they never bend or forsake principle in exchange for trade concessions or in response to economic blackmail. Fortunately the facts indicate otherwise. But the concessions demanded of the Soviet Union so far have been relatively modest. Moreover, the Soviet Union is so large and has such abundant natural resources that except for grain, it is relatively self-sufficient. It is nowhere near as vulnerable to the trade lever as, say Poland. There, General Wojciech Jaruzelski, the head of the Polish Communist party, openly admitted while visiting Moscow that "Poland is in a very grave economic situation. Our situation is also being significantly complicated by the economic sanctions introduced by the American administration as well—under its pressure—by the governments of the other capitalist countries."[13] Presumably this remarkable acknowledgment was intended in large part to generate sympathy, and more important, funding from the Soviet Union, but the fact remains that it was an unusual confession to make publicly.

The trade weapon can inflict damage. But it can also lead the victim to efforts to avoid a similar attack in the future. After the second grain embargo against the Soviet Union was declared in January 1980, the Soviets resolved to free themselves as much as possible from dependency on the United States. Because no one can provide the Soviet Union with as much corn or feed grain as they need, they must continue to import some grain from the United States in order to maintain their livestock herds; but wherever possible, they are seeking either to increase production at home or find sources of supply other than the United States. In particluar, they have signed long-term supply agreements with Argentina and Canada in the hope that they will have to come to the United States only as a supplier of last resort. The result is that whereas the United States regularly provided the Soviet Union with over 50 percent of its imported grain from 1972 through 1979 (the only exception was the 1974-1975 crop year) and frequently over 70 percent of its imports, in the 1980-1981 crop year the American percentage of sales fell to 24 percent and in 1981-1982 it was expected to total only 32 percent.[14] The likelihood is that the Soviets will continue to do all they can to find alternate sources of supply. The United States has enormous leverage at its disposal, but once a lever is pulled, there is an ever-decreasing likelihood that the United States can pull that lever again. This phenomenon can be described as the Iranian deposit syndrome. After the Iranians took over the American embassy in Teheran, the United States confiscated billions of dollars of Iranian assets deposited in American bank branches at home and overseas. This seemed a natural and appropriate step for the United States to take, and it was. Having observed how the United States reacted, however, other members of OPEC decided to reduce their exposure to American authorities and have begun to move some of their deposits to non-American banks. Inevitably such reactions reduce America's future ability to respond in the same way.

Accordingly, when the United States decides to use economic weapons in the future, not only is it vitally important to pick targets carefully but to decide well in advance the purpose of any such action. It must ensure that demands on the Soviet Union are realistic. What does the United States expect the Soviets to do and by when? What happens if they do not respond: remove the trade embargo and return to normal operations without any concessions whatsoever? That can be counterproductive. For example, President Reagan's unilateral decision to lift the grain embargo in April 1981 with no concessions sought from or offered by the Soviet Union made a mockery of the whole principle. It also served to discredit the United States when it called for a subsequent trade embargo by its allies to protest the declaration of martial law in Poland in December 1981.

Policy for the Future

One of the first tasks for the future is to seek some way to agree about how to use American exports and imports as a weapon against the Soviet Union. All too often the United States ends up using such tools as weapons against itself or its allies. Given the very wide diversity in attitudes that exist about how the United States should handle the Soviet Union, this will not be easy.

It would be useful if the United States could establish which levers are effective, and for how long, and which levers are not. One difficulty is that everyone tends to insist that nothing should be done that affects his or her livelihood. Farmers argue that grain embargoes cause the Soviet Union to buy elsewhere so that they are the ultimate losers. To some extent that is true, but so far overall Ameican grain exports have not fallen too sharply; when Argentina steps in to substitute for American sales to the Soviet Union, the United States moves in on the markets abandoned by the Argentinians. That picking up of abandoned Argentinian sales works well up to a point, at least as long as the Argentinians are unable to produce more than 5 million tons of corn for export. As a result, the Soviets must still come to the United States for the bulk of their corn. The difficulty is that given what they see to be expanded market opportunities, the Argentinians and others who have enjoyed the windfall seek to increase their agricultural output so that they can take advantage of exports to both the Soviet Union and their traditional customers. Should they succeed, the United States will be the loser.

Much the same pattern exists in industry. There are indeed areas of industrial technology where the United States has a monopoly either as to production itself or to the quality of production. The problem is that these areas of leadership continue to be reduced, and when the United States refuses to sell a particular product, the Soviet Union is often prepared to settle for second best. Moreover, the export opportunity provided by the sale to the Soviet Union has sometimes provided foreign competition with a convenient way to upgrade their technology. In effect, they use the sale to help finance their break-in costs. As a result, the Soviets help finance the technological experimentation of U.S. competitive rivals. The ultimate loser generally turns out to be the American manufacturer. For example, when the American government prohibited the shipment of Caterpillar pipeline tractors, Komatsu, the Japanese competitor, which used to have no share of the market prior to 1980, eked out a 25 percent share in mid-1980. By 1982, it had increased its share to 75 percent.

At the same time it is necessary to acknowledge that the sale of American technology does improve Soviet strategic capabilities. Prior to the construction of the Kama River Truck Plant, the Soviets lacked the necessary number of diesel tank transports to move their tanks rapidly across long distances to Western Europe. Now they seem to have that ability. They also have an improved capability of monitoring American submarine positions because of the more sophisticated electronic floating buoys they have been able to build. These buoys use semiconductor transistors copied from American models. In the same way, American equipment has made it possible for the Soviet Union to increase the accuracy of its missiles. It may be that as microprocessor technology proliferates, it becomes all but impossible to prevent the Soviet Union from obtaining the equipment it wants. It is said facetiously that some of the computer games now being sold in American discount stores embody a technology that is more advanced than what is permitted to be sold to the Soviet Union. However true such an assertion may be, there is no doubt that it has become very difficult to police any trade policy intended to protect United States security. Even if there should be a breakthrough that will allow the United States to police its policy more effectively, it would still have to come up with some definition of what that security policy should be. There is no doubt that sales of American and Western machinery often add to Soviet military capability. The trick is to find some way to regulate the sale so that in the process the United States does not suffer more than the Soviet Union does.

Similar arguments have been made about the extension of credits to the Soviet Union and Eastern Europe. Without such credits or without the United States or Germany stepping in to guarantee or redeem such credits, the Soviet Union would be unable to divert so much of its wealth to military expenditures. Some have gone so far as to argue that the United States can act unilaterally and cause a default and thus a crisis in a way that it cannot do in agriculture and industry. But there is considerable difference of opinion. There are many, including, not surprisingly, members of the banking community, who argue that the declaration of such a default will cause a collapse not only in the East but in the West. It they were forced to write off their loans to Eastern Europe, several banks in Austria and Germany might collapse, which in turn could set off calls for the transfer of funds among the Western banking community, currently not too secure. Unless the various Western governments stepped in with public funds to prop up their own banks, this could set off a landslide reminiscent of the worldwide banking disaster precipitated by the collapse of the Credit Anstalt in 1931.

Admittedly capitalist trade and credits do increase Soviet military capabilities. But given the fact that the United States apparently has lost the ability to insist on a unified response from its allies, is it possible to design an effective trade strategy? The prospects are not particularly bright.

The first place to start is at home. Something must be done to resolve differences between the Pentagon, which tends to oppose trade, and the Departments of Agriculture, Commerce, and State, which tend to support trade. These interdepartmental disagreements in part reflect differences of opinion within the United States itself. Under the circumstances, it may be that no such overall agreement on restricting exports will ever be reached, but at least some limited compromise may be possible. Perhaps future actions should also focus on restricting imports from the Soviet Union. The West Europeans in particular may find this difficult given that petroleum constitutes over 50 percent of their imports from the Soviet Union and that when a first effort was made to do this in the spring of 1981, the list of affected imports was cut sharply from what had been initially proposed. Nonetheless, this is something worth exploring.

Interagency forums already exist for the discussion of such issues within the administrative branch of the American government. Moreover, even if a policy within the American government can be temporarily agreed to, the likelihood is that it will not be a long-lasting arrangement because of continuous changes in Soviet behavior, as well as in Soviet and U.S. allies' technology. Yet such consultations seem to be very important. Moreover, such forums should include those outside the administration, such as senators and congressmen. One of the most frustrating aspects of the whole relationship is that not only do U.S. policies shift with changes of behavior in the Soviet Union but with different U.S. administrations. A long-standing bipartisan committee consisting of representatives of the major political factions might help reduce, although it probably will never eliminate, the magnitude of the fluctuations in U.S. trade policies with the Soviet Union. The United States has ongoing congressional involvement in representation to the United Nations, and there are a few joint congressional committees with representatives from both houses. Certainly such an arrangement would not be change proof, but it would be unlikely to make matters worse.

Only if the United States can create an internal consensus can it hope to establish a common policy with its allies. What were its allies to think when, on the one hand, the Department of Defense was doing its best to prevent the construction of the Soviet-West European Yamberg-Urengoi pipeline, and on the other, the State Department and the Department of Commerce, in sympathy with the European arguments, seemed to take a more tolerant attitude?

If anything, the American opposition to the building of the Yamberg-Urengoi natural-gas pipeline makes a good case study of what not to do. Given the importance of the project, it was unlikely that the West Europeans would abandon it, no matter how much pressure the United States might apply. Among the considerations, the building of the pipeline represented a good opportunity to provide jobs in Western Europe for the export of pipe and other supplies. In addition, the goal was to diversify the sources of supply as much as possible. Many Europeans recognize the danger in having to rely on the Soviet Union for the delivery of natural gas. In their minds, are supplies from the Soviet Union any less reliable than supplies from Iran, Iraq, or Algeria? Yet many Europeans recognized the dangers such a deal might create. Therefore, rather than generate needless antagonism from allies by opposing the pipeline completely, the United States instead should have urged them to move ahead with the pipeline but with extra storage and stand-by capacity. More important, it should have urged them to coordinate their efforts in order to ensure no subsidy in the interest rate for the loan they were providing for the pipeline. If the United States had tried to coordinate interest-rate policy instead of opposing the whole project, it may have spared itself and its allies needless friction. It might also have been able to hammer out a meaningful credit policy rather than wasting its efforts fruitlessly in blind opposition.

The prospects of designing a mechanism for working out such disagreements within the U.S. government are not much better than the chances of reaching an agreement among its allies. For years, the allies have tried to establish some degree of consensus through COCOM, which meets periodically in Paris. The results have been less than encouraging. The tendency is to adopt the least restrictive proposal. Nor given the poor economic climate in Western Europe where the temptation to sell products to the Soviet Union is sometimes the only business opportunity in sight, is there much support for adopting tight controls. Admittedly, the fact that the West Europeans were able to move so fast to impose very stringent trade and financial controls on Argentina after its invasion of the Falkland Islands suggests that unified action against the Soviet Union is not impossible. But then the Argentinians have fewer troops and missiles than the Russians, and they are farther away. Nor were the Europeans unaware that exports to Argentina from Western Europe are significantly smaller than those destined for the Soviet Union. While there are those in Western Europe who feel that selling to the Soviet Union, especially on such generous credit terms, is ultimately self-destructive, unlike the unity of action against Argentina, there seems to be little chance that the governments now in power will change their trade policy toward the Soviet Union. Only if the Soviet Union decides on some particularly aggressive act is there much prospect for a harder stance. Certainly the Soviet Union is capable of such an act, but at the same time, in the minds of many Americans, the West Europeans seem to have become more and more tolerant of what constitutes an egregious act.

The Trade Lever May Be Ineffective But It's All We Have

With time, the use of trade as a lever by the United States has diminished as American superiority and monopoly in technology and agricultural production have diminished. Other countries now have demonstrated the capability and sometimes the desire to counter American wishes, reducing the flexibility of American policymakers in using trade as a prod against the Soviet Union.

Yet although trade may not be as suitable as it once was as a lever influencing Soviet behavior, there nonetheless are times when the Soviets commit an act that cries out for protest. So far transgressions such as the invasion of Afghanistan and the intimidation of Poland have not warranted a declaration of war by the United States on the Soviet Union. Still, most Americans would argue that it would be wrong to ignore Soviet actions or go about business as if everything were normal. Looking about for some mechanism to express concern, it is only natural that the United States tends to fall back on trade restrictions. There is no doubt that in the past such restrictions have seemed not only moral and proper but there is also evidence that withholding trade or the threat of doing so has served to influence Soviet policy. With time, however, as U.S. technological superiority has diminished, trade as an instrument has become less effective. As the potential damage from a U.S. trade embargo diminishes, it has become more difficult to influence Soviet policy. Nonetheless, out of frustration, it often seems that except for a declaration of war, restricting trade and banning cultural exchanges are about the only mechanisms of disapproval left.

Since the Soviets will probably continue to transgress and involve themselves in Third World countries in ways that the United States would find to be antisocial and repugnant, there is every likelihood that there will be renewed calls for the use of a trade weapon in the future as well. Under the circumstances, the United States should try to work out in advance which of its actions will be most effective and where. At the same time, however, it should also determine where its allies will not join with it and where it will be the least effective. In this way perhaps it can come closer to adopting policies with a specific prohibition for a specific purpose and for a specific time frame.

Notes

1. U.S. Senate, Committee on Foreign Relations, *East-West Trade* (Washington, D.C.: U.S. Government Printing Office, 1964), pt. I, II, III.

2. U.S. Senate, Committee on Banking and Currency, *East-West Trade* (Washington, D.C.: U.S. Government Printing Office, June 1968).

3. Henry Kissinger, *Years of Upheaval* (Boston: Little, Brown, 1982), pp. 985-986.

4. For a more detailed discussion of the renewal of the Slavophile-Westernizer debate, see pp. 166-168 of Marshall I. Goldman, *The Enigma of Soviet Petroleum: Half Empty or Half Full?* (Boston: George Allen & Unwin, 1980).

5. *Pravda*, April 6, 1966, p. 7.

6. Ibid., February 28, 1981, p. 5.

7. *Trud*, April 17, 1981, p. 2; *Sotsialisticheskaia industriia*, October 4, 1981, p. 2.

8. A.P. Alexandrov, "Rech' A.P. Alexandrov," *Vestnik*, Akademii Nauk SSSR, no. 4, 1981, p. 5. See also *Pravda*, June 2, 1981, p. 3.

9. Z. Alexander, "Immigrants to Israel from the USSR," *Israel Yearbook on Human Rights* (1977), 7:268-335.

10. Senator Henry M. Jackson, news release, January 26, 1975, p. 3.

11. Stanley J. Marcus, "New Light on the Export-Import Bank," in Paul Marer, ed., *U.S. Financing of East-West Trade* (Bloomington, Ind.: International Development Center, Indiana University, August 1975), p. 267.

12. *New York Times*, April 17, 1982, p. 1.

13. Ibid., March 2, 1982, p. A-5.

14. Walter Saunders, vice-president, Cargill, presentation at Arden House, New York, March 6, 1982.

Index

Selected Reports and Publications of the California Seminar on International Security and Foreign Policy

Executive Committee
David Elliot, California Institute of Technology
Marvin L. Goldberger, California Institute of Technology
Donald Rice, The Rand Corporation
Albert D. Wheelon, Hughes Aircraft Company
Albert Wohlstetter, European-American Institute for Security Research
Charles Wolf, Jr., The Rand Corporation

Co-Chairmen
David Elliot
Charles Wolf, Jr.

Executive Director
James Digby

Selected Reports of the California Seminar

Number   5   Marshall, Andrew, *Bureaucratic Behavior and the Strategic Arms Competition.* October 1971 ($2.75)

    20   Iklé, Fred. *Can Nuclear Deterrence Last Out the Century?* January 1973 ($2.75)

    35   Brown, Thomas. *What is an Arms Race?* October 1973 ($2.75)

    44   Leites, Nathan. *Once More About What We Should Not Do Even in the Worst Case: The Assured Destruction Attack.* June 1974 ($2.75)

    52   Rowen, Henry. *Implications of Technologies of Precision for Japanese Security.* July 1975 ($3.00)

    54   Saeki, Kiichi, and Charles Wolf, Jr. *Complementary and Conflicting Economic Interests in Japan-U.S. Relations.* July 1975 ($3.00)

California Seminar on International Security and Foreign Policy, Post Office Box 925, Santa Monica, California 90406.

180

Number   63 Imai, Ryukichi. *The Outlook for Japan's Nuclear Future.* October 1975. ($3.00)

          75 Wolf, Charles, Jr. *Weapons Standardization, "Offsets," and Trade Liberalization in NATO.* September 1977. ($3.75)

          76 Burt, Richard. *Nuclear Proliferation and Conventional Arms Transfers: The Missing Link.* September 1977. ($3.75)

          77 Ellsworth, Robert. *New Imperatives for the Old Alliance.* December 1977. ($3.75)

          78 Digby, James. *New Weapons and the Dispersal of Military Power.* September 1978. ($3.75)

          79 Albrecht, Mark and Roger George. *Congress and the All Volunteer Force: How to Affect Defense Budgets Without Really Trying.* October 1978. (Student paper.) ($3.75)

          80 Caterina, Vincent. *Future Air Combat Environments: An Analysis of USAF Tactical Aircraft Entering the Inventory.* With comments by Thomas J. McDonnell. February 1979. (Student paper.) ($3.75)

          82 Payne, Keith B., C. Johnston Conover, and Bruce William Bennett. *Nuclear Strategy: Flexibility and Stability.* March 1979. (Student paper.) ($3.75)

          83 Hassner, Pierre. *The Left in Europe: Security Implications and International Dimensions.* April 1979. ($3.75)

          84 York, Herbert, and G. Allen Greb. *The Comprehensive Nuclear Test Ban.* June 1979. ($3.75)

          85 Ramet, Pedro. *Sadat and the Kremlin.* February 1980. (Student paper.) ($3.75)

          86 Brown, Raymond L. *Anwar al-Sadat and the October War: Factors Contributing to the Egyptian Decision to Go to War, October 1970 to October 1973.* March 1980. (Student paper.) ($3.75)

          87 Mossavar-Rahmani, Bijan. *Revolution and Evolution of Energy Policies in Iran.* July 1980. ($3.75)

          88 Khalilzad, Zalmay. *The Return of the Great Game: Superpower Rivalry and Domestic Turmoil in Afghanistan, Iran, Pakistan and Turkey.* September 1980. ($3.75)

          89 Peele, Gillian. *British Foreign Policy and The Conservative Party.* October 1980. ($3.75)

          90 Gardner, H. Stephen. *Soviet International Economic Relations: Recent Trends in Policy and Performance.* February 1981. ($3.75)

          91 Campbell, Robert. *Soviet Technology Imports: The Gas Pipeline Case.* February 1981. ($3.75)

Number   92   Hanson, Philip. *Soviet Strategies and Policy Implementation in the Import of Chemical Technology from the West, 1958-1978.* March 1981. ($3.75)

          93   May, Michael M. *War or Peace in Space.* March 1981. ($3.75)

          94   Hodgden, Louise. *The MX Missile System: The Decision-making Process and Implications for Arms Control.* April 1981. (Student paper.) ($3.75)

          95   Kiser, John W. *Barriers to Increasing the Export of Manufactures from the USSR: Prospects for Change.* May 1981. ($3.75)

          96   Caldwell, Dan. *Soviet-American Crisis Management in the Cuban Missile Crisis and the October War.* July 1981. ($3.75)

          97   Elliot, David. *Decision at Brussels: The Politics of Nuclear Forces.* August 1981. ($3.75)

          98   Wolf, Charles, Jr. *Beyond Containment: Reshaping U.S. Policies Toward the Third World.* September 1982. ($3.75)

          99   Sherwood, Elizabeth D. *American Foreign Policy Toward West European Communism: The Italian and French Cases.* March 1983. (Student paper.) ($3.75)

Book

Number   81   Wohlstetter, Albert, Victor Gilinsky, Robert Gillette, and Roberta Wohlstetter. *Nuclear Policies: Fuel Without the Bomb* (Foreword by Robert F. Bacher). January 1979 ($16.50) [Available only from Ballinger Publishing Company, 54 Church Street, Harvard Square, Cambridge, Massachusetts 02138.]

About the Contributors

Marshall I. Goldman currently holds the position of the Class of 1919 Professor of Economics at Wellesley College. He is also associate director of the Russian Research Center, Harvard University. In 1977, he served as a Fulbright-Hayes visiting lecturer at Moscow State University. His most recent books include *The Enigma of Soviet Petroleum: Half Empty or Half Full?* and *The USSR in Crisis: The Failure of an Economic System.*

Jean-Marie Guillaume is the nom de plume of a French analyst in government service who is a graduate of the Ecole Nationale d'Administration.

Philip Hanson is a Reader in Soviet economics in the Centre for Russian and East European Studies, Birmingham University, England. In 1971-1972 he worked as senior research officer at the Foreign and Commonwealth Office, London. In 1977 he was a visiting professor at the University of Michigan. His most recent book is *Trade and Technology in Soviet-Western Relations* (1981).

John P. Hardt is associate director for senior specialists and senior specialist in Soviet economics at the Congressional Research Service. He is also adjunct professor in economics at both George Washington and Georgetown universities.

Ed. A. Hewett is a senior Fellow at The Brookings Institution, Washington, D.C. He is the author of *Foreign Trade Prices in the Council for Mutual Economic Assistance* and has written articles on Soviet and East European foreign trade and the Hungarian economy. He is currently working on a book entitled *Energy, Economics and Foreign Policy in the USSR.*

Josef Joffe is a senior associate at the Carnegie Endowment for International Peace and a Professorial Lecturer at the Johns Hopkins School of Advanced International Studies in Washington, D.C. He also is a member of the International Institute of Strategic Studies in London. Dr. Joffe was previously senior editor of the West German weekly, *Die Zeit.* He has contributed many articles on international relations, strategy, arms control, and German foreign policy to scholarly publications and professional journals such as *Foreign Affairs* and *Foreign Policy.* He received the Ph.D. from Harvard University.

Kate S. Tomlinson, formerly a senior research assistant at the Congressional Research Service, is a consultant. She has worked for Wharton Econometric Forecasting Associates and the Office of Technology Assessment, U.S. Congress.

About the Editor

Abraham S. Becker is a senior economist and associate director of the National Security Program at The Rand Corporation, Santa Monica, California. He is the author of *Soviet National Income 1958-1964: National Accounts of the USSR in the Seven Year Plan Period* and *Military Expenditure Limitation for Arms Control: Problems and Prospects*. In 1974 and 1976 he served as the U.S. member of the United Nations Expert Group on the Reduction of Military Budgets. Since 1978 he has been director of the Working Group on International Economics and U.S. Foreign Policy of the California Seminar on International Security and Foreign Policy.